PATHS TO UNITY

PATHS
TO
UNITY

American Religion Today and Tomorrow

2o

by RONALD E. MODRAS

Sheed and Ward: New York

For my Mother and Father,
a Holy Father named John,
and all who rejoice in the coming of his spirit.

For their assistance and critical advice in preparing these pages, grateful acknowledgement is due to Jane Wolford, Barry and Lori Wilkinson, Nancy Dunn, Paul Black, Gerald Chojnacki, and the staff of the Institute for Continuing Education.

R. E. M.

Contents

Contents

Introduction

Today, in many parts of the world, under the inspiring grace of the Holy Spirit, multiple efforts are being expended through prayer, work, and action to attain the fullness of unity which Jesus Christ desires. This sacred Synod, therefore, exhorts all the Catholic faithful to recognize the signs of the times and to participate fully in the work of ecumenism.

—VATICAN COUNCIL II,

DECREE ON ECUMENISM, NO. 4[1]

"There is now incontrovertible evidence that mankind has just entered upon the greatest period of change the world has ever known . . . A fresh kind of life is starting." Pierre Teilhard de Chardin was speaking of the passing of the Age of Nations and the birth of a new spirit of communality among men. He could have been speaking as well of the passing of the Age of Schisms and the birth of a new spirit of communality among Christians. We have been privileged to witness in our day what may prove to be the most significant event in Christian history since the 16th century, the growth and development of the ecumenical movement.

In the priestly prayer which Jesus offered at his Last Supper, we find both his yearning desire for oneness among those who follow him and the singular motive for that oneness:

[1] Excerpts from the Constitution, Decrees, and Declarations of the Ecumenical Council are taken from *The Documents of Vatican II,* published by Guild Press, America Press, Association Press, and Herder and Herder and copyrighted 1966 by The America Press. Used by permission.

That they may all be one; even as thou, Father, art in me, and I in thee, that they also may be in us, so that the world may believe that thou hast sent me. (John 17:21)[2]

And St. Paul shared these same feelings when he exhorted the neo-Christians at Ephesus to value and preserve the unity for which Christ had prayed:

I therefore, a prisoner for the Lord, beg you to lead a life worthy of the calling to which you have been called, with all lowliness and meekness, with patience, forebearing one another in love, eager to maintain the unity of the Spirit in the bond of peace. There is one body and one Spirit, just as you were called to the one hope that belongs to your call, one Lord, one faith, one baptism, one God and Father of us all, who is above all and through all and in all. (Eph. 4:1–6)

Despite the explicit wishes of Jesus Christ, the exhortations of St. Paul, and much echoing and reechoing of both through the ages, the history of the Christian Church has been marred time and again by internal discord and schism. The oldest schism still extant is that of the Nestorians, a separation that occurred in 451. In 1054 there took place the Great Schism which divides to this day the Orthodox Churches of the East from the Roman Catholic Church. In the 16th century the Church was further fragmented by the Protestant Reformation. This disintegration of Christian unity, tragic in itself, invariably became the source of rancor, discord, and sectarian hatred—all in the name of God and to the scandal and disgust of men who wanted no part of this wrangling fellowship.

Voices were raised deploring the schisms which divided the Church; prophetic voices called Christians to a return to the unity for which Christ had prayed. They met little response, however, until our own day, in which it became increasingly apparent that Christian unity is absolutely necessary if "when the Son of man comes," he is to "find faith on earth" (Luke 18:8). Among the purposes outlined by Pope John XXIII for convoking Vatican

[2] The Scripture quotations are from the Revised Standard Version of the Bible, New York, Nelson, 1946, 1952; copyrighted 1946 and 1952 by the Division of Christian Education of the National Council of Churches and used by permission.

Council II, one of the foremost was "to invite the separated [Christian] communities to seek again the unity for which so many souls are longing in these days throughout the world."

The Second Vatican Council, in its Decree on Ecumenism, not only set down principles for Catholic participation in the ecumenical movement but encouraged the full participation of all Catholics in working toward Christian unity. The Decree opens with an unequivocal affirmation:

Promoting the restoration of unity among all Christians is one of the chief concerns of the Second Sacred Ecumenical Synod of the Vatican. (Introduction, No. 1)

It goes on to exhort that the ecumenical concern of the Council be diffused throughout the world:

This sacred Synod is gratified to note that participation by the Catholic faithful in ecumenical work is growing daily. It commends this work to bishops everywhere in the world for their skillful promotion and prudent guidance. Concern for restoring unity pertains to the whole Church, faithful and clergy alike. It extends to everyone, according to the potential of each, whether it be exercised in daily Christian living or in theological and historical studies. (Nos. 4 and 5)

Especially significant in this call to ecumenical action is the statement: "Concern for restoring unity pertains to the whole Church, faithful and clergy alike." Many Catholics are inclined to believe that ecumenism is a proper interest and activity for experts alone, for clergymen and theologians. The Council rejected this opinion on the very good grounds that ecumenism is the proper concern of the entire Church, of all its members, of the people of God. As Pope Pius XII put it, "Laymen and laywomen must become increasingly aware of the fact that they do not simply belong to the Church. They are the Church."

Lay involvement in the ecumenical movement is imperative for the achievement of Christian unity. Catholics, Orthodox, and Protestants will become one Christian Church only when the laymen who make up these Churches desire, with as much intensity as Christ, that "they all may be one . . ." This demands personal

4 *Paths to Unity*

involvement in ecumenical affairs. It demands grass-roots ecumenism.

To be effective, however, grass-roots ecumenism must first be informed. Vatican II urged Catholic laymen "to take an active and *intelligent* part in the work of ecumenism," and intelligent participation requires education and study. *Paths to Unity* is a somewhat rash attempt to answer the need for a layman's introduction to the many and varied aspects of ecumenism and the ecumenical movement.

I refer to this book as rash, because of the breadth of its scope. It draws from history, theology, and contemporary religious sociology, and attempts to present these materials concisely without doing injustice to basic clarity or accuracy. It necessarily avoids delving into the full implications of some of the questions and problems raised in these pages, but it does so with the hope that this general introduction will stimulate the reader to further reading in greater depth.

This book arose from the notes prepared for the course "Focusing in on Ecumenism," part of an adult-education program in the Archdiocese of Detroit, the Institute for Continuing Education. It is presented here, as the course was presented there, not for the ecumenical experts, but for would-be ecumenists—primarily but not solely for American Catholics, for students, adult study groups, discussion groups, and people concerned about Vatican II, Christianity, and our world today.

Paths to Unity is presented with the frank hope that not only will it prove informative and explanatory, but that it will encourage personal awareness and participation in the great movement toward Christian unity. And, most specifically, it is presented with the author's hope—and prayer—that it may encourage and guide Catholics in fuller participation in ecumenical dialogue and encounter, that it may prove an effective stimulus in the growth of grass-roots ecumenism.

1 / The Meaning and History of Ecumenism

The greatest event of our century in the field of religious history is the Ecumenical Movement. When the political upheavals that we have experienced will be no more than paragraphs in history books, the Ecumenical Movement will still be bearing fruits.

—GEORGE TAVARD,
Protestant Hopes and Catholic Responsibility

Before January 25, 1959, when Pope John XXIII announced to the world his intention to convene a council, only a handful of Catholics could have offered a respectable definition of the word "ecumenical." Since that celebrated day, ecumenism has passed from the dusty confines of a theological dictionary to being almost public property, the next thing to a household word. But it did not happen without question and some confusion. When Pope John first brought up the idea of an ecumenical council, there were some who thought he was proposing an international congress, one that would bring together representatives of all the Christian communities of the world to discuss and draw up some form of Christian union. The misunderstanding was cleared up shortly thereafter, when it was explained that "ecumenical" was being used in the technical, historical sense of a council at which would participate all the Catholic bishops of the world in communion with the Bishop of Rome.

The Meaning, Aims, and Means of Ecumenism
Meaning

Ecumenism is that aspect of the theology and activity of the Christian Church which pertains to the ecumenical movement. The word "ecumenical" is derived from a Greek word meaning the "inhabited world." It was originally defined as "general, worldwide in extent or influence." In virtue of this primary meaning, an ecumenical council is one representative of the Church throughout the world. But the ecumenical movement has developed so considerably in this century that it has since given the word a narrower, more specific connotation.

Strictly speaking, the ecumenical movement is defined as the effort and activity of Christians in various Churches to promote the restoration of Christian unity. By establishing relationships between Christian Churches, the ecumenical movement seeks to heal the schisms, i.e., the formal separations, which divide them one from another. In practice, it consists of the efforts of both individual Christians and Christian Churches to help one another become more Christ-like, to realize more fully the Christian ideal after which they all strive. Vatican Council II, in its Decree on Ecumenism, defined the ecumenical movement in this way:

Everywhere, large numbers have felt the impulse of grace and among our own separated brethren also there increases from day to day a movement fostered by the grace of the Holy Spirit, for the restoration of unity among all Christians. Taking part in this movement, which is called ecumenical, are those who invoke the Triune God and confess Jesus as Lord and Savior. They join in not merely as individuals but also as members of the corporate groups in which they have heard the gospel, and which each regards as his Church and, indeed, God's. And yet, almost everyone, though in different ways, longs that there may be one visible Church of God, a Church truly universal and sent forth to the whole world that the world may be converted to the gospel and so be saved, to the glory of God. (Introduction, No. 1)

More broadly speaking, the ecumenical movement refers to mutual efforts at understanding and cooperation not only among

Christians but with those of other faiths as well. In this wider sense, it fosters an attitude of openness to all men, a respect for their beliefs, a willingness to understand their beliefs with sympathy and fairness, and a desire to cooperate with them in the service of mankind. This broader understanding of ecumenism implies a climate for dialogue and cooperation between Christians and Moslems, Buddhists, Hindus, and even those who profess no religion at all. In a special way, because of their common historical roots, it implies communication and collaboration between Christians and Jews.

Aims

The aim of the ecumenical movement is *the visible unity of the Christian Church.* So general a description of the aim of ecumenism places it somewhere on the level of virtue and mother love; it's rather difficult for a Christian to be against it. But Christian unity is so broad a notion that it is obviously open to various and perhaps even contradictory interpretations. Defining what Christian unity *is* requires first a clarification concerning what Christian unity is *not.*

1. The aim of ecumenism is *not simply a return to Rome.* For too long we Catholics have been interested in Christian unity, but only on our own terms. We were accustomed to thinking about the road to unity as being a one-way street. Our attitude had been one of a kindly parent willing to forgive and forget, to welcome back the erring prodigal. The colonnade on either side of the square in front of St. Peter's Basilica in Rome symbolized graphically the opened arms of the Catholic Church, ready and anxious to receive back into the fold all who had wandered astray.

Such largess on the part of the Catholic Church was really quite unecumenical. Orthodox and Protestants were asked to assume the burden of total guilt for our separations and to abandon characteristics and traditions of their faith which were especially dear to them. They were expected to capitulate completely and admit that the Catholic Church is in undisputed possession of the entire truth. Few Catholics were willing, much less ready, to take an objective look at the reasons people had severed themselves from the visible communion of the Catholic Church.

The return-to-Rome attitude was corrected by Vatican Council II when it described the Church as an itinerant pilgrim. This implies that the Church is not in complete possession of the truth, but is led by the Holy Spirit in search of it. It implies that the road to union is not a one-way street but, rather, a twofold movement toward Jesus Christ. In discussing the aim of ecumenism as it is described in the conciliar decree, Father Yves Congar put it this way:

This document does not speak about the "return" of "heretics" and "schismatics" but of a movement, not only in the direction of separated Christians toward the Church, but also of the Catholic Church toward the other Christians. Unity will thus be a meeting in which the Catholic Church will give the separated Christians what they lost when they left it. But it will also receive the really Christian heritage which has been produced by the separated Christians during the centuries of separation, under the impulse of the Holy Spirit. (*Herder Correspondence,* II, 2, p. 111)

Ecumenism for the Catholic Church implies reform of ourselves and our ways of thinking and acting, many of which are out of joint with the Biblical source of our faith and with the needs of the world today. This was the primary intention of Pope John in calling the Council: *aggiornamento,* renewal. He stated as much in his encyclical *Ad Petri Cathedram:*

The main purpose of the Council will be to promote the development of the Catholic Faith, the true reform of the morals of the Christian people and the better adaptation of the discipline of the Church to the necessities and methods of our time.

Instead of expecting Orthodox and Protestants to come back home like erring sheep, Catholics need to work for the renewal and reform of the Church so that it may more clearly express the intentions of Christ. While Catholics believe that the united Christian Church of the future will involve such fundamentals as the Papacy and universal episcopacy, this does not rule out a very different and reformed Papacy or a renewed collegial episcopacy.

The reform which the Council initiated, however, does not do violence to the essential nature of the Church. Unfortunately, there are many Catholics who have confused that which is essential in Christianity with ideas and practices that are peripheral. Delineating the two, the essential from the nonessential, is one of the more sizable tasks these days for ecumenists and theologians alike. Ecumenical reform of the Church does not imply a betrayal of the past; in many instances it involves a return to it. Pope Paul VI, in his opening address at the Second Session of the Vatican Council, expressed this very thought:

The reform at which the Council aims is not a turning upside down of the Church's present way of life or a breaking with what is essential and worthy in her tradition but it is rather an honoring of tradition by stripping it of what is unworthy or defective so that it may be rendered firm and fruitful.

2. Ecumenism does *not* aim at *a super-Church*. The unity of a universal Church does not require the uniformity of all viewpoints, liturgical services, or religious practices. To establish such a uniformity would be to create a monolithic monstrosity. It would rob both Christianity and mankind of the many-splendored expressions of faith and love which the human heart can and needs to fashion. The faith is one; but there is more than one way to understand it, more than one theology. God is one; but there is more than one way to find him or worship him. Love is one; but there is more than one way to express it.

The unity for which the ecumenical movement strives must take into account the diversities of mentality and culture among peoples, not only of different nations, but also of different communities and even localities within the same country. Not only must it recognize the dignity of the individual person and his conscience, but it must also take cognizance of the rights and prerogatives of the local Churches, congregations, and dioceses which make up the universal Church. The precept of St. Augustine would seem appropriate as a criterion; "In essentials, unity; in other things, liberty; in all things, charity." But what are the essentials? That's another question, not quite so easy to answer; and that is precisely the problem.

3. Ecumenism does *not* aim at *mere coexistence*. Christian unity is more than simply agreeing to disagree, more than mutual open-mindedness or tolerance. Although it recognizes the rightful role played by local Churches, ecumenism does not accord them such complete autonomy that they become entities complete unto themselves. No Church, like no man, is an island. The accomplishment of the Church's missionary task demands communal rather than individual or parochial activity. It requires the sharing by all Christians of their religious resources for clearer preaching of the gospel and more effective ministry to the needs of society today. It was the love and not mere tolerance of the early Christians for one another that attracted the attention of society two thousand years ago. At the risk of seeming sanguine, it might work again.

Describing what the aim of ecumenism is not is much easier than defining what it is, particularly since there is considerable disagreement as to the precise nature of the Christian unity for which it strives. Protestant ecumenists, notably those of the World Council of Churches, are willing to leave wide open the question of the exact form which Christian unity will take. They describe it as the unity which Christ desires for his Church at such a time and in such a way as he wishes. The Catholic Church, however, in its conciliar Decree on Ecumenism, explicitly sets up its own unity as the goal to be achieved:

For it is through Christ's Catholic Church alone, which is the all-embracing means of salvation, that the fullness of the means of salvation can be obtained. (Decree on Ecumenism, No. 3)

Some Protestants have expressed resentment at this claim that the Catholic Church must occupy the center of the ecumenical stage. Critics of this claim have countered, not without some justification, that Christ himself should be recognized as the center of ecumenical encounter. They also maintain that, because of the ignorance and sinfulness of their members, all of the Christian Churches are eccentric.

Fortunately, a common effort toward achieving Christian unity does not demand total agreement as to the precise definition of that unity. Churches may entertain reservations about one another's aims and ecclesiological positions, and yet engage in ecumenical activity as brothers in Christ. Despite disagreement as to the exact nature of the remote, eventual aim of ecumenism, Catholics, Orthodox, and Protestants can work for the attainment of more immediate goals. While hoping for the eventual unity of all Christian Churches, we can begin today to think together, talk together, to work and pray together. The success of ecumenical effort does not depend solely upon the achievement of corporate unity. Our endeavors are meaningful and productive by the very concern we have for one another in striving to help one another to become more Christian.

Means

The means for achieving Christian unity inspire relative agreement among ecumenists, whether Catholic, Protestant, or Orthodox, although there are differences of opinion as to which are the more important. Without implying any hierarchy of importance, the means for attaining Christian unity may be listed as: (1) The *elimination of prejudice* and unfair judgment toward other Churches; (2) *dialogue* leading to a more accurate knowledge and appreciation of their teachings; (3) *cooperation* in ministering to the needs of society; (4) *reform,* that "change of heart" that will lead to greater union with Christ and therefore with all Christians; (5) *concern for the needs of other Churches;* and (6) *prayer* offered to God together for the grace of reconciliation.

The Second Vatican Council, in its Decree on Ecumenism, described in these words the means which will foster Christian unity:

The "ecumenical movement" means those activities and enterprises which, according to various needs of the Church and opportune occasions, are started and organized for the fostering of unity among Christians. These are: first, every effort to eliminate words, judgments, and actions which do not respond to the condition of separated brethren with truth and fairness and so make mutual relations between them more difficult; then, "dialogue" between competent experts from different Churches and Communities. In their meetings, which are organized in a religious spirit, each explains the teaching of his Communion in greater depth and brings out clearly its distinctive features. Through such dialogue, everyone gains a truer knowledge and a more just appreciation of the teaching and religious life of both Communions. In addition, these Communions cooperate more closely in whatever projects a Christian conscience demands for the common good. They also come together for common prayer where this is permitted. Finally, all are led to examine their own faithfulness to Christ's will for the Church and, wherever necessary, undertake with vigor the task of renewal and reform. (No. 4)

Contrary Attitudes

An explanation of ecumenism, of its methods and aims, can be further clarified perhaps by contrasting its spirit to a number of attitudes contrary to it. These contrary attitudes are hostility, indifference to our divisions, and doctrinal indifferentism.

Hostility has long marked relationships among separated Christians. We had just enough religion to hate one another and not enough to love one another. Misguided loyalties and muddled thinking nurtured hatred and outright violence among men who thought of themselves as championing the cause of Jesus Christ. Although not as common as it once was, sectarian hostility among Christians still occasionally raises its head, but now it does so in more subtle forms than before. It looks for what is wrong in other Churches, emphasizing differences between them in terms of opposition. It attributes unworthy motives to people of other Churches, doubting their integrity and rejoicing in their difficulties. Hostility for other Churches is obviously opposed to the most basic tenets of Christian charity.

Indifference to our divisions is more common today among Christians than hostility, but it is no less contrary to charity. This is the attitude which confronts the divisions among Christians with apathetic nonchalance. It says, in so many words, "Am I my brother's keeper? Let them take care of themselves. So long as they will leave us alone, we can leave them alone." Among Catholics, this attitude of indifference often shows itself in the belief that responsibility for our divisions lies solely with the other

Churches; it considers Orthodox as "schismatics" and Protestants as "heretics"—and both with the obligation to make efforts to return to the Catholic fold. In fact, however, the words "schismatic" or "heretic" can be attributed only to Christians who have deliberately or maliciously severed themselves from the Church or rejected what they know to be the truth. These terms cannot be applied to Christians whose only offense is that of being loyal to the spiritual heritage of their fathers. Just as it is no credit to any person to have been born of Catholic parents, so too it is no discredit to any person to have been born of Orthodox or Protestant parents. The responsibility for the origin of our divisions is shared by Catholics, Orthodox, and Protestants alike. The responsibility for the healing of those divisions falls to all of us alike. Indifference to the schisms which separate Christians today disregards the explicit wishes of Jesus Christ and ignores the need for a united Christian witness in order to make Christ relevant to the world. Indifference contradicts obedience to Christ.

Doctrinal indifferentism is the attitude which believes that one religion is as good as another. It thereby implies that one religion is as worthless as another. It lacks respect for the nature of truth and the importance of religious doctrine, ignoring the Christian belief that God revealed himself in history and made his mind and will known to us. Counterfeit currency and the genuine article are not the same thing, even if the former is used in good faith. Doctrinal indifferentism maintains that what a person believes is not really important, so long as he lives a good life. It overlooks the fact that a man usually bases the actions of his life precisely on what he believes. Doctrinal indifference contradicts the Biblical injunction of St. Paul: "If any one is preaching to you a gospel contrary to that which we preached to you, let him be accursed" (Gal. 1:9).

Counterfeit Ecumenism

These attitudes contrary to the ecumenical spirit sometimes give rise to activities which may appear on the surface to be ecumenical but which in reality are counterfeit, viz., compromising doctrines

of faith and camouflaged proselytism. Genuine ecumenism should
not be confused with either one of them.

Compromising doctrines of faith is sometimes referred to as
false irenicism or unionism. It attempts to achieve union at any
price, even that of neglecting or distorting traditional teachings of
the Church. It prefers to concentrate solely upon social action in
common as a means toward unity, taking for its motto "Doctrine
divides, service unites."

A genuine ecumenical spirit would prefer disunity to a make-
believe merger that ignores essential differences of doctrine. Such
a union could not be anything but superficial. The Church is
primarily a community of faith; even before the first disciples of
the apostles were called Christians, they were called "believers."
Honest ecumenical dialogue demands facing up to the differences
and disagreements among Christians concerning doctrine. The
Vatican Council spoke out strongly against any attempts at achieving a cheap union at the cost of doctrinal compromise:

This most sacred Synod urges the faithful to abstain from any super-
ficiality or imprudent zeal, for these can cause harm to true progress
towards unity. Their ecumenical activity must not be other than fully
and sincerely Catholic, that is, loyal to the truth we have received
from the apostles and the Fathers, and in harmony with the faith
which the Catholic Church has always professed, and at the same
time tending toward that fullness with which our Lord wants His
body to be endowed in the course of time. (Decree on Ecumenism,
No. 24)

For a Catholic to change the teaching of the Church in ecumenical discussion simply for the sake of agreement is dishonest. It is
a misrepresentation of the Church's two-thousand-year-old tradition. It would likewise be hypocrisy to dwell solely upon points of
agreement and pretend that unmentioned areas of disagreement are
not there or else do not matter. But, at the same time, it is important to note that our similarities by far outnumber and outweigh our differences. Formidable as they are, the walls that
separate Christians do not reach to heaven.

Without compromising doctrines of faith, however, we can
approach our differences with much less controversy and much

more charity in an effort to understand each other. Ever since Martin Luther posted his ninety-five theses challenging all-comers to debate, Protestant-Catholic relations had been marked by polemics. Much effort and ingenuity was spent on the art of one-upmanship, while few attempts were made to really get down to facts and understand the other side. Ecumenical dialogue is a relatively recent phenomenon, but already it has demonstrated that quite often our differences do not so much contradict as complement one another. Disagreements have often proved to be more apparent than real, owing to the varying emphases, mentalities, and points of view that Catholics and Protestants have held in approaching the same topic.

This does not imply that the doctrinal differences that divide Christians are simply a matter of semantics and that dialogue will erase all our schisms. But ecumenical dialogue is helping us to see precisely where those differences lie; it is causing us to take a broader, more encompassing view of our own faith. And it is teaching us more about that faith. The Catholic Church has never claimed to have a monopoly on truth. There is a great deal that Catholics can learn about Jesus, the Church, and the wonderful works of God from Orthodox and Protestants—and vice versa. If a Catholic fears that, with all this dialogue, the Catholic Church is becoming too Protestant, he might be interested, if not consoled, to learn that many Protestants are complaining that their Churches are becoming too Catholic.

Camouflaged proselytism is likewise a form of counterfeit ecumenism. It is not that the Church is no longer interested in receiving converts, for Christians have a mandate from Christ to carry the good news of salvation to all men. The Church, of its very nature, is missionary; and the Catholic Church, no less than any other Christian Church, holds itself ready to receive into its ranks individuals who believe in conscience that the Holy Spirit is leading them to make that step. But ecumenism is not a missionary technique. Although it does not contradict convert-work, ecumenism is something very different from it. Ecumenism recognizes that the schisms which divide Christians cannot be healed solely on the basis of individual conversions.

Ecumenism strives for the corporate reunion of dedicated Chris-

tians into one Church; convert-work strives for the individual renewal in grace of those countless millions who are only vaguely
related to traditional Christianity, the nonpracticing Christian, the
unchurched, the unbaptized. There is no conflict between the two
efforts. It would be well for us to remember, however, that conversion is preeminently a work of the Holy Spirit, who gives grace
wherever he wills. A man responds to the impulse of the Holy
Spirit by following his conscience as to how he can best love and
serve God. And his conscience must be respected. It is better for
a man to live as a devout, believing Protestant than as a lax
Catholic. Conversely, it is better for a man to live as a faithful
and loving Catholic than as a lax Protestant.

Our mission as Christians is not a matter of conquering souls
for Christ. Our task is to be instruments of grace, to attract men
to Christ by reflecting him in our lives, by rendering the world an
example of Christ-like service. There is a non-Christian world of
vast proportions, not only in Africa and Asia, but in our own
American cities, indeed, within our very congregations. These
people will never accept Christ until we Christians all convert,
until we all have a real change of heart by rejecting selfishness and
sectarianism, until we truly embrace the example of Christ, of his
love and service. Ecumenism aims not at making Catholics out
of Protestants or Protestants out of Catholics; it works to help all
of us, individuals and Churches alike, to become more Christian.

The History of the Ecumenical Movement

Early Attempts

Ecumenical encounters are not altogether recent phenomena. High-
level attempts at reunion between Orthodox and Catholics were
made in the 13th century at the Second Council of Lyons and
in the 15th century at the Council of Florence. Both efforts proved
abortive, however, because they involved only bishops on either
side of the schism. Neither the lower clergy nor the people of the
Eastern Churches were prepared for reunion with Catholics, and
when the plan was formulized on paper, they rejected it. History
has thus taught a compelling lesson of the absolute necessity of
grass-roots ecumenism.

Shortly after the Protestant Reformation, efforts were made at theological dialogue between Catholics and Evangelical Protestants, with the hope of arriving at some sort of common understanding. The Diet of Regensburg in 1542 was the outstanding example of such colloquies. It involved some of the foremost Protestant and Catholic theologians of the day, and their discussions centered upon the nature of faith, a basic issue of contention in the 16th century. In a serious effort to achieve a reconciliation of views, both the Protestant and Catholic delegates finally arrived at an understanding of faith which satisfied the Reformers and yet accorded with traditional Catholic teaching. Back in the 16th century, however, passion and prejudice overcame understanding, and the Catholic delegates were reproached for giving in to the Lutherans on important dogmatic issues. Any further official attempts at reaching some sort of theological concord came to an abrupt halt with the Council of Trent, which militantly defended any Catholic position attacked by Protestants.

Subsequent dialogues between Catholics and Protestants were of an unofficial nature, conducted purely on an individual basis. In the 17th century, for example, Bishop Bossuet of France corresponded with the German philosopher Leibniz in an effort to reconcile Catholic and Protestant viewpoints. None of these enterprises, however, achieved any permanent results.

In the 19th century the Protestant Church of England experienced a Catholic revival by way of the Oxford Movement. One of the aims of this revival was a corporate reunion between Anglicans and Catholics. While it did not succeed in achieving such a union, the Oxford Movement did result in the formation of a strong Anglo-Catholic party within the Church of England. At this time there developed within Anglicanism the so-called "branch theory"; it maintains that the universal Catholic Church consists of three main branches—the Roman Catholic, the Anglo-Catholic, and the Eastern Orthodox.

In 1908 Father Paul Wattson, an Anglican friar, began popularizing the Chair of Unity Octave, a practice of eight days of prayer for Christian unity. He and his community entered the Catholic Church in 1909. Known as the Society of the Atonement or the Graymoor Fathers, they have devoted themselves ever since to the work for Christian unity. The Church Unity Octave (January 18–25), although it did evince interest in the cause of Christian unity, was pre-ecumenical in that it was based on the theme of unity through submission to the Holy See. In this form, Catholics could take part in the practice, but other Christians could hardly be expected to pray for their submission to Rome. Father Paul Couturier, in Lyons, France, expanded the vision of the Octave so that all Christians could pray together. He laid heavy emphasis upon the need of "spiritual ecumenism," the practice of common prayer for Christian unity. He founded the *Week of Prayer for Christian Unity,* which has subsequently replaced the earlier concept of the Octave. It is endorsed and encouraged by both high-level Protestant and Catholic leadership.

From 1921 to 1926 a series of conversations took place between Anglicans and Catholics at the residence of Cardinal Mercier, the Archbishop of Malines, Belgium. Known as the Malines Conferences, these discussions concentrated upon theoretical, dogmatic questions; there was no attempt to negotiate an Anglican-Catholic reunion. The dozen or so delegates endeavored, not to persuade or convince one another, but rather simply to acquire mutual information and clarification of one another's theological positions. The Malines Conferences reached no definite conclusions, but they were noteworthy for the important lesson that they taught: theological dialogue between Christian Churches was possible.

Protestant Ecumenism in the 20th Century

The beginnings of the ecumenical movement as we know it today can be traced back to 1910 and the World Missionary Conference held at Edinburgh, Scotland. It grew out of the awareness by Protestant missionaries of the scandal which Christian disunity was presenting to the cause of evangelization. Their competing for converts was resulting not only in a duplication of resources but also in confusion to the natives of the mission lands. While not the first of its kind, the Edinburgh Conference was the first such meeting which could be called ecumenical both in geography and spirit. The delegates became convinced of the absolute necessity of a united witness to Christ and affirmed their belief that an organically united Church was the will of Jesus Christ. Out of the conference there arose the International Missionary Council, established for the coordination of Protestant missionary activity.

One of the organizers of the Edinburgh Conference, however, had more in mind than the coordination of missionary endeavors. He was Bishop Charles Brent, an Episcopal bishop in the Philippines and, later, of Western New York. He proposed discussions among Protestant Churches aimed at achieving theological and organizational unity. American Protestants were ready for such a movement, and such groups as the Young Men's Christian Association (YMCA) and the World's Student Christian Federation had already fostered a climate favorable toward Christian unity. Following Bishop Brent's proposal, the Episcopal Church of the United States appointed a commission to bring about "a conference for the consideration of questions touching on the faith and order [government] of the Church." Despite quick and enthusiastic support, it took ten years before representatives of the Churches could meet for a preparatory meeting at Geneva in 1920. In 1927, at Lucerne, Switzerland, the "Faith and Order Movement" had its first world conference. Although its method was largely one of comparing the theological viewpoints of the participating Churches, it showed that various Churches could converse on doctrinal issues.

In 1919, in a meeting at The Hague, Nathan Söderblom, the Lutheran Archbishop of Upsala, Sweden, proposed a meeting of the Churches to promote Christian cooperation on the level of life and work. The ravages of World War I gave his plea for united Christian service a note of urgency, and in 1925 at Stockholm the "Life and Work Movement" held its first world conference. The Stockholm meeting marked the first instance that representatives of the Eastern Orthodox Churches participated with Protestants in an ecumenical conference. The Life and Work Movement expounded an activist ecumenism that avoided doctrinal discussion and concentrated instead on interdenominational Christian cooperation in confronting contemporary problems of a political, economic, and social nature.

Protestant ecumenism continued to develop in the first part of this century along two distinct lines. The Faith and Order Movement dealt with theological questions; the Life and Work Movement concerned itself with social action. Despite their divergent approaches to the problems of Christian disunity, however, both movements found themselves crossing each other's concerns. At the Faith and Order Conference held at Edinburgh in 1937, an amalgamation of the two movements was proposed. The outbreak of World War II prevented any further action until 1948. In that year, at Amsterdam, Holland, the Faith and Order Movement united with the Life and Work Movement to form the World Council of Churches.

The *World Council of Churches* (WCC), when it was founded in 1948, was composed of members of 148 Churches, including representatives of Eastern Orthodoxy. It has grown since that time to a membership of over 200 Churches; among these is the largest of the Orthodox Churches, the Russian Orthodox Church, which joined in 1961.

The World Council of Churches is not a super-Church; it does not legislate for its members. Neither is it an agency for negotiating mergers between Churches, although it has served to bring Church leaders together and this, in turn, has led to a number of mergers. A former General Secretary of the World Council, W. G. Visser 't Hooft, has described the World Council in this way:

It is a fellowship of Churches which acknowledge Jesus Christ as God and Savior and which desire to enter into constructive relations with each other. It is a platform for serious conversation about the issues of unity, a means for cooperation in matters of common concern, an organ of common witness when it is given to the Churches to speak together to the world.

The World Council serves as a framework for dialogue and mutual assistance for its member Churches. It does so, abstracting from the varying viewpoints which its members might have concerning one another's authenticity. A statement issued by its Executive Committee in 1964 put it in these words:

Although the Churches may have reservations concerning one another's ecclesiological position, they are ready to engage in this conversation on equal terms. It is a conversation in which all are expected to listen as well as to speak, to receive as well as to give, and in which existing differences and tensions are frankly faced.

The Churches in the World Council believe that the member Churches should recognize their solidarity with one another, render assistance to each other in case of need, and support one another in their witness to Christ and in their evangelistic and missionary task, and wherever it is possible to do so, take common action and render common witness on the basis of consultation and agreement with one another.

The headquarters of the World Council of Churches is in Geneva, Switzerland. Its Central Committee, consisting of one hundred members representing various Churches, meets annually. Its highest authority, however, is vested in the General Assembly, which meets once every six years. At such a General Assembly in 1961 at New Delhi, the delegates voted to accept as a basis for membership in the World Council a belief in the Trinity as well as the Lordship and divinity of Jesus Christ. Dr. Visser 't Hooft, a Dutch Calvinist, guided the WCC as its General Secretary from its beginnings in 1948 until 1966, when he was succeeded by an American Presbyterian, Dr. Eugene Carson Blake.

The World Council of Churches by no means exhausts contemporary Protestant ecumenical endeavor. In 1960 Pastor Max Lackmann, a German Lutheran, co-founded the *League for Evangelical-Catholic Reunion*. This group was organized to advance the cause of a corporate union of Evangelical (Lutheran) Churches as a distinct rite within the Catholic Church.

In 1947 the Church of South India was formed, a merger of four Churches—United Presbyterian, Episcopalian, Methodist, and United Church of Christ. On December 4, 1960, Dr. Eugene Carson Blake, speaking at Grace Episcopal Cathedral, San Francisco, proposed a merger of the same four Churches in the United States. His proposal was seconded by Bishop James Pike, who followed him in the pulpit. The original four Churches were joined by another two, the Disciples of Christ and the Evangelical United Brethren, and there was established the *Consultation on Church Union*. The purpose of the Consultation was to explore the possibilities and procedures of a merger, the establishment of a united Church which would be, in the words of the participants, "truly catholic, truly evangelical, and truly reformed." The Blake-Pike plan seeks to unite the "catholic," i.e., sacramental emphasis, with the "evangelical," i.e., Biblical, and the "reformed," i.e., spontaneous. In 1965 the Consultation on Church Union was opened to other Churches, and has since included a number of other Churches in the merger talks.

Catholic Ecumenism in the 20th Century

The initial reaction of the Catholic Church to the Protestant ecumenical movement was one of hesitance and cautious suspicion. In 1919 Pope Benedict XV expressed keen interest in the movement and gave it his encouragement, but a Vatican decree was nevertheless issued forbidding Catholics to participate in ecumenical congresses except with the express permission of the Holy See. In 1928 Pope Pius XI published the encyclical *Mortalium Animos* in which he took the ecumenical movement severely to task for the direction it was taking at that time. He criticized those Protestant ecumenists who avoided theological discussion on the grounds that "doctrine divides, service unites." He encouraged the theological discussion of doctrines that Christians share in common, asserting that "unity of faith is the principal means that must unite the disciples of Christ."

Despite the "watch and wait" attitude of Catholic officialdom, there were a number of Catholic ecumenists who began individually to lay the groundwork for Catholic participation in the ecumenical movement. In France, Dom Lambert Beauduin established a monastery of monks of both Byzantine and Latin rites to prepare by study and prayer for Orthodox-Catholic reunion. In Germany, Father Josef Metzger founded in 1939 the *Una Sancta Confraternity* in order to pray for peace among Christians and build bridges of intellectual and spiritual understanding between separated Christian confessions, "emphasizing that which unites rather than that which divides." The *Una Sancta* gatherings were unhappily halted by World War II, and Father Metzger himself was killed in 1944.

With the pontificate of Pope Pius XII, the attitude of the Catholic Church toward ecumenism took a decidedly positive turn. In 1949 the Vatican issued an instruction entitled *Ecclesia Catholica*. It acknowledged that the ecumenical movement was awakened "under the inspiring grace of God," and entrusted bishops with the task of fostering ecumenical discussions by competent priests. The instruction required, however, that for Catholics to participate, such meetings had to be under Catholic sponsorship. Limited as it was, this instruction served as the charter for Catholic ecumenism until the advent of Pope John XXIII, Pope Paul VI, and Vatican Council II.

On January 25, 1959, the Feast of the Conversion of St. Paul and the last day of the Week of Prayer for Christian Unity, John XXIII announced his intention to summon an ecumenical council. Although the immediate purpose of the council was to be Catholic renewal and reform, its remote goal was to provide an "inspiration to seek that unity for which Jesus Christ prayed so ardently."

On Pentecost of 1960, Pope John announced the establishment of the *Secretariat for Promoting Christian Unity*. Under the leadership of Augustin Cardinal Bea, the Secretariat maintains relationships with non-Catholic Christian Churches throughout the world. During Vatican Council II the Secretariat supplied these Churches with authoritative information concerning the work of the Council, received and assessed their suggestions, and, where feasible, applied them. As a result of the labors of the Secretariat for Christian Unity, numerous official non-Catholic observer delegates were not only present at the Council but contributed to it; every single document promulgated by Vatican II was in some way affected by the suggestions of these observer delegates. In the wake of the Council, the Secretariat continues to function by directing and coordinating Catholic ecumenical activity throughout the world.

The success of the Secretariat for Christian Unity led Pope Paul VI to establish in 1964 a *Secretariat for Non-Christians*. Its purpose is to study non-Christian religions, maintain communications with them, and cooperate with them in the attainment of humanitarian goals. In 1965 Pope Paul instituted the *Secretariat for Non-Believers* in order to study and reflect upon the phenomenon of contemporary atheism and the problems it sets for the Christian religious conscience.

Pope Paul VI has shown himself to be a man sensitive to the ecumenical significance of symbolic gestures. In January 1964 he made a pilgrimage to the Holy Land where he met with Patriarch Athenagoras, Ecumenical Patriarch of all Eastern Orthodoxy. There, at the birthplace of Christ, the Pope and the Patriarch expressed their fraternal affection with an embrace, and declared their mutual concern for the cause of Christian unity. On December 4, 1965, at the Basilica of St. Paul's Outside the Walls, where Pope John first announced the Council, Pope Paul participated with several bishops and non-Catholic observer delegates in a "prayer service for promoting Christian unity." Three days later, on December 7, shortly before the close of the Council, Pope Paul, in solemn ceremonies at St. Peter's in Rome, and Patriarch Athenagoras, in his cathedral in Istanbul, both abrogated the nine-century-old excommunications which in 1054 had marked the beginning of the schism between East and West. This mutual abrogation had no real or theological effect, since the parties involved have been dead for nearly a thousand years and since the validity of the excommunications was doubtful in the first place. But certainly the gesture of the mutual abrogation had considerable symbolic value for Catholics and Orthodox alike.

Ecumenism in the Documents of the Second Vatican Council

The Second Vatican Council marked a definite turning point for ecumenism within the Catholic Church. Prior to the Council, apprehension or at best ambivalence characterized the official attitude toward the unity movement. The Johannine spirit of openness to the world and our times, however, infected the entire Church; it expressed itself at Vatican II in wholehearted acceptance of the ecumenical movement and the desire that every Catholic be part of it.

Almost all of the documents promulgated by the Second Vatican

Council have some significance for the ecumenical movement. Four of them, however, deserve special consideration here: the Dogmatic Constitution on the Church, the Declaration on Religious Freedom, the Pastoral Constitution on the Church in the Modern World, and, of course, the Decree on Ecumenism.

Dogmatic Constitution on the Church

The Dogmatic Constitution on the Church is considered the document most basic to the rest of the Council. Almost all else that came out of Vatican II flowed from it like a corollary. In clarifying the nature of the Church, particularly in highlighting the mystery of the Church, the Constitution did away with the overemphasis on the visible, juridical nature of the Church characteristic of Catholic theology since the Reformation. Without defining the meaning of membership in the Church, the Constitution describes the Church as a communion of life with Jesus Christ in which all validly baptized persons are sharers; it thus recognized that Orthodox and Protestants, along with Catholics, have been incorporated into the Church and share in its blessings. Also of immense ecumenical significance is the document's affirmation of the collegiality of bishops; it thus dissipated the unfortunate misunderstanding of the Church as a Papal monarchy.

Declaration on Religious Freedom

The Declaration on Religious Freedom is not by any means a revolutionary document. It states principles that modern society has come to accept as truisms, affirming that every man, because of his dignity as a human person, has an inviolable right to religious freedom. The document is significant in that it eliminated the long-standing ambiguity of a double standard—freedom and equality for the Catholic Church when it is a minority, and privilege for it when Catholics constitute the majority. In upholding the inherent freedom of the individual conscience, the Declaration opened the way toward new confidence in ecumenical relationships, particularly with Protestants, for whom religious freedom is of central importance. The document makes it clear that Catholics are bound to respect the faith and religious con-

victions of others, whether individuals or religious bodies. It
declares that all have the right, not only to immunity from religious coercion, not only to profess their faith openly and express
it in public acts of religious worship, but also to give witness to
their faith and thus, in a responsible manner, to seek converts.

Pastoral Constitution on the Church in the Modern World

The Pastoral Constitution on the Church in the Modern World
typifies the spirit of Vatican II perhaps better than any other
document. It reverses the hostility and entrenched defensiveness
that had characterized the Church's attitude toward the world
since the Council of Trent. It calls upon all Catholics to open
themselves to all men, to engage with them in dialogue, to
serve them—and to serve with them—as a sign and instrument
of solidarity. Gone are the polemics, the condemnations, the
exhortations to flee the world or even conquer it for Christ.
The message of this document pertains not only to Catholic attitudes; it pertains to the attitudes of all Christians toward all men.

Decree on Ecumenism

The Decree on Ecumenism is both a charter and a mandate for
Catholic involvement in the movement for Christian unity. It
calls for the full participation of Catholics in the ecumenical
movement and provides a number of basic principles to act as
guidelines for such participation. The following are some of the
chief principles enunciated by the Decree regarding the meaning,
aims, and methods of the ecumenical movement.

   1. Blame for the schisms which separate Christians must be
shouldered equally by all.

From her very beginning there arose in this one and only Church of
God certain rifts . . . which the apostle [Paul] strongly censures as
damnable. . . . But in subsequent centuries more widespread disagreements appeared and quite large Communities became separated from
full communion with the Catholic Church—developments for which,
at times, men of both sides were to blame. However, one cannot im-

pute the sin of separation to those who at present are born into these Communities and are instilled therein with Christ's faith. (No. 3)

St. John has testified: "If we say that we have not sinned, we make him [God] a liar, and his word is not in us" (1 Jn. 1:10). This holds good for sins against unity. Thus, in humble prayer, we beg pardon of God and our separated brethren, just as we forgive those who trespass against us. (No. 7)

2. Some degree of unity already exists between Catholics, Orthodox, and Protestants; because of our faith and baptism, we are already brothers in Christ.

For men who believe in Christ and have been properly baptized are brought into a certain, though imperfect, communion with the Catholic Church. Undoubtedly, the differences that exist in varying degrees between them and the Catholic Church—whether in doctrine and sometimes in discipline, or concerning the structure of the Church— do indeed create many and sometimes serious obstacles to full ecclesiastical communion. These the ecumenical movement is striving to overcome. Nevertheless, all those justified by faith through baptism are incorporated into Christ. They therefore have a right to be honored by the title of Christian, and are properly regarded as brothers in the Lord by the sons of the Catholic Church. (No. 3)

3. Our similarities far outweigh our dissimilarities; yet our differences are considerable.

We are indeed aware that among them views are held considerably different from the doctrine of the Catholic Church even concerning Christ, God's Word made flesh, and the work of redemption, and thus concerning the mystery and ministry of the Church and the role of Mary in the work of salvation. But we rejoice to see our separated brethren looking to Christ as the source and center of ecclesiastical communion. (No. 20)

. . . when Christians separated from us affirm the divine authority of the sacred Books, they think differently from us—different ones in different ways—about the relationship between the Scriptures and the Church. In the Church, according to Catholic belief, an authentic teaching office plays a special role in the explanation and proclamation of the written word of God. (No. 21)

Baptism . . . constitutes a sacramental bond of unity linking all who
have been reborn by means of it. But baptism, of itself, is only a beginning, a point of departure, for it is wholly directed toward the
acquiring of fullness of life in Christ. . . . The ecclesial Communities
separated from us lack that fullness of unity with us which should
flow from baptism, and we believe that especially because of the lack
of the sacrament of orders they have not preserved the genuine and
total reality of the Eucharistic mystery. (No. 22)

And if in moral matters there are many Christians who do not always
understand the gospel in the same way as Catholics, and do not admit
the same solutions for the more difficult problems of modern society,
nevertheless they share our desire to cling to Christ's words as the
source of Christian virtue . . . (No. 23)

4. Non-Catholic Christian Churches are truly Churches; God
uses them as instruments of grace and salvation, bringing men
closer to himself through them.

Moreover some, even very many, of the most significant elements or
endowments which together go to build up and give life to the Church
herself can exist outside the visible boundaries of the Catholic Church:
the written word of God; the life of grace; faith, hope, and charity,
along with other interior gifts of the Holy Spirit and visible elements.
All of these, which come from Christ and lead back to Him, belong
by right to the one Church of Christ. (No. 3)

. . . Catholics must joyfully acknowledge and esteem the truly Christian endowments from our common heritage which are to be found
among our separated brethren. It is right and salutary to recognize
the riches of Christ and virtuous works in the lives of others who are
bearing witness to Christ, sometimes even to the shedding of their
blood. For God is always wonderful in His works and worthy of
admiration. . . . Whatever is truly Christian never conflicts with the
genuine interests of the faith; indeed, it can always result in a more
ample realization of the very mystery of Christ and the Church.
(No. 4)

5. Despite the real, although imperfect, union which exists
among Christian Churches, no fullness of union can exist without
the Catholic Church.

. . . our separated brethren, whether considered as individuals or as Communities and Churches, are not blessed with that unity which Jesus Christ wished to bestow on all those whom He has regenerated and vivified into one body and newness of life—that unity which the holy Scriptures and the revered tradition of the Church proclaim. For it is through Christ's Catholic Church alone, which is the all-embracing means of salvation, that the fullness of the means of salvation can be obtained. (No. 3)

6. Ecumenism for Catholics demands working for the reform of the Church.

Every renewal of the Church essentially consists in an increase of fidelity to her own calling. Undoubtedly this explains the dynamism of the movement toward unity.

Christ summons the Church, as she goes her pilgrim way, to that continual reformation of which she always has need, insofar as she is an institution of men here on earth. Therefore, if the influence of events or of the times has led to deficiencies in conduct, in Church discipline, or even in the formulation of doctrine (which must be carefully distinguished from the deposit itself of faith), these should be appropriately rectified at the proper moment.

Church renewal therefore has notable ecumenical importance. Already this renewal is taking place in various spheres of the Church's life: the biblical and liturgical movements, the preaching of the word of God, catechetics, the apostolate of the laity, new forms of religious life and the spirituality of married life, and the Church's social teaching and activity. All these should be considered as favorable pledges and signs of ecumenical progress in the future. (No. 6)

There can be no ecumenism worthy of the name without a change of heart. . . . Let all Christ's faithful remember that the more purely they strive to live according to the gospel, the more they are fostering and even practicing Christian unity. For they can achieve depth and ease in strengthening mutual brotherhood to the degree that they enjoy profound communion with the Father, the Word, and the Spirit. (No. 7)

This change of heart and holiness of life, along with public and private prayer for the unity of Christians, should be regarded as the soul of the whole ecumenical movement, and can be rightly called "spiritual ecumenism." (No. 8)

7. The means for fostering Christian unity are prayer, study, and Christian cooperation.

Prayer

In certain special circumstances, such as in prayer services "for unity" and during ecumenical gatherings, it is allowable, indeed desirable, that Catholics should join in prayer with their separated brethren. Such prayers in common are certainly a very effective means of petitioning for the grace of unity, and they are a genuine expression of the ties which even now bind Catholics to their separated brethren. . . .

As for common worship, however, it may not be regarded as a means to be used indiscriminately for the restoration of unity among Christians. Such worship depends chiefly on two principles: it should signify the unity of the Church; it should provide a sharing in the means of grace. The fact that it should signify unity generally rules out common worship. Yet the gaining of a needed grace sometimes commends it.

The practical course to be adopted, after due regard has been given to all the circumstances of time, place, and personage, is left to the prudent decision of the local episcopal authority, unless the Bishops' Conference according to its own statutes, or the Holy See, has determined otherwise. (No. 8)[1]

Study

We must come to understand the outlook of our separated brethren. Study is absolutely required for this, and should be pursued with fidelity to truth and in a spirit of good will. When they are properly prepared for this study, Catholics need to acquire a more adequate understanding of the distinctive doctrines of our separated brethren.

[1] Local ecumenical commissions have now been established in many dioceses, and several of these commissions have already issued specific guidelines for interfaith worship and common prayer. General guidelines have also been suggested by the National Conference of Catholic Bishops, Committee on Ecumenical and Interreligious Affairs, 1312 Massachusetts Avenue, N.W., Washington, D.C. 20005.

. . . Of great value for this purpose are meetings between the two sides, especially for discussion of theological problems, where each can deal with the other on an equal footing. (No. 9)

When comparing doctrines, they [Catholic theologians engaged in ecumenical dialogue] should remember that in Catholic teaching there exists an order or "hierarchy" of truths, since they vary in their relationship to the foundation of the Christian faith. Thus the way will be opened for this kind of fraternal rivalry to incite all to a deeper realization and a clearer expression of the unfathomable riches of Christ . . . (No. 11)

Cooperation

Before the whole world, let all Christians profess their faith in God, one and three, in the incarnate Son of God, our Redeemer and Lord. United in their efforts, and with mutual respect, let them bear witness to our common hope, which does not play us false. Since in our times cooperation in social matters is very widely practiced, all men without exception are summoned to united effort. Those who believe in God have a stronger summons, but the strongest claims are laid on Christians, since they have been sealed with the name of Christ.

Cooperation among all Christians vividly expresses that bond which already unites them, and it sets in clearer relief the features of Christ the Servant. Such cooperation, which has already begun in many countries, should be ever increasingly developed, particularly in regions where a social and technical evolution is taking place. It should contribute to a just appreciation of the dignity of the human person, the promotion of the blessings of peace, the application of gospel sciences in a Christian spirit. Christians should also work together in the use of every possible means to relieve the afflictions of our times, such as famine and natural disasters, illiteracy and poverty, lack of housing, and the unequal distribution of wealth. Through such cooperation, all believers in Christ are able to learn easily how they can understand each other better and esteem each other more, and how the road to the unity of Christians may be made smooth. (No. 12)

The Mystery of Unity and Disunity

The Church is "a people made one with the unity of the Father, the Son, and the Holy Spirit." With these words, the Second Vatican Council defined the nature of the Church as a community. The very word "church" signifies an assembly or gathering, a bringing together into union the people of God. Oneness with God and with one another not only constitutes the nature of the Church, but it also implies the Church's dynamic character and mission.

Christians are united to God and to one another by several bonds or ties. Faith is the first and most fundamental of these bonds: "And without faith it is impossible to please [God]" (Heb. 11:6). Love serves to complete and vitalize faith: "If I have all faith, so as to remove mountains, but have not love," St. Paul wrote, "I am nothing" (1 Cor. 13:2). Baptism is the external expression chosen by Christ whereby a man's faith and love become united into the faith and love of the entire Church: "He who believes and is baptized," Jesus said, "will be saved" (Mark 16:16). The effect of faith, love, and baptism is grace, the overwhelming gift of God giving himself to men in the person of the Holy Spirit, making us sons of the Father and brothers to Jesus Christ: "You have received the spirit of sonship" (Rom. 8:15). The Church is essentially, therefore, a community of faith, love, baptism, and grace—a spiritual kingdom, internal and invisible.

But in order to be truly human, Christians express their supernatural and invisible union with Christ and with one another in a human fashion, externally, with visible ties. These external bonds of unity are the same for the Church today as they were when St. Luke described the early Christians in Jerusalem as "devoted . . . to the apostles' teaching and fellowship, to the breaking of bread and the prayers" (Acts 2:42). This external unity of the Church both expresses and reinforces its internal unity. It is both sign and cause of union and, as such, it is sacramental. It finds its ultimate expression in the sharing of the Eucharist.

The Church is not a static reality, however, which merely enjoys its oneness. It is a dynamic community, with the mission of both extending and intensifying itself. The Church renders perpetual the work of Christ's redemption by calling all men to the oneness of faith, love, and baptism. In other words, the Church acts as an instrument of reconciliation. Christ has given to his Church a share in his own mission: "As the Father has sent me, even so I send you" (John 20:21). In the words of the Vatican

Council, the Church has "the task of bringing all men to full union with Christ." Like the mustard seed, the leaven, the field of grain, the Church "grows visibly in the world through the power of God." But the Church's growth is also meant to be intensive. The New Testament is filled with the exhortations of Christ and the apostles to greater faith and love, disposing a man thereby to an increase of grace, an intensification of his union with God and all Christians in Christ. "Speaking the truth in love, we are to grow up in every way into him who is the head, into Christ" (Eph. 4:15); we are to "grow in the grace and knowledge of our Lord and Savior Jesus Christ" (2 Peter 3:18). And, in the words of the Vatican Council, "By the power of the gospel, the Holy Spirit makes the Church grow, perpetually renews her, and leads her to perfect union with her Spouse."

Despite many promising signs, the union of Christians with Christ in our 20th-century world is still imperfect and incomplete. The Church suffers from separations caused by selfishness and sin, separations of Christians from Christ, separations of Christians from one another. The Christian life is a dynamic process of decreasing in selfishness, so that Christ can increase his unifying presence in grace. The mere fact that we can increase in our union implies that this union is not yet complete, that some sort of separation still exists. While scripture leaves no doubt that Christ desired and prayed for unity in his Church, the history of Christianity is marred by factions and schisms, by selfishness and sinfulness. Why does God permit these to occur and to continue? Several reasons offer themselves as possibilities.

1. A man's entrance into the Church does not take away his freedom. The Church is human as well as divine; it is made up of men. God made men free, and he respects their freedom. As a result, a Christian, like any man, is free to sin, to separate himself from God and the Christian community. This separation constitutes its own punishment, self-inflicted but also just. Witnessing the ravages of the 16th-century Reformation, Pope Adrian VI pronounced the schism a terrible but deserved punishment visited upon the Church because of its sinfulness. The sinfulness of our own day, our own insufficiency of faith and love, contribute to the prolongation of that schism.

2. In order to follow in the footsteps of Christ, the Church is required to take up its cross. Certainly there is no heavier or more painful burden that the Church must bear than its own division. Schism is a cross, a sign of contradiction to what the Church is meant to be. Echoing the words of St. Paul, the Church is "crucified with Christ" (Gal. 2:19). Schism, like any suffering, even Christ's redemptive suffering, is not a good in itself; yet it can be offered to God, in love and submission, with patience and faith, for the eventual reconciliation of all men with God.

3. Schism, like all sufferings, too, can teach lessons which the Church needs to learn—lessons of humility, utter dependence upon God, and wisdom. In developing to so great an extent apart from one another, the mystical tradition of Orthodoxy, the prophetic tradition of Protestantism, and the priestly tradition of Catholicism have suffered grievously. But they have also gained insights which they very well might never have obtained otherwise. These are insights which we can now share with one another.

Despite our attempts to find meaning in our schisms, ultimately they remain a mystery. With Job we ponder the question why even good men suffer. But God still writes straight with crooked lines. God can draw good even out of evil, even out of sin. The schisms which separate Christians baffle us, much the same way the schism between Israel and the early Church baffled St. Paul: "O the depth of the riches and wisdom and knowledge of God! How unsearchable are his judgments and how inscrutable his ways!" (Rom. 11:33). But mystery should not snuff out hope. It was St. Paul too who wrote, "For we know that in everything God works for good with those who love him" (Rom. 8:28).

Conclusion:

Anyone who is serious about being Christian in this 20th century has been burdened at once with both a history and a hope. We have inherited a history remarkable for the loftiness of its ideals—but marked, too, by infidelity to those ideals, even to the point of scandal. Honest candor compels us to acknowledge that not only our fathers but we ourselves have proved disloyal to the ideals of Christian brotherhood and unity which Christ meant to characterize his Church. But the schisms which divide Christianity are not so complete that we cannot talk to each other. And here is the hope we have inherited, a hope that communication will bring about understanding, that from understanding there will come love. And there is no limit to what God can do with love.

Ecumenical dialogue and encounter will not provide a panacea to all the Church's ills, but it can provide a beginning toward the healing of those ills. The Decree on Ecumenism states: "We must come to understand the outlook of our separated brethren. Study is absolutely required for this, and should be pursued with fidelity to truth and in a spirit of good will." With some idea of the meaning and the mystery, the aims and the history of ecumenism, an attempt will now be made to understand the history, faith, and religious life of those with whom we Catholics live in today's pluralistic society. A sincere effort has been made to be accurate, to pursue this understanding "with fidelity to truth." Of a certainty, it was done "in a spirit of good will."

Suggested Reading

Alting von Geusau, Leo G. M., ed. *Ecumenism and the Roman Catholic Church*. Newman, 1966.

Baum, Gregory. *The Catholic Quest for Christian Unity*. Paulist, 1962.

Bea, Augustin Cardinal. *The Way to Unity after the Council*. Herder, 1967.

Brown, Robert McAfee. *The Ecumenical Revolution*. Doubleday, 1967.

Brown, Robert McAfee, and Gustave Weigel. *An American Dialogue*. Part I, Ch. 2, "Preliminaries," Ch. 6, "Ecumenism"; Part II, Ch. 7, "Envoie." Doubleday, 1960.

Congar, Yves. *Dialogue between Christians*. Newman, 1966.

Dulles, Avery. *The Dimensions of the Church*. Newman, 1967.

Horton, Douglas. *Toward an Undivided Church*. Association Press, 1967.

Leenhardt, Franz J. *Two Biblical Faiths: Protestant and Catholic*. Westminster Press, 1964.

Persson, Per Erik. *Roman and Evangelical*. Fortress Press, 1964.

Sheerin, John B. *The Ecumenical Movement and American Catholicism.* Hawthorn, 1966.

Skydsgaard, K. E. *One in Christ.* Alex C. Kildegaard, tr. Fortress Press, 1957.

Tavard, George H. *Two Centuries of Ecumenism.* New American Library, 1962.

———— *Understanding Protestantism.* Ch. 10, "Ecumenical Dimension." Paulist, 1964.

2 / Judaism and Christianity:
The Olive Tree and the Branch

. . . some of the branches were broken off, and you, a wild olive shoot, were grafted in their place to share the richness of the olive tree . . . (Rom. 11:17)

The ecumenical movement is concerned primarily with the achievement of Christian unity, the elimination of all schisms dividing those who profess Jesus Christ to be Lord and Savior. But ecumenism also implies a climate, an attitude of openness to and respect for those who are not Christian. It involves both a willingness to understand their faith and a desire to cooperate with them in the service of mankind. In this broader sense, Christians are able to enter into ecumenical dialogue with those who do not accept Jesus as the Christ. Because of the wealth of spiritual heritage which they hold in common, Christians are especially encouraged to establish such communication with Jews.

The benefits which can derive from Jewish-Christian dialogue are many and mutual. When Pope Pius XII remarked that "spiritually, we are all Semites," he was pointing to the many and deep roots which the Church has in Jewish history, doctrine, and religious life. To be a Christian means to be a "Messianist," a disciple of a Jew who by his birth, breeding, manner of life, and mode of teaching was wholly and unreservedly a *Ben B'rith,* a "Son of the Covenant." No Christian can truly understand his own religion unless he understands the Judaism which Jesus practiced. The more Christian a man becomes, the more Semitic will be his faith. Such understanding, together with a brotherly cooperation in meeting the needs of society today, can lead to a new chapter in the history of the Church and the Synagogue, one which will do honor to the God of Abraham, Isaac, Jacob, and Jesus Christ.

The History of Judaism

The Patriarchs and God's Promise

From Ur of the Chaldees, covered today by the dust of four thousand years, there came Abraham, revered as a Patriarch by Jews, Christians, and Moslems. By all of these faiths it is believed that God entered into human history, revealing himself to Abraham as the one true God and promising to him a family which would multiply more numerous than the "stars in the sky and the sands on the shore." The generations from Abraham to Isaac to Jacob to his twelve sons were recounted down the centuries until finally recorded in the first book of the Hebrew Bible, known to Christians as the Old Testament.

The Book of Genesis relates how the small Semitic clan came to settle in Egypt; the book of Exodus recounts their escape from servitude there several centuries later, now a people made up of twelve tribes. Israel's exodus from Egypt was followed by the most momentous event in all its history, its election by God as his very own people. The faith of every believing Jew today is based upon the *B'rith,* the Covenant, which God made over three thousand years ago with Israel, whereby Israel became God's chosen people. And to this day the most frequently uttered prayer of every Jew is the great *Shema,* "Hear, O Israel, the Lord is your God, the Lord alone."

Moses, who was instrumental in leading Israel out of Egypt, was also the great mediator between God and Israel in the relating of the *Torah,* or Law, the first five books of the Bible, known as the five books of Moses. To these five books were eventually added the subsequent history of the Israelites, their conquest of the Promised Land, their unification into a kingdom, and their golden age under Kings David and Solomon. Prayer-poems, love songs, proverbs, and the sermons of the prophets all came to be added to the original Mosaic Torah, and all came to be revered as the inspired word of God. The defeat of Israel by its neighbors and subsequent deportation to other lands impressed upon them their di. ?rentness, their chosenness. In this Diaspora, they found in their sacred scripture a source of religious and cultural solidarity. The Jews eventually came to be regarded by their neighbors as the "people of the Book."

Throughout the Hebrew Bible there exists a certain polarity, a vision which strains in two directions. One looks back to the past, to the faith and traditions of the Patriarchs, to the Covenant and Law of Moses. The other looks forward to the future, to the promise made by God to Israel of the Messianic age, in which universal justice and peace would prevail and all men would come to know and worship the one true God. Particularly with the political defeat of Israel and the cessation of the monarchy, Jews both in Palestine and scattered abroad in the Diaspora began to await more intensely the fulfillment of God's promise. They looked forward to the coming of the Messiah, who would usher in a new era. For Christians the fulfillment of that promise came in the person of Jesus Christ.

Rejection of Jesus as the Messiah

It is a fact of history and a mystery of faith for Christians that the great masses of the Jewish people at the time of the apostles did not accept Jesus as the Messiah. For St. Paul, a Pharisee devoted to the Law and to his ancestral traditions and a convert to Christianity, it was a source of personal anguish: "I could wish that I myself were accursed and cut off from Christ for the sake of my brethren, my kinsmen by race" (Rom. 9:3).

Jesus did not fulfill the expectations of Israel for several reasons. For one, a new order of things was anticipated: the end of oppression, universal peace and justice, the cessation of all sin. For another, the Messiah was expected to be simply a man; the Christian claim that Jesus was the Son of God made man offended the sensibilities of most Jews, for whom God could not be a trinity and for whom an incarnation in any material form was totally contrary to God's absolute otherness.

To St. Paul, however, it was ultimately God's will that the Jews did not accept Jesus as the Christ; here was a mystery beyond comprehension, but not beyond acceptance: "O the depth of the riches and wisdom and knowledge of God! How unsearchable are his judgments and how inscrutable his ways!" (Rom. 11:33).

St. Paul made it clear, despite the separation which was widening between the early Church and the Synagogue, that Jews and Christians were still brothers, worshipers of the same God: "For there is no distinction between Jew and Greek; the same Lord is the Lord of all and bestows his riches upon all who call upon him. For, 'every one who calls upon the name of the Lord will be saved' " (Rom. 10:12–13). Paul also emphasized the fact that God had not rejected Israel, that the Jews are still heirs of God's promise: "For the gifts and the call of God are irrevocable" (Rom. 11:29).

Judaism did not come to an end with the Old Testament. Indeed, the Jews do not accept the Mosaic Covenant as being old but ever new, the one and only testament. The fall of Jerusalem some forty years after Christ did not put an end to Jewish life or the development of its faith. But it did deprive the Jews of any homeland they could call their own and left them a minority in any land they settled. This minority status, together with their self-imposed segregation from the religious and cultural milieu in which they lived, made the Jews a very visible and vulnerable prey to suspicion and persecution. The next fifteen hundred years of Jewish history are both a scandal and a source of bitterness, marked by an anti-Semitism which to this day has not been laid to rest.

Anti-Semitism

The history of anti-Semitism is one of which most Christians are blissfully ignorant. Because it comprises so great a part of their history, however, Jews are painfully aware of the pogroms and persecutions which have marked the last twenty-three centuries of their existence. Anti-Semitism is by no means solely a Christian attitude; but because of its prominence during the height of the Church's influence, many Jews have equated anti-Semitism with Christianity. A betterment of Jewish-Christian relations today is inconceivable without a realistic appraisal of the bitterness which marred them for so long.

Anti-Semitism did not begin with the Christian era. Some eighty-eight years before the birth of Christ, mob assaults were made upon the Jews of Alexandria in Egypt, then the largest colony of Jews outside of Palestine. The first real pogrom occurred there in 38 A.D. The Greco-Roman world resented the aloofness, sense of superiority, and claim of uniqueness which Judasim exhibited toward its Hellenistic conquerors. By retaining their distinctive characteristics and refusing to give up their identity, the Jews—a sizable minority of about five million persons at the time of Christ, about one-eighth the population of the entire Roman Empire—set themselves off from the Greco-Roman world.

In addition to their visible aloofness, Jews, even before the time of Christ, had provoked resentment and anger by a new and concentrated missionary outlook. Militant proselytizing had brought many Gentiles to identify themselves with the Jewish community and the worship of one God. This influence was sufficiently great to create a sense of rivalry between the proud conquerors and the politically negligible Jewish minority; and the very idea of a rivalry further irritated the Greco-Roman majority. Separatism was an essential part of Jewish religion and mores, a separatism based upon a conviction of superiority. In turn, Jewish intolerance of religious or cultural defilement wounded Roman sensitivities, generating reactions of contempt, anger, and even hatred.

The advent of Christianity upon the Gentile world should have resulted in the irradication of anti-Semitism. Once they encountered Christ, Gentiles should have risen above their previous anti-Jewish bias. Unfortunately, they did not. Instead, they received but another excuse for its existence. Jewish involvement in Christ's crucifixion became a new rationalization for resenting the Jews. It came to be forgotten that Jesus, his mother Mary, the apostles, and most of the early Church were all Jews. Instead, the small band of Jewish priests and rabbis who were influential in Christ's conviction and execution came to be considered as representative of the entire people. Then too, the early Church suffered hostility from the Synagogue, with persecutions at times instigated by Jews. And the refusal of the Jews to accept Jesus as the Messiah came more and more to be regarded as blindness and malice. All these factors became additional sources of resentment against Jews. Judaism's missionary zeal further evoked fears among Christians, who saw Judaism as a rival of their own universalist aspirations.

The fourth century was a time of triumph for the Church, defeat for the Synagogue. As Christianity came to be accepted as the official religion of the Roman Empire, the status of Jews began to deteriorate. Under the new Christian empire, privileges which they had previously enjoyed were withdrawn from the Jews. Forbidden to own slaves, lest they make converts of them, the Jews were thus deprived of earning a living from agriculture. Public office was closed to them, because it did not seem fit for "unbelievers" to rule over Christians. The refusal of the Synagogue to join the Church was a source of scandal to Christians and a source of worry to their pastors. Outstanding bishops of the Church, including St. Gregory of Nyssa, St. Ambrose, and above all, St. John Chrysostom, denounced the Jews as "slayers of the Lord, enemies of God, advocates of the devil, and haters of goodness." Compulsory baptism became a common practice after a time, until censured severely by Pope Gregory the Great in the sixth century. Thanks to Pope Gregory and his immense influence on subsequent centuries, there was inaugurated with respect to Jews a "policy of humanity, equity, and relative protection." But there were always exceptions.

In 1096 ill-organized hordes of monks, nobles, knights, and peasants set off from their homes to free the Holy Land from the unbelieving Turk. With "God will it" upon their lips, the First Crusade set out to combat the enemies of God in the East. Enroute, however, the militant zeal of these would-be missionaries came to be directed toward the unbelievers right in their midst, the Jews. Despite the protests of local bishops, entire Jewish communities were compelled to accept baptism or death. Mob action was reinforced by religious fanaticism; massacres ensued, resulting in the death of up to ten thousand Jews. When the Crusaders finally arrived at Jerusalem in 1099, they found the Jews of that city assembled in a synagogue, which they then set ablaze.

During the subsequent Middle Ages, Jews became quite active

in money-lending, an occupation closed to Christians who were forbidden to collect interest. This did not in any way endear them to either the Christian clergy or populace. Although many Jews were able to acquire considerable wealth, they periodically suffered confiscation, cancellation of debts owed to them, and physical abuse—now for reasons not only religious but also economic. Libelous stories of Jews engaging in the ritual murder of infants became popular during this period and gave them a Satanic image. When the Black Death swept Europe in the mid-14th century, taking with it one-third of the population, Jews were blamed for poisoning the wells and, in some localities, were put to death at the stake. Even outside of the pogroms, in times of relative peace, the lot of the Jews at the hands of Christians was not a happy one. They were compelled to wear a distinctive badge or dress, singling them out from the rest of the community. They were obliged to gather regularly to listen to sermons by friars who would extol Christianity and denounce the errors of Judaism. They were required to live in a ghetto, segregated from the rest of the populace, and often enough expelled from their homes with scant notice. The Jews of the Middle Ages found their only hope and protection in the Popes, many of whom upheld Jewish rights, set penalties for attacks on synagogues, and decreed that Jewish clergy should be accorded the same privileges as Christian clergy. Pope Martin V, in a decree, said:

. . . we command that they [the Jews] be not molested in their Synagogues; that their laws, rights and customs be not assailed; that they not be baptized by force, made to observe Christian festivals, or to wear new badges, and that they not be hindered in their business relations with Christians.

Yet time and the forces of suspicion, fear, and hatred too often proved stronger than a sense of justice or tolerance. In the 14th century in France, one hundred thousand Jews were arrested in one day and orders were given that they be deported within a month. In 1492 King Ferdinand deported three hundred thousand Spanish Jews—the entire Jewish community, which had predated

Christians in Spain—and confiscated all their property. Thousands of Jews sought refuge in Poland, where they were permitted considerable independence. Here they attained a prominence and measure of self-government which they had not enjoyed since before the destruction of Jerusalem. But when the Eastern Orthodox Cossacks allied themselves with the Tartars in the 17th century and invaded Poland with anti-Roman-Catholic fanaticism, they reserved their fiercest atrocities for the Jews. From 1648 to 1658 the Jews of some seven hundred communities were massacred, a toll of five hundred thousand lives.

Jews usually mark their emancipation from religious and cultural servitude with the French Revolution and the spread of democratic ideals throughout Europe. The demise of Christian influence over the political affairs of Europe did not coincide altogether, however, with the demise of anti-Semitism. We have no cause to judge self-righteously the crimes of the past. Our own generation has witnessed the greatest holocaust of all. The popular appeal of Hitler's Nazism and its ability to attract and unite the various and disparate segments of German society can be explained in great part by its fierce anti-Semitism. Before the fall of the Third Reich, six million Jewish lives were sacrificed in the most scientific and calculated attempt at genocide ever conceived.

The persecution of Jews is both a sin and a shame which can never rest easy upon the Christian conscience. That so much of it was perpetrated in the name of Christ, himself a Jew, is a scandal. In the light of the Biblical and dogmatic foundations which have often been claimed in anti-Semitic calumnies, the Second Vatican Council felt constrained to invoke the supreme teaching authority of the Catholic Church to reject once and for all the doctrines that the Jews were responsible for the death of Christ and that they have been rejected or accursed by God:

True, authorities of the Jews and those who followed their lead pressed for the death of Christ . . .; still, what happened in His passion cannot be blamed on all the Jews then living, without distinction, nor upon the Jews of today. Although the church is the new people of God, the Jews should not be presented as repudiated or cursed by God, as if such views followed from the holy Scriptures. . . . The Church repudiates all persecutions against any man. Moreover, mindful of her common patrimony with the Jews, and motivated by the gospel's spiritual love and by no political considerations, she deplores the hatred, persecutions, and displays of anti-Semitism directed against the Jews at any time and from any source. (Declaration on Non-Christian Religions, No. 4)

It should be made clear that Vatican Council II did not presume in any way to absolve or exonerate Jews from guilt for Christ's crucifixion. It did not absolve, because absolution was not needed. Rather, the Council declared them innocent of any responsibility beyond that shared by the entire human race.

Confronted for the first time by the chronicle of Christian anti-Semitism, a Catholic inevitably reacts with embarrassed amazement and no little discomfort. It is not a history to be proud of. But even as today's Jews are not guilty of Christ's death, neither are today's Christians guilty of the anti-Jewish persecutions of the Middle Ages. The responsibility, whether of Christians or of Jews, is neither collective or retroactive. "The son shall not suffer for the iniquity of the father" (Ezek. 18:20). Nevertheless, it can be reasonably regretted that there was not given at Vatican Council II some word or gesture of Christian sorrow for the sinful lack of Christ-like charity toward Jews in the past. Such a symbolic act would certainly not have been devoid of significance.

The Talmud

The Jewish response to their misfortunes was the *Talmud,* a vast religious literature which directs and inspires Jewish life even today. The Talmud was formulated over a period of some seven hundred years, from 200 B.C. to 500 A.D., but its oral traditions go perhaps as far back as Moses. The Jewish exile of 500 B.C. witnessed the inauguration of two new institutions within Jewish life, the Synagogue and the Rabbinate. Even after the exile both institutions continued to flourish, particularly in the Diaspora, but even in Palestine. When the destruction of Jerusalem in 70 A.D. witnessed the end of both the Temple and the Priesthood, leadership and the task of preserving Judaism fell to the Rabbinate.

Rabbinic Judaism is recorded in the more than six thousand pages of the Talmud, the teachings of over two thousand rabbis who lived in Palestine and Babylonia. At first these teachings and traditions were oral; they were not committed to writing so as not to rival in any way the Torah, the Hebrew Bible. Eventually, however, recording these many traditions became an absolute necessity lest they be lost, and in 200 A.D. the first written compilation was edited and codified, the Mishnah. About the year 500 A.D. a second compilation of subsequent religious discussions and developments was made, the Gemara. The two compilations were gathered together to form the Talmud, the basic document of Rabbinic Judaism.

Two forms of literature are to be found in the Talmud. One is *halakah* (literally, "walking"), a record of the 613 commandments to be found in the Hebrew Bible and the application of these laws to various and changing circumstances. It is the practical application of the humanitarian ideals of the Torah to everyday life. The other form of literature found in the Talmud is *haggadah* (literally, "story"), ranging from prose and poetry passages on philosophy, theology, medicine, and mathematics to homely stories meant to inspire and edify.

The Talmud made possible the accommodation of Judaism to the hostile world which it had so often to face—a world of exile and dispersion. Its study was considered to be one of the greatest virtues a Jew could have. When the rest of Europe suffered from illiteracy during the Dark Ages, Jews continued to pore over the Talmud and thus maintained a tradition of both literacy and scholarship. To have one's son become a gifted Talmudic student was the devout wish of every Jewish parent. The Talmud proved to be the unshakable rock of Jewish survival, defying all the ordeals of the Diaspora. It established patterns of living that encompassed the entire life-situation of the Jewish community, enabling Jews to exist as a culture within an alien environment. It has been said that "more than the Jewish people preserving the Talmud, the Talmud preserved the Jewish people." If the Jews were the "people of the Book," the Talmud was the "Book of the people."

Judaism Today

Although the religious life of Jews today has its roots in the Rabbinic Judaism of the Talmud, it is more directly the product of the modern temper which Jews began to acquire in the early 19th century when the spirit of the Enlightenment began to affect the Jews of Western Europe. Many rabbis were willing to build bridges linking the new knowledge generated by scientific inquiry to Jewish religious thought. Attempts were made to update traditional Judaism, to bring it more into accord with the contemporary Western landscape. They resulted in the establishment of Reform and Conservative Judaism as alternatives to Orthodox Judaism.

In Eastern Europe the spirit of the Enlightenment did not reach the Jews until the second half of the 19th century. There a new phenomenon began to spread among the Jews of the Russian empire, a romantic expression of nationalism, which resulted in *Zionism*—a movement which held that, since the Jews formed a separate nationality, they had a right to a separate nation, a publicly recognized state of their own. Theodor Herzl, in his book *The Jewish State,* fired the hearts of his Jewish compatriots with a wild dream of their own homeland back in Palestine. In 1948 the establishment of the State of Israel saw the realization of that dream and the inauguration of what is termed by some as a new development in the history of the Covenant.

Orthodox Judaism—or Traditional Judaism, as its leaders prefer to name it—regards as authoritative and binding both the written law of Moses and the oral law of the Rabbinate as contained in the Talmud. It believes that every question facing man today can be answered in the light of these ancient teachings and insists that any other approach contradicts authentic Judaism and will lead to eventual assimilation of the Jewish people. Orthodox Jews adhere to belief in the literal revelation of the Torah and to the need to submit in every instance to the teachings of the Talmud.

Orthodox Jews are characterized by an almost instinctive tendency to meet every life-situation with what is called a "Torah-true approach." Since the principles and precedents of Jewish law and tradition must be mastered in order to be applied to each situation, Orthodox Jews place a strong emphasis upon education and religious scholarship. When questions of profound difficulty arise, the Orthodox Jew turns to his rabbi for a judgment. Strict adherence to the Talmudic interpretations of the Torah makes considerable demands upon Orthodox Jews, particularly in observing Kosher dietary practices and refraining from work on the Sabbath. Orthodox Jews retain their belief and expectation of a personal Messiah.

After many years of decline, Orthodox Judaism is experiencing something of a resurgence in its membership. The basic strength of Orthodox Judaism, however, is seen not so much in its number of adherents as in its witness to all Jews of the fullness of their tradition, even among those who do not always accept all of its teachings.

Reform Judaism believes that the forms of religion which reflect particular historic or cultural situations should change as life changes. The discoveries of science, history, and comparative religion gave rise to the Reform movement within Judaism in the mid-19th century, chiefly in Germany and the United States. Reform Judaism broke with the Rabbinic tradition and denied the binding authority of the Torah and the Talmud on questions of ceremonial and ritual law. In denying the supernatural authority of the Bible, Reform Judaism came to emphasize instead the ethical teachings of the prophets. At the center of its theological interest was Israel's mission and vocation to give to the world "ethical monotheism." Reform Judaism has given up the belief in a personal Messiah and has replaced it with the expectation of an earthly kingdom in which universal justice and peace will prevail. It does not accept a literalist interpretation of the Bible and prefers to be selective in what is considered human and what is considered divine in the scriptures.

Reform Jews have been noted for radical experimentation in almost every sphere of Jewish religious practice. Their houses of worship are generally called temples rather than synagogues, and here the prayers are in English as well as Hebrew. For a time the Saturday Sabbath, hallowed by tradition, was almost replaced by worship on Sunday mornings instead. The Kosher dietary laws are generally not observed by Reform Jews. Neither do they refrain strictly from work on the Sabbath and holy days, although many Reform Jews still observe the ritual of lighting candles on Friday evening and the ceremonies related to the Biblical festivals.

Reform Judaism still tends to be liberal and experimental in its approach to religion; but it has retraced some of its earlier departures, reintroducing in recent years much that is traditional. Its humanist and naturalist approach to God and religion are gradually being replaced by more traditional Jewish theological attitudes. Today the most significant differences between Orthodox and Reform Judaism are concerned not with religious belief but with ritual practices.

Conservative Judaism occupies the center between Traditional and Reform Judaism. While many Jewish scholars agreed with the purposes of Reform Judaism in accommodating its spirit and practice to the contemporary world, they felt that it had over-emphasized the universal elements in the Jewish past to the detriment of that which was uniquely Hebraic. The Conservative movement arose as an attempt to preserve historical Judaism, even in its present situation, by emphasizing the distinctively Jewish elements of tradition.

Unlike the Reform movement, Conservative Judaism believes that Rabbinical law is binding; but, unlike Traditional Judaism, it also believes that the law is susceptible to change. Depending upon the local congregation, Conservative Jews sometimes resemble Traditional Jews, while at other times they lean more closely to the Jews of the Reform. Along with Traditional Jews, they emphasize the importance of the Torah and of Israel's supernatural role in religious history. With the Reform Jews, they share an emphasis on the ethical teachings of the prophets and a concern for social justice.

All three branches of modern Judaism hold more in common than their divisions seem to indicate. Each group has its own interpretation of Jewish tradition. There are differences in ceremonial practices and, in some instances, even in religious beliefs. Yet Jews in all three of these branches, and even Jews who no longer believe in God or observe the Law, all have one thing in common: association with the Jewish community. It is this association, more than any creed or religious practice, which makes a person a Jew.

Judaism does not have an official creed, since there is no central religious body authorized to establish one. But it does have its own unique attitudes about God, man, and the world; these attitudes comprise the Spirit of Judaism.

The Spirit of Judaism

God

"Hear, O Israel, the Lord, our God, the Lord is One"—this statement of belief, recited three times daily in prayer, is the central religious affirmation of Judaism. Belief in and worship of the One God is one of the great contributions of Judaism to the world. God, for historical Judaism, is not a vague force or abstract principle. He has a name. He is a person. But beyond this, for a Jew, there is little which can be known about God in himself, for he is spiritual, ineffable, totally beyond man's conceptive ability. A reverential agnosticism characterizes Judaism, an unwillingness to accord God a bodily form or to admit that a physical form could ever represent him.

Although in himself God is three times holy, that is, completely transcendent and unknowable to us in himself, yet God can be known in his actions, in his relationships with man. For God has revealed himself to men, and he has shown himself to be a redeemer. When God revealed in the Ten Commandments, "I am the Lord, your God," he added, "who led you out of Egypt." Jewish emphasis upon God's saving activity, especially at the Exodus, disproves the erroneous but prevalent belief that, unlike Christians who concentrate on God's goodness and mercy, Jews concentrate upon his justice and wrath. Some of the most exalted descriptions of God's love for men are to be found in the Hebrew scriptures. In the festive commemoration of any Jewish historical event, it is God—and not Moses or some other hero—who is hailed as the Savior of Israel. Beyond this Judaism is unwilling to go. It is reluctant to speculate about God except in terms of what he is not. The rabbis have traditionally been religious existentialists rather than speculative philosophers, more concerned about what God does than what he is.

In the light of these Jewish emphases, it is understandable why Jews find it difficult to accept the divine sonship of Jesus Christ and the implied Christian doctrines of the Trinity and the Incarnation. Jews admit that God can and has entered into human history, but not human flesh. The Messiah, according to traditional Judaism, will be a man, not a God-Man. Orthodox Jews still await the Messiah, a personal messenger from God who will restore Israel to its former glory and usher in universal peace. Conservative and Reform Jews by and large do not expect a personal Messiah, but do look forward to a Messianic age, not necessarily outside of human history, when ethical perfection will prevail for all men. Jews tend, therefore, to look upon Jesus not as Son of God, Savior, or Messiah, but simply as Rabbi who at best helped prepare the world to worship the One God and to accept the Messianic age once it does come.

Man

Judaism tends to be man-centered. More than being ethical monotheism, it is monotheistic ethics. The very first book of the Torah, Genesis, relates not only that God created man in his image but that God gave to man dominion over all the rest of creation. According to Rabbinic teaching, God placed in man a potency to imitate his justice and mercy and a mission to complete God's creation of the universe. The precepts of the Torah are an aid to conform human behavior to the divine plan. The 613 *mitzvoth,* or laws, were given to men, not to make them holy, but to enable them to fulfill God's will. Judaism believes that man, in fulfilling these commandments, gives expression to his belief both in God and in the meaningfulness of human life.

Judaism has no doctrine of original sin. It admits in man, along with a tendency toward good, a tendency toward evil, which leads to sin and which in turn requires repentance. But its outlook is generally one of moral and cosmic optimism: "And God saw everything that he had made, and behold, it was very good" (Gen.

1:31). Sin is not viewed as an alienation from God, since Judaism does not accept the doctrine of grace and personal union with God. But Jews do believe that the covenant between God and Israel binds them all to God and that obedience to his law brings about an experience of his nearness greater than that given to any other people. This covenant, rendering the Jews as God's chosen people, constitutes for them not only a privilege but also a burden: the necessity of being more faithful and obedient to his law. Otherwise, God will punish them more severely than he would another people. Yet, Jews believe, God will never totally reject them.

Christians have tended to hold that with the advent of Jesus Christ, God's covenant with Israel came to an end. We forget Christ's statement that he had come "not to destroy the Torah but to fulfill it." When St. Paul affirmed, in regard to his fellow Jews, even those who did not accept Jesus as the Messiah, that God is faithful to his promises ("the gifts and the call of God are irrevocable" [Rom. 11:29]), he was simply repeating the promise made by God through Isaiah: "Can a woman forget her child . . . Even these may forget, yet I will not forget you" (Isaiah 49:15). For Jews, their covenant with God is not old but ever new; the Hebrew Bible is not an Old Testament but, rather, an inspired living sacred scripture. In the light of this covenant, and as affirmed by St. Paul, Christians cannot regard Jewish life and worship as mere empty form. God remains present in his gifts to Israel. "The Christian Church is not dependent on a second covenant made with it alone, but on the single original covenant in which, by the grace of Jesus Christ and the hard labor of the Apostle Paul, the Church enjoys a share—along with the Jewish people" (Leonard Swidler and Marc Tanenbaum, *Jewish-Christian Dialogues,* p. 7).

The World

Judaism is primarily a religion of the here and now, not the hereafter. It believes in the doctrines of resurrection and immortality, holding that in God's universe nothing precious is ever lost and therefore that life does not end with death. But Jewish theology is extremely reticent about dwelling upon the subjects of death, judgment, heaven and hell, and refuses to speculate about their nature. The Talmud advises men against trying to penetrate beyond the boundaries of this world. It teaches that "one hour of repentance and good works in this world is better than the whole life of the world to come." Judaism concentrates on this world and how it can be made into a better place to live. The kingdom of God, which mankind is meant to build with God's help, is, in Judaism's view, definitely of this world. Man's tasks and responsibilities are centered here. He is to hallow life and raise it to its highest estate, thereby cooperating with God in ruling the earth and carrying it forward to its completion.

The Jewish Community

In the light of the foregoing, it can readily be seen that doctrines contained in Jewish theology are not considered by themselves or as ends in themselves. They are oriented toward practice. Judaism is a life, a life dedicated to expressing in human action the basic belief that man's life in this world has a meaning, because God exists and gives it meaning. But even this basic belief does not fully express the spirit of Judaism. As summarized by Rabbi Robert Gordis: "He who understands Judaism from within knows that the Jewish group cannot be subsumed under alien and inappropriate categories. The usual terms 'religion,' 'nationality,' or that most bloodstained of words, 'race,' are not applicable to the Jewish community" (J. Bruce Long, ed., *Judaism and the Christain Seminary Curriculum*, p. 129). What is most consistently to be recognized as "Jewish," whether or not an individual Jew seeks out the values and rites of the Synagogue, is some positive manifestation of loyalty to and identification with the Jewish people. Judaism is a life, and it is the Jewish people who make it what it is.

Jewish Life and Worship

The Synagogue

The Synagogue arose in Jewish life out of a need for a "portable sanctuary," when the Temple of Solomon was destroyed in 586 B.C. and the Jewish people found themselves in exile from their homeland. The exiles sought to bind themselves together in religious devotions, particularly the reading and study of the scriptures. Since neither priesthood nor altar were permitted outside Jerusalem, the activities of the Synagogue from the very first were centered in the congregation. Even after the return to Jerusalem and the rebuilding of the Temple, the Synagogue remained as a Jewish religious institution, functioning as a house of prayer, a house of study, and a house of assembly.

The synagogue serves as a center for congregational prayer three times a day, morning, afternoon, and evening. Any male Jew may lead these services. They are collected, along with the other formal prayers of Jewish worship, in the official prayer book of Judaism, the *Siddur*. The central prayers of the Siddur are the 150 Psalms. Prayer, for the Jew, is the "service of the heart" and usually reflects the oneness of God, his love for Israel, and his fidelity to his promises.

The structure of most Jewish services is built around the prayer "Hear, O Israel, the Lord, our God, the Lord is One," together with a prayer entitled the "Eighteen Benedictions." In Orthodox and Conservative congregations most of the services are still conducted in Hebrew, although the reading from scripture and the sermon are in English. Such services do not require the presence of a rabbi. A congregation of ten men or boys who have made their *bar mitzvah,* i.e., who have passed their thirteenth birthday, is all that is required.

The synagogue is also a "house of study." The very word for "synagogue" in Yiddish is *schule,* which means "school." The reading and teaching of the Torah became the central feature of Jewish public worship, so much so that the study of the Torah became as important as prayer itself. Every synagogue, no matter how humble, inevitably has a library-study hall where not only the sacred books are available, but also books dealing with the philosophy, theology, history, and jurisprudence of Judaism. Scholarship has traditionally prevailed as an outstanding characteristic of the Jewish people.

The synagogue also serves as a "house of assembly." Here matters of public and communal concern are discussed. In the early synagogues courts of law met to adjudicate questions and redress wrongs. Today the synagogues serve as civic and cultural centers within the Jewish community where the human needs of members are considered no less important than their spiritual needs.

A visit to a synagogue will impress the stranger with the absolute absence of images and the scarceness even of symbols. It was feared that these might become objects of worship and thus jeopardize the essential spirituality of the Torah. The center of the sanctuary is the Ark, an enclosure which contains the Torah scroll. A light burns perpetually before the Ark symbolizing the eternity of faith. Upon entering a Conservative or Orthodox synagogue, all men, whether Jewish or not, are expected to cover their heads with a *yarmulke,* a skullcap. It is a sign of respect which arose out of the East and, in a synagogue, denotes an attitude of reverence in the presence of God. Also worn by Jewish men at a synagogue service is the *tallith,* a prayer shawl with fringes at its four corners, worn like a stole and reminiscent of the outer garb worn in ancient Palestine. Except in some Reform congregations, instrumental music is never found in the synagogue, although almost all of the readings and prayers of the services are chanted. Musical instruments are prohibited as a sign of national mourning for the loss of the Temple. Chanting the liturgy and leading the congregation in singing is the task of the *hazan,* the synagogue cantor.

The Rabbi

The spiritual leader of a Jewish congregation is the rabbi. He is the authoritative heir of both the Biblical prophet and priest, although he is neither. His office goes back to the First Exile and the establishment of the Synagogue, when his function was to teach and apply the oral Torah begun at Mt. Sinai and developed through the centuries. The New Testament refers to them as scribes, the name which they had until the destruction of Jerusalem, when they came instead to be called rabbis.

The word "rabbi" means "teacher," and this best describes his function, namely, to act as a teaching elder and interpret the laws and traditions of Judaism for the congregation. The rabbi is not a priest, since he performs no ritual on behalf of the congregation. Neither is he a minister, since he is not recognized as a divinely authorized instrument of grace. He is a layman, but one graduated from an authorized Rabbinical academy and recognized by the scholar-teachers there to be one of them.

Since each congregation is autonomous, it elects its own rabbi without reference to any outside authority. His ritual functions are no greater than that of any other adult male in the congregation, except for the instruction, which it is his task to deliver. The affairs of a congregation are usually managed by a board of trustees, which customarily seeks the counsel of the rabbi but operates independently of his or any other jurisdiction. The principle of voluntarism undergirds the relationship of the rabbi to the congregation in all instances. His authority is primarily one of moral influence.

The Jewish Home and Family

Even more basic to Jewish religious life than the Synagogue is the home. In the Synagogue Judaism is learned; in the home it is lived. A continuing series of religious activities permeates the Jewish household throughout the year and from birth to death. Here, or in a hospital, on the eighth day after birth, a Jewish boy is circumcised and signed thereby as a "Son of the Covenant." Here the Sabbath rest is greeted with the lighting of candles and the various holy days of the Jewish calendar are observed. Here the deceased members of the family are remembered and prayer is offered for their repose. So central is the home to Judaism that it is even symbolized at the Jewish wedding service by the wedding canopy under which the bride and groom stand as they share their vows and two cups of wine, a sign of life's goodness.

Several ritual objects will be found in the Jewish home. On the right side of the doorpost is the *mezuzah*, a small wood or metal container into which is placed a parchment scroll on which is printed in Hebrew the *Shema*, "Hear, O Israel . . ." It is a reminder to all who enter and leave of their religious obligations. A candelabrum, a braided candle, and a box of spice are used by the woman of the house at the beginning and the end of the

Sabbath. The *Menorah,* a nine-branched candelabrum, is used for Hanukkah, the Feast of Lights, in the winter. During Passover, in the springtime, special dishes are used, especially for the *Seder,* the Passover meal, for during this time only unleavened bread, *matzah,* is eaten. In the homes of Orthodox Jews, the laws of Kashruth are also observed. Pork is not eaten, nor oysters, clams, lobster or shrimp, nor indeed any fish without fins or scales. Separate dishes are used for meat and dairy foods. The Kosher dietary laws are meant to hallow mealtime and remind the Jew of his debt of gratitude for God's goodness.

In Judaism a man's highest station is believed to be achieved through married life. Marriage is considered a duty, and celibacy is frowned upon. The first commandment of the Torah is "be fruitful and multiply" (Gen. 1:28). Judaism recognizes divorce, but it must be admitted that the frequency of divorce among Jewish families is far lower than the average in this country; and so too is the incidence of juvenile delinquency and mental illness. The strong bonds of Jewish homelife can be credited for these enviable statistics.

The Sabbath and Jewish Holy Days

Although other nations celebrated holy days in conjunction with the seasonal cycle of nature, the Jews were the first to add to this concept the commemoration of history, namely, God's saving action in time. The Jewish Sabbath and festivals marked not only the passing of the seasons but also the historical events in the life of Israel, along with a renewed communitarian commitment to the Covenant to which they gave rise.

Even though it occurs weekly, the Sabbath is the most significant of all Jewish religious commemorations, with the exception of Yom Kippur. The Sabbath, like all Jewish days, begins at sundown the previous evening. From Friday evening to Saturday evening, the time is "set aside" for peace, rest, and family togetherness. The Sabbath is thus "set aside" to remind Jews that they, as God's chosen people, are "set aside."

The High Holy Days of the Jewish calendar occur in the autumn, beginning with Rosh Hashanah, the Jewish New Year, and ending with the most solemn day of the entire year, Yom Kippur, the Day of Atonement. The spirit of these days is self-examination, confession, and repentance, climaxing with a twenty-four-hour fast on Yom Kippur.

Among the Jewish festivals is Sukkoth, also called the Feast of Booths or Feast of Tabernacles, a harvest-thanksgiving holy day commemorating the sojourn of the Jews in the desert for forty years before their entrance into the Promised Land. Pesach, or Passover, occurs in the spring and recalls the liberation of Israel from Egypt; it is marked by the *Seder,* a ritual meal including unleavened bread, wine, and bitter herbs in memory of the Exodus. Shabuoth, or Pentecost, follows fifty days later and commemorates the giving of the Torah by God to the Jewish people. Another feast which in recent years has been given greater, more festive observance because of its proximity to the Christmas holidays is Hanukkah, commemorating the recapture and rededication of the Temple after it had fallen into the hands of unbelievers.

Jewish-Christian Dialogue

Even a superficial knowledge of Judaism is enough to indicate how thoroughly Jewish are the origins of Christianity. The entire Bible is of Jewish origin, the New Testament as well as the Old. Jesus was a devout practicing Jew, as were his Mother, Joseph, Peter, Paul, the apostles, and most of the early Church. The Gospels testify as to how thoroughly Jewish practice and ritual permeated Christ's life. They tell of his circumcision, presentation in the Temple, and *bar mitzvah.* They tell how Jesus participated in synagogue services as a young rabbi and indicate how thoroughly Rabbinic in method were his teachings and parables. His Last Supper, commemorated in every Catholic Mass, was a *Seder,* a Jewish Passover meal. Bread, wine, water, oil, the Ten Commandments, the Psalms, Amen, Alleluia—all go back to our roots in Israel. We worship the God of Abraham, Isaac, and Jacob. And we believe in the words of Jesus Christ, who said that "salvation is from the Jews" (John 4:22).

The bishops of the Second Vatican Council encouraged Christians to enter into ecumenical encounters in a special way with Jews:

Since the spiritual patrimony common to Christians and Jews is thus so great, this sacred Synod wants to foster and recommend that mutual understanding and respect which is the fruit above all of biblical and theological studies and of brotherly dialogues. (Declaration on Non-Christian Religions, No. 4)

Such encounters can certainly serve to promote the renewal which is going on within the Catholic Church, particularly in regard to biblical and liturgical studies.

Here in the United States, there are particular practical reasons for Jewish-Christian dialogue, since both communities are intimately involved with one another on the social, civic, and cultural level. And on this level there exist some serious differences which demand thoughtful and respectful consideration.

Most Jews take a strong position in favor of strict separation of Church and State. They are especially adamant against governmental aid to religiously oriented schools and the introduction of religious instruction into the public school. Catholics, on the other hand, tend to prefer close cooperation between Church and State as a means of maintaining the commonweal. Because of their vast system of education, Catholics are resentful that their tax dollars do not go toward the support of their schools. It is important for both Catholics and Jews to see the historical and theological reasons for these divergent views. Many Catholics believe that Jews are against religion in general and Christianity in particular, that they are in league with secularists. The fact is that Jews fear a loss of their minority rights when Church and State become too close.

Jews also seem to differ with Christians on many other questions, such as public morality and censorship. All such areas deserve ecumenical discussion in hopes of compromise—or, at least, friendly controversy and better understanding.

Conclusion:

The benefits which can accrue to all participants in Jewish-Christian dialogue are many. Christians have already been enriched by the history and traditions of Judaism, and we can continue to learn from its wisdom and profit from its piety. We can gain much from Judaism's traditional insistence on the spirituality, personality, and transcendence of God; its emphasis on the dignity of man; its vision which looks to the future without ignoring the here and now for the building up of the earth. Ecumenical discussion may well begin to heal the wound of resentfulness inflicted upon Jews by their tragic history. The direction for Jewish-Christian relations has been indicated clearly by the late Pope John XXIII:

There is a great difference between one who accepts only the Old Testament and one who joins the New to it as supreme law and guide. This distinction, however, does not suppress the brotherhood that springs from their common origin, for we are all sons of the same heavenly Father; among us all there must be ever the brightness of love and its practice.

Suggested Reading

Brown, Robert McAfee. *The Ecumenical Revolution*. Doubleday, 1967.

Flannery, Edward H. *The Anguish of the Jews*. Macmillan, 1965.

Glock, Charles Y., and Rodney Stark. *Christian Beliefs and Anti-Semitism*. A scientific study of the ways in which the teachings of the Christian Churches shape American attitudes toward the Jews. Harper, 1966.

Hertzberg, Arthur, ed. *Judaism*. Washington Square Press, 1963.

Long, J. Bruce, ed. *Judaism and the Christian Seminary Curriculum*. Loyola University Press, 1966.

Rosenberg, Stuart E. *Judaism*. Paulist.

Swidler, Leonard, and Marc Tanenbaum. *Jewish-Christian Dialogues*. Part of the Grass-roots Ecumenism Program. National Council of Catholic Men (Washington, D.C.), 1966.

3 / The Orthodox Churches of the East

The two most ancient churches, the Orthodox and the Catholic, should fall into one another's arms, weep over their past, and then, purified by the tears of contrition, appeal to the Divine Power and through their reconciliation give their peoples the joy of the Lord.
— METROPOLITAN PANTELEIMON,
Greek Orthodox Bishop of Chios

From 1925 to 1934 Archbishop Angelo Roncalli was papal representative to Bulgaria; from 1935 to 1944 he served in the same capacity to Turkey and Greece. During that time he came to know and respect, and assuredly to love, the Eastern Orthodox. He saw the depth of their faith and learned to value the richness of their traditions. When later he became Pope John XXIII and summoned an ecumenical council for the renewal of the Roman Catholic Church, it was undoubtedly with a view to the eventual reunion of all Christian Churches. There is little doubt that Pope John's primary hopes for a Christian reunion lay in the direction of the East.

Recent years have seen a growing improvement of relations between the Catholic West and the Orthodox East. In 1964 Pope Paul VI made a pilgrimage to the Holy Land, and there he met with the Ecumenical Patriarch of the East, Athenagoras. In 1965, toward the end of Vatican Council II, joint statements were made by both Pope Paul and Patriarch Athenagoras, lifting the bans of excommunication that had been exchanged by their 11th-century predecessors. These symbolic gestures of brotherhood and mutual forgiveness have highlighted the need for Roman Catholics to learn more about the Orthodox Churches of the East, their history, spirituality, and traditions. The very word "catholic" is of Greek origin, and it means "universal." Yet Roman Catholics have been considerably less than universal in presuming that their approach to Christianity is the most ancient, the most appropriate, and even the only one. Some 130 million Christians live within the spirit and tradition of the Eastern Orthodox Churches, a spirit which goes back to the apostles and a tradition formulated by some of the greatest saints and theologians in the Church's two-thousand-year history. Roman Catholics have by and large been unaware of Eastern Christianity, and they have been the poorer for it. Establishing closer ties with the Orthodox will mean for Roman Catholics an enrichment of their own faith. It will mean a fuller, more catholic appreciation of the Christian way of life. Above all, it will mean that Catholics and Orthodox alike will be led to realize the urgent need for both traditions to come together in a living synthesis that will preserve the Christian authenticity of both.

For the sake of Christian unity and for the sake of his own personal growth in faith and holiness, every Catholic, together with Pope John XXIII, would do well to turn to the East. In the words of the Second Vatican Council:

All should realize that it is of supreme importance to understand, venerate, preserve, and foster the exceedingly rich liturgical and spiritual heritage of the Eastern Churches, in order faithfully to preserve the fullness of Christian tradition, and to bring about reconciliation between Eastern and Western Christians. (Decree on Ecumenism, No. 15)

The History of the Eastern Churches

Early Developments

From the moment that the Spirit of Pentecost filled the disciples in the Upper Room, the Church began to spread. As would be expected, its initial growth centered around the area nearest to its birthplace, the Eastern Mediterranean. St. Luke's book of Acts is filled with the names of cities where the apostles laid the foundations for Christian churches—Antioch, Corinth, Philippi, Ephesus. Here the apostles began to establish Christian traditions, and the early martyrs shed their blood in witness to Christ. Here Jewish Christianity met with the philosophy and culture of Greece and struggled to translate its message into new concepts, new words. Here Christianity developed a vast religious civilization all its own. From certain populous cities in particular, missionaries spread out to convert the neighboring countryside. These cities became centers of Christianity in the East; their traditions and religious rites came to influence the rest of the Eastern churches, and their bishops came to be called *Patriarchs,* Fathers. These cities were Jerusalem, Antioch, and Alexandria.

In 330 A.D., shortly after he had proclaimed Christianity an official religion of the Roman Empire, the Emperor Constantine moved the capital of the Empire from Rome to a small town in what is now Turkey. The name of the town was Byzantium, but the Emperor saw fit to rename it after himself, Constantinople, the "city of Constantine." This political maneuver split the Empire into two spheres, East and West. As capital of the Empire, Byzantium became the "New Rome," and its political influence soon led to its acquiring of great religious influence as well. Its bishops, too, soon obtained the title of Patriarch, and its traditions, customs, and religious practices became normative for most of the churches in the Eastern Empire's jurisdiction.

The history of the Church's early growth in the understanding and expression of its faith is located almost entirely in the East. It is a tumultuous history, marked by controversy, struggle, and even bloodshed. When Arius, a priest of Alexandria in Egypt, began preaching that the Second Person of the Blessed Trinity was not divine but merely a creature, the entire Church became disrupted by the most serious heresy it had to face to that date. The Emperor summoned the bishops of the Church to a council, and this gathering of bishops is now recognized as the first ecumenical council in the Church's history. In 325 at Nicaea, in what is now Turkey, some 318 bishops, most of them from the East, condemned Arianism and proclaimed that to be a Christian one had to believe that the Son of God is equal to, and indeed of the same nature as, the Father. In reaction to Arianism, Christians in the East have tended ever since to emphasize strongly the divinity of Jesus Christ, his majesty, and awesomeness. The magnificent images of Christ as the Pantocrator give expression to the deep faith which the East has in Christ's supreme glory.

In 381 a second ecumenical council was called, this time in Constantinople. About 185 bishops, all of them from the East, upheld that the Holy Spirit is divine and is to be "adored with the Father and the Son." A strong basis for this decision was the "divinizing" activity of the Holy Spirit upon every baptized and believing Christian. The influence of the Holy Spirit upon the Church and upon every individual in it remains a basic element in Eastern theology and spirituality. The decisions of this council, as well as those of the one held earlier at Nicaea, were confirmed by the Bishop of Rome, the Pope. And the creed which they formulated became a standard of belief for all Christians. Even today the Nicene Creed is an official creed of Catholics, Orthodox, and some Protestants.

Although written in Greek, the New Testament was the product, for the most part, of men who were Jews and who therefore thought in Semitic concepts and patterns. To the Greek Church fell the task of translating those concepts, defining them, and making them meaningful to the prevalent philosophy of the day without thereby distorting their basic meaning. It was a difficult task, often an agonizing one. After developing the Christian doctrine on the Trinity, the Eastern Church turned to the mystery of the Incarnation. Once again doctrine developed in an atmosphere of controversy. When Nestorius began teaching that in Jesus Christ there were two persons, divine and human, as well as two natures, the third ecumenical council was called in 431 at Ephesus. The Nestorians claimed that Jesus was two persons and that Mary was Mother of only the human person. In response to this heresy, the council declared that Jesus was but one divine person, existing with two distinct natures, one divine, the other human. It further proclaimed that Mary was not only the Mother of Christ but, since Christ is God, the very Mother of God, *Theotokos*. Subsequently, Eastern Christianity has been characterized by an intense devotion to Mary, and she is rarely venerated in the East under any other title than Mother of God. A fourth ecumenical council in 451 at Chalcedon further defined the relationship between person and nature in Christ, emphasizing that his humanity and divinity were separate and distinct. At this council the teaching of Pope Leo I provided the basis for the council's final doctrinal decisions, and the Pope was hailed by the Eastern bishops with the affirmation that "Peter has spoken through Leo."

The incarnation of Divinity in the person of Jesus Christ eventually became symbolized by pictorial representations of Christ, Mary, and the saints. In the East the image of a sacred person was considered itself a sacred thing, an extension of the mystery of the Incarnation. When the Iconoclasts, literally the "image breakers," equated the use of sacred images as tantamount to idolatry, another ecumenical council was called in 787 at Nicaea. The council declared that images could not be worshiped but could be used and venerated, not because they were holy in themselves but because of what they represented.

The teachings of the first seven ecumenical councils, all of which were held in the East, constitute the essential faith of the Orthodox Churches. Not all the churches of the East accepted the teachings of the Councils of Ephesus and Chalcedon. To distinguish themselves from these dissidents, the churches which did accept these conciliar teachings began referring to themselves as "orthodox," literally those possessing the "correct teaching." The Orthodox Churches, however, do not admit of any authoritative statement of belief *subsequent* to those first seven councils. According to the Orthodox, only an ecumenical council can be competent to make such a statement; and the Eastern Churches admit that the schism between East and West prevents them from having any council of bishops which could claim to be truly ecumenical, truly worldwide in scope. Likewise, since subsequent councils have been held without the full collaboration of the Orthodox East, they were not, according to the Orthodox, truly ecumenical and therefore not universally authoritative.

The doctrines defined at these seven ecumenical councils, the liturgy, the spirit, the very life of Eastern Christianity, resulted from the meditation and reflection of some of the greatest saints and scholars the Church has ever known. Basil, Gregory of Nyssa, Gregory of Nazianzen, John Chrysostom, Athanasius, Ephrem, Cyril of Jerusalem—all are revered as Fathers, Doctors, and saints of the Church in both East and West. Their teachings have elucidated the faith and inspired the devotion of Christians throughout the world. To the East, too, goes the credit for the origin and development of monasticism. St. Anthony and St. Paul, the Desert Fathers of Egypt, St. Basil and St. Pachomius—these great men laid the foundations for ascetical theology and religious life, giving rise to a tradition which has given numerous saints to both East and West. The Bishops of the Second Vatican Council expressed their high regard and gratitude for the benefactions of the East to Western Christianity:

> From the glorious days of the holy Fathers, there flourished in the East that monastic spirituality which later flowed over into the Western world, and there provided a source from which Latin monastic life took its rise and has often drawn fresh vigor ever since. Therefore Catholics are strongly urged to avail themselves more often of these spiritual riches of the Eastern Fathers, riches which lift up the whole man to the contemplation of divine mysteries. (Decree on Ecumenism, No. 15)

From the East, too, came one of the greatest missionary endeavors ever recorded in Christian history. Saints Cyril and Methodius led a host of missionaries who carried the faith from Constantinople and its environs to Bulgaria, Serbia, Poland, and Russia. These apostles to the Slavic peoples brought with them not only the faith but an alphabet and a civilization, one that has perdured through a thousand years, influencing the lives of millions of people. But it was a civilization and a culture very different from that of the Latin West, and it is this cultural difference more than any religious divergence which led to the tragic schism between Catholics and Orthodox.

Schism between East and West

The establishment of Constantinople as the imperial city of the East marked the beginning of Byzantine civilization and culture. Constantinople flowered into a center of wealth, political power, and religious influence. At the same time the West began to suffer political and cultural decline. Masses of barbarian invaders disrupted the political structure of the Western half of the Empire, and there were ushered in the so-called Dark Ages. To the Catholic Church fell the task of assimilating and educating the immigrants and creating a new civilization.

Differences of culture led to differences of theology, as both East and West came to approach the same religious truths from divergent viewpoints. Maintaining the tradition of the Greek philosophers, the Eastern Church was strongly inclined to subtle, speculative thinking. The Catholic West, on the other hand, maintained the tradition of ancient Rome with its talent for government and jurisprudence. Thus Christianity took two very different paths. The Greek mind, idealistic, sensitive, imaginative, given to poetry and speculative thought, was mirrored in the Orthodox East. Roman thought, clear, cold, decisive, productive of jurists, administrators, and conquering warriors, indelibly marked the Catholic West. Eventually linguistic differences aggravated the cultural split. After the barbarian invasions, relatively few Latins understood or spoke Greek, and the Greeks had no desire to learn a language which they scorned as barbaric and crude. Interpreters had to be hired to translate important documents; their errors, whether intentional or not, increased misunderstandings.

When the political structure of the Roman Empire fell in the West, the emperor in the East came to be regarded as the protector of all Christendom. When in 800 the Pope crowned Charlemagne as the new head of a new Western Empire, his action was taken as an insult to both the Byzantine emperor and the entire East. A political rivalry subsequently arose between the kings of France and the Byzantine emperors for the title of heir to the ancient Roman emperors. This political rivalry intensified a religious rivalry which had already arisen between the Pope and the Patriarch of Constantinople. The Patriarch, as head of the Church in the "New Rome," claimed an authority second only to that of the Pope. And although the Orthodox Churches recognized that the Bishop of Rome occupied the see of primacy in all Christendom, they did not view this primacy from the same viewpoint as did the West.

For a short period of time in the ninth century, East and West were split over what has been called the Photian Schism. Patriarch Photius accused the West of tampering with the ancient creeds by adding the word *Filioque*—a reference to the Holy Spirit proceeding from the Father "and the Son." The schism was healed and peace was restored betwen the Eastern and Western Church, but the damage had been done: the supreme authority of the Bishop of Rome had been challenged.

About two hundred years later, another Byzantine Patriarch, Michael Cerularius, began another attack against the Latin Church, this time against some of its ceremonial practices, namely, using unleavened bread at Mass and suppressing the use of "alleluia" during Lent. In 1054 Pope Leo IX sent Cardinal Humbert as his legate to answer the Patriarch's charges and reaffirm the supreme authority of the Roman See. The Cardinal, although noted for his piety and zeal for reform, lacked the diplomatic tact for such a mission. In the heat of controversy, he excommunicated the Byzantine Patriarch. Michael and a synod of bishops countered with a sentence of excommunication of their own, leveled against Cardinal Humbert. No formal declaration of schism was declared, nor was an attempt made to excommunicate the Pope. This incident, however, is commonly regarded as the beginning of the final rupture between Roman Catholicism and Orthodoxy.

A more devastating blow to Catholic-Orthodox relations took place 150 years later. On their way to deliver the Holy Land from Moslem domination, Catholic Crusaders from the West marched through the lands of the Byzantine Empire. Exemplifying neither Christianity nor knighthood, the Fourth Crusade, led by the Venetian fleet, attacked, captured, and plundered Constantinople in 1204. Wives, daughters, and women religious were raped; churches were sacked; the Blessed Sacrament was strewn in the streets. Added to these atrocities was the dethronement of the Byzantine Patriarch and his replacement by the "Latin Patriarchate of Constantinople." Pope Innocent III strongly decried the outrages of the Fourth Crusade, but he did permit the Latin domination of Byzantium to continue as a *fait accompli,* hoping it might lead to reunion of East and West. Instead, a bitter resentment and national hatred intensified the religious and cultural differences between Constantinople and Rome. The Crusaders eventually lost their hold on Byzantium, but the East has not forgotten to this day the abuse and humiliation it suffered at the hands of these "Roman Catholics."

Attempts at reconciliation between East and West were not wanting, even after the onslaught of the Crusaders. The threat of Moslem conquest by the Turks inclined the Eastern emperors toward alignment with the West. It was considered the lesser of two evils. The Second Council of Lyons in 1274 and the Council of Florence in 1439 attempted formal reunion of the two Christian traditions. They both failed, however, because they involved only princes and prelates, not the priests and people. They served only to finalize the schism between Roman Catholicism and Orthodoxy, and to bring about its formal recognition. In 1453 the City of Constantinople fell once again, this time to the invading Turks. The "city of Constantine" was renamed Istanbul, and its Patriarch became a mere figurehead over Orthodoxy. His title of leadership over the Eastern Churches was claimed by the bishop of Moscow, now the Patriarch of the "Third Rome." Despairing of ever entering into an ecumenical union with the entire Orthodox East, the Catholic Church began to receive individual local and national bodies of separated Easterners into Catholic unity. The most noteworthy example of this was the Union of Brest-Litovsk, which in 1595 brought the Orthodox bishops and people of the Ukraine, Lithuania, and Poland into union with the Holy See. These Eastern Catholics number some eight million Christians today. Sometimes referred to as "Uniates" (a term that has a history of derision and might best be avoided), they are members of the Eastern Rites of the Catholic Church.

Subsequent History

The history of Orthodoxy after the fall of Constantinople has been one of constant splintering into national and even subnational, local Churches. Orthodoxy has concentrated on the deepening of its interior life, often to the detriment of external unity. Semi-autonomous, cut off from one another by national boundaries, the Orthodox Churches have failed to bring about real unity among themselves. Only the loosest conception of a federation can be said to bind them. Increased communication with Western Europe over recent years, however, has helped the Orthodox to realize how indispensable they are to one another. In 1961 the Russian Orthodox Church joined the World Council of Churches. This association has helped the Orthodox to realize how much more they have in common with Catholics than with Protestants, particularly in the area of doctrine. It has also compelled the World Council of Churches to give more serious consideration to the question of revealed dogma. The invitation to the Orthodox Churches to send observers to Vatican Council II occasioned Patriarch Athenagoras' summoning of a Pan-Orthodox Conference at Rhodes in November 1964. Representatives of fourteen Orthodox groups agreed at this conference not to send observers to the Vatican Council, but promised to work for Catholic-Orthodox dialogue by "creating favorable circumstances" for it. Such recent developments portend greater unity among the Orthodox Churches themselves as well as a new era of East-West relations.

The great number of Eastern Churches may well be confusing to a Western Christian. There are Syrian Churches, whose traditions go back to ancient Antioch, and Coptic Churches, whose origins go back to Alexandria. There are also the Eastern Catholic Churches whose traditions go back to the Fathers but which, like the Maronite Church of Lebanon, never separated themselves from the Catholic communion, or else rejoined that union. The largest and most influential of the Eastern Churches, however, are the Orthodox Churches, whose origins go back to Byzantium and whose traditions have been adopted by numerous other Eastern Churches. Today some 130 million Christians belong to the Orthodox tradition; it is their spirit, their belief and practices, which most typify Eastern Christianity today.

Beliefs and Practices of the Eastern Churches

Theology and Doctrines

Christianity, Catholic and Orthodox, took its origins from the East. The first seven ecumenical councils developed and expressed the Church's understanding of God's revelation through some of the stormiest centuries in the Church's history. The teachings of these seven councils are the common patrimony of both East and West.

As a result, Orthodox and Catholics, although they may differ in approach, substantially agree in what they hold to be God's revelation to men.

Both Orthodox and Catholics believe that the foundation for the Christian faith is the Word of God as it is found in scripture. They also believe alike that scripture has been interpreted by the tradition of the Church. Catholics and Orthodox hold together to the mystery of one God in three persons, the mystery of God's Son made man for our redemption, and the mystery of the Holy Spirit uniting and sanctifying the Church. Together Orthodox and Catholics believe in the seven sacraments as man's encounter with God through Christ. Together both East and West uphold the tradition of apostolic succession. Together both believe in the communion of saints, the union of all believing and baptized Christians in Christ. Together both honor Mary as Mother of God and Queen of Saints; the East especially is noted for its filial and unswerving devotion to Mary. And Catholic and Orthodox Christians stand together in their profession of the beliefs proclaimed in the Nicene Creed.

The differences between Catholic and Orthodox beliefs are difficult to define, precisely because the East traditionally tends to avoid dogmatic definitions. Perhaps this is the greatest difference of all between them. Catholic theology, with its penchant for clear, neat, scholastic definitions and distinctions, and Catholic jurisprudence, with its heavy emphasis on law, order, and central administration, are both quite foreign to the Orthodox mind. For Eastern Christians the Church is primarily a society of believers. While it is truly a visible entity, it is essentially mystical and invisible, inspired by the Holy Spirit. The whole Church, according to the Orthodox, is infallible; priests and laymen share in this infallibility as well as bishops, and the mind of all of them is expressed in an ecumenical council, one at which Orthodox and Catholic bishops alike deliberate.

As a result of their more mystical approach to the nature of the Church, Orthodox Christians, unlike Catholics, do not accept the *juridical* primacy of the Pope. They admit that the Pope is Bishop of Rome, Patriarch of the West, and, as the successor of St. Peter, the "first among equals." They accord him, in other words, a primacy of honor among bishops, but not a primacy of jurisdiction. They do not believe that he speaks with the protection of infallibility, except in conjunction with all the bishops of both East and West in an ecumenical council. They do not believe that he has the authority to enter into the ordinary, internal matters of a local church. They accuse Roman Catholics of juridicism, of making law the whole basis for Christian unity and arbitrarily subordinating the rights and powers of individual bishops to the whims of the Bishop of Rome. The theological objections of the Orthodox Churches to the primacy of the Pope are certainly colored by a nationalism which tends to view the Pope as a foreign political ruler. Eastern Christians have a strong, innate fear of Western leadership, a fear that unity with the West would ultimately mean the loss of their identity as Orthodox.

Another difference between East and West, deserving note because of the controversy it engendered, centers around one word, "*Filioque*." The Nicene Creed, accepted as normative for both East and West, professed the belief that the Holy Spirit "proceeds from the Father." When the custom arose in the Western Church to add the word *Filioque,* "and the Son," expressing the belief that the Holy Spirit proceeds from the Father and the Son, the Eastern Churches accused the Catholic West of a tampering with the ancient creed. They resented the addition of any word whatever, and they questioned the orthodoxy of the Catholic belief. The Eastern Fathers had traditionally taught that the Holy Spirit proceeds from the Father and through the Son. A compromise was reached between Catholic and Orthodox theologians when it was explained that the meanings of "and the Son" and "through the Son" were essentially the same. The Catholic Church does not consider the addition of the word an addition to the creed, but simply an explanatory clarification which the East may or may not use, as it wishes.

Further differences between East and West arose from the refusal of the Orthodox Churches to accept as authoritative the teachings of any ecumenical councils after the first seven. This does not mean that they necessarily reject the teachings of later councils as false; it rather means that they do not accept them as doctrinally defined as having been revealed by God. Thus there are some differences between Catholic and Orthodox beliefs concerning Mary's immaculate conception and purgatory.

On the question of Mary's immaculate conception, there is a certain lack of unanimity among Orthodox, even though the doctrine was rather generally held in the East until the 15th century. Many Orthodox believe that Mary was free from sin from the first instant of her conception; others hold that she was cleansed in her mother's womb later. Today, however, most Orthodox incline to the opinion that Mary was cleansed from sin when the Angel announced to her that she was to be the Mother of Christ.

Many Orthodox deny that they believe in purgatory; nevertheless, all the Eastern Churches uphold the tradition of praying for the dead. The objection of the Orthodox regarding purgatory is the all-too-common Catholic image of purgatory as a place of punishment by fire. Their objection is well-founded, since the Church has never authoritatively declared either that purgatory is a place or that it consists of fire. The Catholic Church officially teaches that purgatory is a state of purification, without defining how this is accomplished. St. Thomas Aquinas was of the opinion that the souls in purgatory are purified by love; this is the teaching of the Orthodox East.

Aside from the disagreement between Orthodox and Catholics concerning Papal primacy, the outstanding differences between East and West are not matters of doctrine but, rather, of emphasis and approach. The Orthodox object to the Catholic tendency of analyzing, defining, and compartmentalizing. The enduring foundation for Eastern theology is the tremendous mystery of the Trinity. The emphasis on God as an unfathomable mystery is a tradition of the East. He is unknowable, unapproachable, utterly transcendent.

Jesus Christ, for the Orthodox East, is essentially the Son of God, risen from the dead, and seated at the right hand of the Father in glory. Rarely is his humanity, or his passion, emphasized. Jesus' resurrection is central to Orthodox faith and life. Whether in the Greek or Slavic languages, Easter is the "Great Day," and every Sunday is called simply "Resurrection." Eastern crucifixes bear no corpus; their churches display no stations of the cross. Entirely foreign to the Eastern Churches would be a devotion to the

Sacred Heart. Jesus for them is not so much Brother or Friend as Kyrios, Pantocrator, Omnipotent Lord. Not only the liturgy but the very spirit of the East is characterized by the Easter Alleluia.

The resurrection of Christ, for the East, is the cause and pledge of our own resurrection, our own divinization, in and through the Holy Spirit who is present everywhere. So exalted is the poetic eloquence of the East in speaking of the transformation, indeed the deification, of all creation by the Holy Spirit that, to our Western ears, they sound like pantheists. This is but one other example of the distinct difference between East and West, their emphasis of the heart over the intellect, the intuitive over the rational, the mystical over the methodic.

Philosophical reasoning has little place in Orthodox theology. Symbolism is the language of the East. Its liturgy abounds in symbolic gestures; its churches are filled with signs. Most of the symbols used in Western Churches are of Oriental origin, the Alpha and Omega, the ICHTUS, the IHS. Particularly characteristic of the Eastern Churches, however, is the veneration of icons, images of Christ, Mary, and the saints, fashioned according to a stylized Byzantine form. Every Eastern church is decorated with icons, as are most Orthodox homes. The Orthodox Christian will bow to an icon, kiss it, light a lamp before it. This kind of veneration may seem exaggerated to the Western mind, but to the Oriental mentality the icon and the person it represents are so intimately linked that, when one contemplates the image, the person is somehow mysteriously present. Although the image is never identified with the person represented, the relationship between an icon and its subject is likened to that between a shadow and its body. Because of this mysterious iconic presence, the image is considered not only as inspirational art but a veritable channel of grace. To the Eastern Churches all creation, but particularly sacred symbols and images, are reflections of heavenly realities, manifestations of divine energy transforming the world.

In considering the differences of theological approach and emphases between the East and the West, Vatican Council II stressed that divergences are to be regarded more as complementary than contradictory:

In the investigation of revealed truth, East and West have used different methods and approaches in understanding and proclaiming divine things. It is hardly surprising, then, if sometimes one tradition has come nearer than the other to an apt appreciation of certain aspects of a revealed mystery, or has expressed them in a clearer manner. As a result, these various theological formulations are often to be considered as complementary rather than conflicting. With regard to the authentic theological traditions of the Orientals, we must recognize that they are admirably rooted in holy Scripture, fostered and given expression in liturgical life, and nourished by the living tradition of the apostles and by the writings of the Fathers and spiritual authors of the East; they are directed toward a right ordering of life, indeed, toward a full contemplation of Christian truth. (Decree on Ecumenism, No. 17)

Sacraments and Worship

The Churches of the East possess the same seven sacraments as the Catholic Church. Generally referred to as "mysteries," they are the same not only in number and kind but also in validity. There are differences as to emphasis and practice, however, and these deserve consideration.

Baptism and Confirmation are administered at the same time in the Eastern Churches. Baptism is administered by total immersion, and is followed by Holy Myron, the confirmation of the neophyte Christian by the priest with oil consecrated by the bishop. It is an Eastern custom that even infants, when they are baptized and anointed with Holy Myron, receive Holy Communion as a nourishment for the new supernatural life they have received.

Differences between East and West also exist in regard to the sacraments of Penance and the Anointing of the Sick. The Orthodox do not ordinarily approach confession as frequently as Catholics; neither are they as detailed in enumerating the numbers and kinds of their sins. They simply make a general statement of sinfulness and sorrow. The sacrament of Anointing is administered in the East not only to those in danger of death but also to the mildly sick. On Wednesday of Holy Week it is often administered even to those who are in good health.

Eastern practices connected with Matrimony and Holy Orders

are quite expressive of the Orthodox mentality. Gone from the marriage ceremony is the Western emphasis on contract and consent. Instead, the ceremony is rich in symbols of union and prayers for happiness. It is the officiating priest who imposes the wedding rings upon the bride and groom. He also places a crown upon each of them and gives them a cup of blessed wine to drink. The matrimonial consent of the parties is merely implied; it is the priest's blessing which is required for the validity of the sacrament. Marriage is considered indissoluble in principle, but in practice the Orthodox Churches do permit divorce and remarriage; once a marriage is dissolved by a civil court, a bishop may declare the marriage dissolved spiritually as well. Regarding Holy Orders, the imposition of hands and a prayer of consecration constitute the rite in the East as they do in the West. The Eastern Churches, however, traditionally permit the ordination of married men to the priesthood. Priests do not marry, but married men are ordained. Celibacy, however, is required for consecration to the episcopacy. Because of this custom, the majority of Eastern bishops are monks with the vow of chastity.

The Mass—or, as it is called, Divine Liturgy—is the culmination of the theology, life, and spirit of the Eastern Churches. Worship, to the Byzantine mind, is man's participation on earth in the liturgy of heaven. In the days of the Fathers the East sought to create a Eucharistic liturgy with the theme of heaven on earth. With a truly remarkable synthesis of poetry, drama, music, and art, the Orthodox world achieved that goal as much as it seems humanly possible. The sacredness and splendor of "heaven on earth" is approached by a generous use of images and symbols, incense and gold. The *iconostatis,* a screen separating the sanctuary from the nave of a Byzantine church, is covered with icons of Christ, Mary, and a number of saints; it not only depicts, but is thought to render, the worshipers actually present to the heavenly court. Most of the Byzantine liturgy is sung. It is never accompanied by musical instruments; instead, priests and people alternate with melodies that vibrate with Easter joy and bring to mind the celestial choirs.

Several Eucharistic rituals in the East differ from those in the West. The ordinary sign of reverence in the Eastern Churches is not a genuflection but a bow. The sign of the cross is made by touching the right shoulder before the left, with the thumb, index, and middle fingers held together as a sign of the Trinity. Upon entering a church, it is customary to go to a table in the center aisle and kiss a crucifix and icon placed there for that purpose. Leavened bread is used in the Eastern Churches, and the people receive Holy Communion under both forms, that of bread and wine.

The prayers and ceremonies of the Byzantine liturgy are credited to St. John Chrysostom. They bear little resemblance to a Roman Catholic Mass; yet all the essentials are the same. The Liturgy of the Word centers around prayers of penitence, litanies of petition, and readings from scripture. The Liturgy of the Eucharist begins with a magnificent call to prayer titled the "Hymn of the Cherubim," reminiscent of the Preface in a Catholic Mass. The *anaphora,* or canon, of the Mass is entirely sung aloud. Its two most solemn moments are the words of institution, recalling Christ's words at the Last Supper, and an *epiklesis,* a prayer to the Holy Spirit requesting divine intervention to change the bread and wine and render Christ present under these forms. Many Orthodox have insisted upon the epiklesis as being necessary for the validity of a Mass. Catholics teach that only the words of institution are absolutely necessary, but, as a matter of fact, do have a prayer similar to an epiklesis. Frequent Communion is not a common practice among the Eastern Churches; neither is daily Mass. Exposition of the Blessed Sacrament is not practiced either, since the Eastern mentality stresses the depth of the Eucharistic mystery by keeping the Sacrament concealed and distant from the faithful. The Eastern Churches have a liturgical year similar to that of the Catholic Church; but they follow the Julian Calendar, so that Easter and all the feasts of the liturgical year fall on days different from those of the Western Church.

The ceremonies of the Eastern Churches are quite different from those of the Catholic Church; they may seem not only foreign but exaggerated to the Western mind. In many instances, however, they are more ancient and dramatic than those of the Catholic Church, and certainly more attuned to the religious spirit of the

East. In speaking of the worship of the Eastern Churches, Vatican Council II made the following statement:

Everybody knows with what love the Eastern Christians enact the sacred liturgy, especially the celebration of the Eucharist, which is the source of the Church's life and the pledge of future glory. In this celebration the faithful, united with their bishop and endowed with an outpouring of the Holy Spirit, gain access to God the Father through the Son, the Word made flesh, who suffered and was glorified. (Decree on Ecumenism, No. 15)

Orthodox-Catholic Dialogue

Mutual Need

It should be readily seen from the foregoing how much Catholics and Orthodox share in common—creeds, sacraments, bishops rightfully claiming descent from the apostles, above all a love for Jesus Christ, and a unique devotion to the Mother of God. Perhaps the one thing they share most in common is that which they both realize least, a genuine need for one another.

The Catholic Church has a real need for the East. Not that it should assume expressions of the Oriental mentality and culture which would be foreign to the Western mind. But there is much within the Orthodox tradition that is universal to human nature, and this is what is needed by the Catholic Church in order to counteract and complement certain of its one-sided extremes. The Catholic Church's penchant for law and order has too often led to legalism and enforced uniformity. In struggling to preserve its independence against political dominance and to prevent further disintegration at the time of the Reformation, the Catholic Church so emphasized the jurisdictional primacy of the Pope that it often denigrated the equally sacred office of the bishops. The teaching of the Second Vatican Council concerning the collegiality of bishops was an important beginning toward counteracting an exaggerated emphasis on the Papacy and restoring the episcopacy to its rightful prominence. Closer communication with the East could greatly further this Catholic restoration, and help advance it from theory to practice. Under the influence of lawyers, the Catholic

Church has too often grown impersonal and cold. The traditions of the Eastern Fathers, preserved in the Orthodox Churches, are peculiarly apt toward lending some of the humanness and warmth which the Catholic Church needs.

The Orthodox, on the other hand, are also in need of much which the Catholic Church can provide. Its admirable devotion to the teachings of the Fathers has sometimes led the East to a traditionalism which refuses accommodation in any way to changing times and circumstances. If the Eastern Churches are not to petrify into an antique curiosity, they must acquire the same spirit of *aggiornamento* which Pope John breathed into the Catholic Church. Furthermore, the Eastern Churches have a tradition of dependence upon political authority, a dependence which has too often led to governmental control. Closer affiliation with the Catholic Church can provide Orthodoxy with the supranational and independent spirit it needs, especially in this age of totalitarian governments. Most important of all, the disintegration of Orthodoxy into numerous and often feuding national and subnational, local Churches could be halted, and the process reversed, by a more universalist, more ecumenical mentality which Catholic-Orthodox dialogue might well engender.

Obstacles

The significance of the meeting between Pope Paul and Patriarch Athenagoras was not lost on the symbol-conscious Churches of the East. But this gesture of fraternal affection between East and West, as beautiful as it was, should not lead to the presumption that Catholic-Orthodox unity is a simple matter. There are still serious obstacles, both theoretical and practical, which have to be resolved. Not the least of these is the existence of the Eastern Churches which have already reunited with the West. There is an unfortunate history of Latinization of these Eastern Catholic Churches, one to which Orthodox have been wont to point with contempt and as a warning to others who toy with the idea of union with Rome. Because of the ignorance and narrow-mindedness of many Roman Catholics, these Eastern Catholic Churches have often been made to feel like a minority

group, inferior to the much larger Latin Rite. The Orthodox
Churches are fully aware of the humiliation which Eastern Catholics have too often been made to suffer at the hands of Latins. To
prevent any such further humiliation and to undo the Latinization
which they have undergone, the Eastern Churches were accorded
their proper regard and their rights were officially recognized by
Vatican Council II, including their right to a certain traditional
autonomy:

. . . this sacred Synod solemnly declares that the Churches of the
East, while keeping in mind the necessary unity of the whole Church,
have the power to govern themselves according to their own disci-
plines, since these are better suited to the temperament of their faithful and better adapted to foster the good of souls. Although it has not
always been honored, the strict observance of this traditional principle
is among the prerequisites for any restoration of unity. (Decree on
Ecumenism, No. 16)

The basis for much of the Latinizing of the Eastern Catholic
Churches was the mistaken notion that somehow the Latin Rite
possessed a precedence over the other rites. The Council rejected
that opinion as false:

Such individual Churches, whether of the East or of the West . . . are
consequently of equal dignity, so that none of them is superior to
the others by reason of rite. They enjoy the same rights and are
under the same obligations . . . (Decree on Eastern Catholic Churches,
No. 3)

The Council further called upon the Eastern Catholic Churches
to become, not obstacles between the Catholic West and the
Orthodox East, but bridges. As a means to achieving this role,
Eastern Rite Catholics are urged to learn their Eastern traditions,
to honor and maintain them:

The Eastern Churches in communion with the Apostolic See of Rome
have a special role to play in promoting the unity of all Christians,
particularly Easterners . . . (Decree on Eastern Catholic Churches,
No. 24)

All Eastern rite members should know and be convinced that they can and should always preserve their lawful liturgical rites and their established way of life, and that these should not be altered except by way of an appropriate and organic development. Easterners themselves should honor all these things with the greatest fidelity. Besides, they should acquire an ever greater knowledge and more exact use of them. If they have improperly fallen away from them because of circumstances of time or personages, let them take pains to return to their ancestral ways. (Decree on Eastern Catholic Churches, No. 6)

Aids

If Catholics and Orthodox are to begin dialogue with a view to eventual unity, the de-Latinization of the Eastern Catholic Churches must be a first major step. Together with this process there must begin an educational process of Roman Catholics as to their indebtedness to the East. The sooner Latin Catholics repent of their arrogant self-importance and turn to the East with a sense of gratitude, the easier a rapprochement will be.

Renewed interest in the Eastern Churches and reverence for their traditions will not only hasten dialogue between Catholics and Orthodox; it will also open to Catholics treasures of spirituality peculiar to the East, and obtainable nowhere else. The Vatican Council urged Catholics to join in prayer with all Christians for the purpose of Christian unity. With the Orthodox Churches alone, however, did the Vatican Council open the possibility of inter-communion.

Although these Churches are separated from us, they possess true sacraments, above all—by apostolic succession—the priesthood and the Eucharist, whereby they are still joined to us in a very close relationship. Therefore, given suitable circumstances and the approval of Church authority, some worship in common is not merely possible but is recommended. (Decree on Ecumenism, No. 15)

The Council went on to permit Catholics to seek the sacraments of Penance, Eucharist, and Anointing from priests belonging to the Eastern Churches separated from Rome, and to permit members of these Churches to receive these same sacraments from Catholic priests, in cases of genuine spiritual benefit when access to a priest of one's own Church is impossible (cf. Decree on Eastern Catholic Churches, No. 27). Inter-communion between Orthodox and Catholics already exists in certain places behind the Iron Curtain.

Conclusion:

The positive, irenic, and even reverential attitude which the Second Vatican Council expressed concerning the Eastern Churches cannot help but give the impression that the Catholic Church regards them not so much as separated but sister Churches. A rediscovery is called for, and it is a mutual re-discovery. The schism between East and West was as unnecessary as it is painful. It is nearly a thousand years old. It is the fervent prayer of both Orthodox and Catholics alike that the millennium of that schism will see East and West gathered around the same altar, praying *Kyrie Eleison*—Lord, have mercy.

Suggested Reading

Dick, P. Ignace. *What Is the Christian Orient?* Newman, 1967.

Englert, Clement. *Catholics and Orthodox, Can They Unite?* Paulist, 1959.

Etteldorf, Raymond. *The Soul of Greece.* Newman, 1963.

Le Guillou, M. J. *The Spirit of Eastern Orthodoxy.* Paulist, 1964.

Meyendorff, John. *Orthodoxy and Catholicity.* Sheed and Ward, 1966.

Meyendorff, John., *et al. The Primacy of Peter in the Orthodox Church.* Faith Press (London), 1963.

Schmemann, R. P. A. *The Historical Road of Eastern Orthodoxy.* Regnery, 1966.

4 / The 16th-Century Protestant Reformation

A Church that would be wholly independent of Rome was never in Luther's program at any time.

—MAX LACKMANN

It was never the will of the Reformers and certainly not of Calvin to form separated Christian Churches.

—MARCEL PRAVAND

History has been variously labeled as bunk, mere gossip, and little more than a chronicle of crimes. Hegel, the 19th-century German philosopher, claimed that no one learned anything from it yet. Despite these and similar charges against history, however, we are still its victims. Disparage history all we like, we cannot disown it. We are the sums of a million moments.

There is probably no clearer example of the power of history than the impression which the 16th century has made upon our own. The schism between Catholics and Protestants which began in 1517 not only endures to this day but continues to color the lives of millions of people. Nearly every phase of human existence, political, social, and economic, has been affected by it. Protestants still react in many ways to the causes which led to the Reformation. The personalities and dispositions of Martin Luther and John Calvin, who spearheaded the Reform, continue to affect the Protestant mentality. And the Catholic Church only recently and with much concentrated effort has attempted to put a stop to its defensive reaction to all that is Protestant. As one historian, John P. Dolan, put it, the Reformation "is an event that is still taking place."

The 16th century was a period much like our own, a time of transition and therefore of tension and unrest. The discovery of America, the invention of printing, the rise of national monarchies—all contributed to reshaping the life-patterns of Europe and changed the course of history. But the most significant event of that century was undoubtedly the Protetsant Reformation. No wonder it was considered probably the most important influence in the history of Western religious thought since the advent of Christianity.

Precisely because it was so crucial and complex an event, the Protestant Reformation has received a more thorough examination from historians than almost any other era in the course of Western civilization. Rarely, however, were these studies conducted without sectarian bias. There is no lack of books recounting the events of the Reformation, but more often than not they convey along with historical facts the religious beliefs and prejudices of the author. For too long has the Reformation been treated in terms of "good guys" and "bad guys," of absolute right and absolute wrong.

It is to the credit of our ecumenical era that contemporary historians have been able to approach the subject of the Reformation with more objectivity and less bias. Protestant and Catholic scholars, together with those who are not Christian at all, have succeeded in attaining a certain degree of unanimity in their assessment of the Reformation. Unfortunately, too many Catholics have received a picture of the 16th century that is not altogether accurate. Historical honesty and the cause of ecumenism require that these misunderstandings be cleared away. Their significance for our day to the ecumenical movement make it necessary for us to consider the causes of the Protestant Reformation, the personalities who became its leaders, and the Catholic Counter-Reformation.

Causes of the Protestant Reformation

October 31, 1517, is usually regarded as the date which marks the beginning of the Protestant Reformation. On that day Father Martin Luther, an unknown Augustinian monk in a small university town in Germany, posted his Ninety-five Theses, challenging all-comers to a debate on the theologically knotty subject of indulgences. The debate never took place. But from this unlikely beginning developed the movement which shook the Church to its foundations and pitted brother against brother in religious combat. The causes of the Reformation are far deeper, more numerous, and more complex than Luther's challenge to a debate. They go back several centuries before the Reformation. The tinder had long been dried. Europe was ready for the fire. It only remained for a Luther to strike the spark.

Several attempts have been made to list the fundamental causes of the Reformation. None of them are totally satisfying. All of them tend to oversimplify. This attempt can be no different, but it may serve to provide a broad overview. Without going either into depth or detail, the causes of the Reformation can be classified under three broad categories: the moral weakness of the Papacy, the reaction against the ideas and ideals of the Middle Ages, and the need of the Catholic Church for reform.

Moral Weakness of the Papacy

In the 16th century the successors of St. Peter did not command the love or loyalty which they do in our own time. Politically the Popes were never stronger. They were a power to be reckoned with, the acting sovereigns over vast tracts of land. Yet they had very little moral influence over the policies of Christian princes or the lives of Christian people. This was due to several causes.

The Avignon Papacy. From 1304 to 1377 the Bishops of Rome did not reside in Rome but in southern France, at Avignon. These Popes were French in nationality, and they kept the College of Cardinals, from which their successors would be chosen, well stocked with Frenchmen. The loyalties of the Avignon Popes were clearly on the side of France. No semblance was made toward impartiality. Consequently, the Papacy became identified with the French Crown which dominated it, and the Popes themselves came to be regarded as little more than chaplains to the French king.

The Great Western Schism. Perhaps no period in its history was quite so dismal for the Catholic Church as the years from

1378 to 1438, the length of the Great Western Schism. It followed upon the return of the Papacy from Avignon to Rome. The death of the Pope the following year necessitated an election of a successor by the College of Cardinals. An Italian was elected, much to the delight of the Romans who wanted the assurance that their bishop would remain with them in Rome instead of southern France. Shortly thereafter, however, the French cardinals claimed they had been pressured in the election; and they declared it null and void. They held another conclave and elected a second pope, a Frenchman. For the next sixty years Christian Europe was divided as two—and, at one time, even three—men claimed to be the validly elected successor to St. Peter.

The Conciliar Theory. As the initial claimants to the Papacy died, their parties elected successors; and it began to appear that two separate lines of Popes would become a permanent institution in the Church. The situation became increasingly intolerable, and no solution was found until the Council of Constance, when one Pope was elected and accepted by all of Europe as the rightful Bishop of Rome. The dual spectacles of the Avignon Papacy and the Western Schism had greatly demeaned the prestige of the Popes. At the same time, the success of the Council of Constance in healing the Schism added to the importance assigned to ecumenical councils. The result was Conciliarism, the theory that an ecumenical council was superior to the Pope and could even depose him from office.

By the time of the 16th century the Conciliar Theory had contributed both disagreement and confusion concerning the primacy of the Pope and the exact extent of Papal authority. It was an issue all the more difficult to determine because of the fact that the Pope was not only a spiritual leader but a temporal prince. Over one-third of Italy constituted the Papal States, and the Popes were not above hiring mercenary soldiers to keep these lands under Papal domain. The Popes of the 16th century were concerned with matters political more than with the supernatural. They devoted their energies more often to maintaining a balance of power between the French kings and German emperors than to teaching the gospel or applying it to the life of the Church. Consequently the Office of Peter lost its supranational character;

the Pope came to be regarded as an Italian prince. It became exceedingly difficult for many Catholics to tender spiritual allegiance to a political rival. Thus Papal politics, loss of prestige, and doctrinal uncertainties concerning the primacy of the See of Peter all paved the way for Luther's rejection of the Papacy.

Reaction against the Ideas and Ideals of the Middle Ages

Times of transition are invariably times of reaction. The viewpoints and values of the immediate past are usually rejected for that which is supposedly modern. This recurring pattern of action-reaction was certainly exemplified by the 15th and 16th centuries; everything that smacked of the medieval was subjected to the sharpest criticism.

The Middle Ages had held up the ideal of a united Christendom. It was a self-contained world in which Church and State, Pope and Emperor, constituted the ultimate spiritual and temporal authorities, with the spiritual enjoying a primacy it occasionally saw fit to exercise. Although the ideal of complete unity was never fully realized, the unity of the Catholic Church in the West was a powerful unitive force during the Middle Ages; Europeans looked upon themselves rather as Catholics than as Frenchmen or Englishmen, Italians or Germans. Not so in the 15th and 16th centuries. In opposition to this ideal of a united Christendom, there arose strong tendencies toward *nationalism*. The decline of the moral influence of the Papacy contributed to an increase in the power of national monarchies. Kings and princes came to be identified with the territories they ruled, and commanded new loyalties. National interests quickly developed into national ambitions; and these in turn precipitated tension, resentment, and conflict. German solidarity had become a force to be reckoned with; Luther knew it when he inveighed against sending German money to build an Italian church.

The medieval period was a God-centered era. Nearly every aspect of its culture from Gothic spires to morality plays bespoke the transcendent, the hereafter. In reaction to this God-centeredness, the 15th and 16th centuries were characterized by a thoroughgoing *humanism,* a radical man-centeredness. The rediscovery of the classical Greek and Latin works of pagan antiquity had led to a profound admiration for all that was pre-Christian. Admiration inspired imitation, and the literature, painting, and sculpture of the Renaissance strived to duplicate the heoric proportions of the classic past. In Italy, especially, imitation of pagan learning often led to imitation of pagan lives. Man, not God, became the measure of all things. The body, not the soul, attracted attention and cultivation. Although humanism was essentially an aristocratic movement, yet its influence permeated society far beyond its conscious sphere. It was a rupture with the past, a critical and even at times contemptuous rejection of the Middle Ages. This rejection could not help but color a humanist's attitude toward the foremost institution of the Middle Ages, the Catholic Church.

The Middle Ages had witnessed a flowering of Catholic philosophy and theology. Thomas Aquinas, Albert of Cologne, Bonaventure, and Duns Scotus all contributed toward the building up of a medieval edifice every bit as towering and formidable as a Gothic cathedral, namely, Scholasticism. But, by the time of the 16th century, Catholic philosophy and theology had declined to a complex tangle of subtle distinctions and rivalry among schools of thought. One of the prevailing systems of thought was *Occamism,* the theological theories of the English Franciscan, William of Occam. The humanism of the times had led to an emphasis upon individualism, and this in turn led to a belief in the radical separateness of men from one another. Because of these atomizing tendencies, Occamism defined the Church as simply the sum of the men who make it up. It further taught that God arbitrarily determines some men to heaven, others to hell. It has been called a "hardly Catholic" theology; yet Occamism held sway over most religious thinkers of the 16th century. In it we find the seeds of Protestant theology.

Need of the Church for Reform

The Catholic Church of the 16th century has been described as a "community no longer dominated by charity." It was sorely in need of reform. As early as 1200, calls were sounded for a return to the simplicity of apostolic times. Popes, ecumenical councils, and saints such as Francis of Assisi appealed for reform of the Church in both its visible head and its members. Criticism was leveled against abuses in the Church from some of its most dedicated partisans. Yet neither criticism nor appeals for reform effected any significant change. Despite genuine holiness on the part of many, despite resolute attempts at reform and some minor successes at it, the situation remained bad and even deteriorated. Medieval man made no adequate distinction between the sacred and the secular, the spiritual and the temporal. Those who were supposed to be men of God believed that they could be at the same time men of the world; their temptations to power and pleasure proved to be almost irresistible.

In 1512 the Fifth Lateran Council was convened in order to bring about reform; it proved ineffective. Ironically it closed in 1517, the same year a German monk from Wittenberg was to initiate his own reforming movement. He didn't say anything that had not been said before. He didn't say anything that everybody did not already know. The Church was in need of reform on every level—Pope, prelates, priests, people, and practices.

Pope. Long before the birth of Luther, the Italian author of political intrigue, Machiavelli, was able to write that "there is no plainer proof that this religion [the Catholic Church] is falling to pieces than the fact that the people who live nearest to Rome are the least pious of any." The Renaissance Popes were patrons of the arts rather than shepherds of souls, humanists as much enamored of pagan antiquity as any prince in Europe. When Leo X succeeded Alexander VI and Julius II in the Papacy, these successive Popes were described by an appraisal not altogether unfair: "First Venus held sway, then Mars, and now Pallas Athena." It was during the pontificate of Leo X that Luther began his reforming movement. And it was Leo who had assumed as a motto: "Let us enjoy the Papacy, for God has given it to us."

In 1537, twenty years after the beginning of the Reformation, a Commission of Cardinals was delegated to investigate the corruption within the Church for the sake of a reform. The following are only some of the evils this Papal Commission pointed out:

the selling of ecclesiastical offices, e.g., that of cardinal, archbishop, or abbot, together with the revenues attached to these
offices; the selling of dispensations, absolutions, and indulgences;
the luxury and immorality rampant at Rome, especially among
the members of the Papal Curia; and, most devastating of all, an
exaggerated theory of Papal authority whereby the Popes were
led to imagine that their will constituted a supreme law. Well after
the Protestant Reformation was under way, when Adrian VI,
from the Netherlands, was elected Pope, he declared:

We know very well that even in the Holy See there have occurred
over the past years many scandals, abuses in spiritual matters, and
violations of the commandments that have become an open scandal
to all. Hence it is not suprising that this sickness has been transplanted
from the head to the members.

Prelates. In the 15th and 16th centuries two qualities were
required of any candidate for the office of bishop: noble birth
and a degree in canon law. A knowledge of theology was not
considered necessary; bishops were regarded more as administrators of ecclesiastical properties than as teachers of the gospel. The
medieval amalgam of the sacred and secular conferred upon
bishops both spiritual and temporal authority, together with the
trappings more befitting a prince than a pastor. Highly indicative
of the unfortunate state of affairs is the fact that the profession
of faith, formerly made by bishops at their consecration, was
replaced by an oath of allegiance.

It is not difficult to see how abuses could easily arise out of the
medieval status of bishops. Absenteeism was a major abuse;
many bishops lived away from their dioceses, visiting them only
occasionally, leaving administrators in their place, but regularly
collecting the revenues. Pluralities were another common abuse;
one man could hold the office of bishop over several dioceses, presumably with no injustice to any of them since he didn't have to
care for any of them personally. Another abuse which arose was
the promising of a diocese to a successor before it was vacant.
This last practice was not unknown to encourage the homicide
of the original holder! It is apparent that all too often men were

attracted to the ranks of the hierarchy less by the desire to serve than by sheer avarice.

Priests. In 1350 an epidemic morbidly known as the Black Death swept Europe. Thousands were stricken; and before the epidemic had run its course, one-third of the population died. Even a greater percentage of priests were stricken, however, since theirs was the pastoral care of the sick and dying. The ranks of the clergy were decimated; and in order to recoup the losses, the intellectual and moral standards for ordination to the priest-hood were drastically reduced. In too many instances priests were ordained who were barely literate and whose characters left some-thing to be desired. There was no seminary system to ensure the proper education of aspirants to the clerical life. A would-be priest simply lived for a while with an experienced cleric, "caught the hang" of it, and then presented himself for ordination.

Priests were not only under-educated; they were underpaid. They received no set salary and, as a result, had to depend upon the generosity of the people for their sustenance. This situation led only too easily to simony, to priests' charging a stipulated price for their services. It was known for priests to ask a fee for anointing the sick and dying; and if the sick person recovered after the sacrament, there was frequently an additional charge.

The scandal offered by the ignorance and avarice of many priests was further compounded by the open practice of con-cubinage. Priestly celibacy was regarded as an ideal, but too often as one that was impractical. Its violation was tolerated with an unwholesome broadmindedness.

People. It is little wonder that the faith of the people in the 15th and 16th centuries often lacked substance. They were too frequently deprived of proper instruction from their pastors in even the fundamentals of Christianity. Such neglect had its effects. Religion for them became largely a matter of externals. Supersti-tion was rampant. Prayers were offered much in the vein of magic formulas. Relics and indulgences were sought more avidly than encounter with Christ in the sacraments.

The late medieval period was also a time of tension in the Church between the people and the clergy, arising from the eco-nomic advantages which the clergy enjoyed. The Church was the richest landowner in all Christendom, especially in Germany, where it is estimated that nearly one-third of the real estate was under ecclesiastical control. Since Church property was tax-exempt, it was necessary for the people to pay all the more in taxes. Tensions as well as resentment further marred the relationship between the people and clergy because of the competition in which the Church engaged. Many monasteries operated not only farms but breweries, wineries, taverns, and bakeries. As if the competition did not foster hard feelings enough, the privileges which these ecclesiastical enterprises enjoyed aggravated already strained relations. The Church's establishments of business were permitted to open on Sundays and feast days, while their lay competitors were compelled by civil law to remain closed.

Practices. When people are poorly educated and religion becomes for them largely a matter of externals, devotional practices can easily become gross misrepresentations of the faith they are meant to express. Thus, in the late Middle Ages, that which is peripheral in Christianity assumed a central importance. Certain acts of piety, orthodox enough in themselves, were exaggerated to the point of becoming grotesque. Devotion to relics, for example, reached a height of absurdity. Such spurious "relics" as a drop of milk from the breast of the Virgin Mary, a piece of the tablecloth used at the Last Supper, or a leaf from the burning bush of Moses were commonplace. At the church in Wittenberg, where Martin Luther first made a name for himself, over 5,000 "relics" were collected, with claims of "indulgences of more than 1,443 years" to be obtained by paying honor to them.

The Eucharist itself, the central act of Catholic worship, was not above abuse. Rather than a sacrificial meal at which one encountered Jesus Christ through scripture and sacrament, the Mass came to be regarded as a panacea for any sickness, whether of body or soul. Regular attendance at the liturgy was supposed to be a guarantee against sudden death and a protection against blindness, starvation, and bodily injury. The elevation of the host and chalice immediately after the consecration assumed a central significance it was never meant to have. Gazing upon the host was thought to be the very essence of Eucharistic worship, and some priests were known to receive larger stipends for holding the host and chalice longer during the elevations. There were even incidents in which lawsuits were initiated in order to insure a more favorable view of the altar during Mass.

The need of the Church for reform in the 16th century is a historical fact. It does no service to either the cause of truth or the Catholic Church to deny this fact or in any way to whitewash it. The Church, by its own appraisal, is human as well as mysteriously divine; it is vulnerable to all the temptations and faults, the heartaches and natural shocks, that flesh is heir to. Yet, shameful as the abuses of that period were, they should not be exaggerated to the extent that the holes appear bigger than the boat. The 15th and 16th centuries gave evidence also of profound faith and spirituality. The corruptions were neither that total nor all-embracing.

In attacking the abuses within the Church, the 16th-century Reformers did not deny that the Catholic Church was the authentic offspring of the Church of the apostles. They accused the Church of being so corrupt, however, and so unfaithful to its apostolic heritage, that it no longer deserved to command either respect or loyalty. They regarded the corruption of morals within the Church as an effect of a corruption in doctrine; and they traced both back to the fourth century and the days of Constantine, when the Church was permitted to leave the catacombs and assume a position of influence and power in society. Desiderius Erasmus, the foremost humanist and intellectual of the 16th century, was not outdone by any of the Reformers as a critic of the abuses present in the Church of his day. Yet he did not accept the Reformers' thesis that the Church was so vitiated by corruption that it thereby forfeited its authority. As he put it, he refused to believe that the Holy Spirit had abandoned the Church for twelve hundred years only to return to set it aright in the person of Martin Luther.

The causes which precipitated the Protestant Reformation did not appear as clear-cut and classifiable in the 16th century as they do to us. Standing alone, none of them would have sufficed to bring about the rupture within the Church. Yet, taken together as a constellation of elements, at a particular time, in a particular set of circumstances, they fused to cause a sequence of events which split Western Christianity into two camps. The success of the Protestant Reformation was due every bit as much, if not more, to political, social, and economic factors as it was to reasons theological and ecclesiastical. One of the leading Lutheran reformers himself, Philip Melanchthon, was constrained to admit that the spread of the Reformation was due not so much to a desire to see the Church reformed as a desire to be freed from obedience to its authority. "They seek not doctrine and religion," he said, "but power and liberty."

It is interesting, too, to note that the Protestant Reformation could never have taken place if it had not been for the invention of printing shortly before by Johann Gutenberg. Not only did printing make Luther's writings easily available throughout Europe; it made the scriptures accessible to every home. The discrepancy between the simplicity of the apostolic Church and the pomp and splendor of 16th-century Catholicism became more apparent with the popularization of the Bible. And Luther was able to replace obedience to Papal and episcopal authority with personal reading of and deference to the scriptures.

The causes of the 16th-century Reformation were many and complex, going back long before 1517. Would they still have resulted in a schism between Protestants and Catholics if there had been no Augustinian monk named Martin Luther teaching sacred scripture at Wittenberg? It's hard to say. What can be said, however, without too much fear of contradiction, is that the course of the Reformation, the shape that Protestantism took, would not have come about were it not for the personality and drive of men like Martin Luther and John Calvin. Every bit as important as the fundamental causes of the Protestant Reform was the character of the men who played leading roles in its development.

Martin Luther

The Historical Facts

Thomas Carlyle, the 19th-century British historian, believed that "the history of the world is but the biography of great men." His observation certainly holds true in the history of the Protestant

Reformation: the course of events which led to the break and those which flowed immediately from it all pertain to the life and person of a Saxon monk.

Martin Luther was born in 1483 in Saxony, Germany. He was a thoughtful young man and a serious student. It was his father's wish that Martin become a lawyer, but young Luther had other inclinations. Both sensitive and pious by bent, he was attracted instead to the religious life. He entered the Augustinian Friars, and in 1507, at the age of twenty-four, Martin Luther was ordained a Catholic priest.

His many talents captured the attention of his religious superiors, and shortly after his ordination Father Luther was promoted to a teaching assignment. Continuing his studies at the same time, he earned for himself, at the youthful age of twenty-nine, a doctorate in sacred theology. When the newly established University of Wittenberg found itself in need of a professor of sacred scripture, Father Luther was assigned to fill the position. Here at Wittenberg two events took place that were to change the course of Luther's life and the Church's history. One was in the quiet of his study, the other in the square before the church door. Both were to make famous, and infamous, the name of Martin Luther, a name to be uttered in his own day in reverence or scorn.

The same sensitivity that had led young Luther to enter the religious life also left him vulnerable as a victim of scruples. For some time, both before his ordination and after, he had striven earnestly to advance in the spiritual life, practicing all manner of ascetical and devotional exercises in order to overcome the doubts he was suffering concerning his own salvation. He was obsessed by feelings of sinfulness and a stark terror of the justice of God. During his studies at Wittenberg, however, in conjunction with his lectures in sacred scripture, Father Luther suddenly gained a new personal insight into the epistles of St. Paul, especially those to the Galatians and Romans. He was reading the Epistle to the Romans, Chapter I, Verse 17, when suddenly he was struck with the force of a revelation: "This is what reveals the justice of God to us; it [the gospel] shows how faith leads to faith, or as scripture says, the upright man finds life through faith." Prior to this time, despite any counsels that he had received to the contrary, Luther had regarded God's justice as a harsh vindictiveness. On reading this particular passage at this particular time, he underwent a moving religious experience. He was exhilarated with relief at the realization that though God is truly just, his justice consists in the merciful pity he shows us by making us holy through our faith in Christ. The word "justice" acquired not only a different meaning for Luther, but this new meaning opened a new horizon to his life.

Besides lecturing at the University, Father Luther also began winning a reputation as a preacher. Some of his strongest sermons were those in which he preached against the abuses concerned with practices regarding indulgences, the remission of temporal punishment due to sin. Several errors about indulgences were then commonplace among the people; they believed, for instance, that an indulgence operated infallibly no matter what the interior dispositions of a person. Furthermore, indulgences in the 16th century could be obtained, not only by offering certain prayers, but also by contributing alms to various good works—a practice which easily led to the appearance of "buying" forgiveness. Such misunderstandings and abuses connected with indulgences were in no way alleviated by the overenthusiastic preaching of men like John Tetzel.

Tetzel, a Dominican, had been entrusted with the task of raising funds for the building of St. Peter's Basilica in Rome. For a donation to this cause, an indulgence was attached, provided that all the usual conditions of contrition and repentance were fulfilled. But Tetzel did not dwell in his preaching upon the interior dispositions required to obtain the indulgence. The money claimed his first interest, and he hawked the indulgences like a mountebank. In 1517 he drew close enough to Wittenberg to raise the moral indignation of the young preacher and professor at the University, Martin Luther. On the eve of All Saints', October 31, Father Luther nailed his celebrated Ninety-five Theses on the door of the castle church and announced his willingness to debate anyone on the value of indulgences. No one took up his challenge. No debate took place. But his theses were printed and, before long, distributed throughout Europe. Most of the theses were not opposed to traditional Catholic doctrine but, rather, were reactions to the abuses connected with preaching and practices regarding indulgences. But they gave Luther a reputation as both critic of the Church and one who dared to challenge its authority.

Luther's challenge was taken as an affront not only to John Tetzel but to the prestige of the entire Dominican Order. The Dominicans set about using their powerful influence to ruin the upstart Augustinian. Pope Leo was reluctant at first to become involved in the matter; it seemed little more than a feud between two religious communities. Luther was becoming more vocal, however, in his criticisms not only of indulgences but of other abuses within the Church and of the Pope himself. At the urging of the Dominicans, Pope Leo sent the foremost philosopher of the day, Thomas Cardinal Cajetan, as his emissary to obtain a recantation from Luther. Luther apologized for the violent outbursts he had made against the Pope, but he refused to retract either his criticisms against abuses or his teachings. He maintained that he would not retract so long as he was convinced he was right. And he would not be convinced otherwise except on the basis of sacred scripture. This was the first real break that Luther made with Catholic tradition. It was to be his essential break. For him the Church itself, interpreting the teachings of scripture, was no longer the foundation for faith; rather, Luther was saying, the basis of faith is the scripture itself as it is read and understood by any believer.

For holding fast to this unorthodox position, Luther was excommunicated in 1521. Such a sentence would ordinarily have left him liable to prosecution by the State; Luther, however, enjoyed the favor of the prince under whose domain he lived, and he escaped the usual punishment meted out to obdurate heretics, burning at the stake. In the same year as his excommunication, Luther was issued a writ of safe conduct and invited to appear before a meeting of leaders of both Church and State in Germany, including the German emperor himself, Charles V. Before this august body Luther held steadfast to the position he had expressed earlier and had repeated now many times: .

Unless I am shown by the testimony of the Scriptures—for I do not believe in popes or councils—unless I am refuted by Scripture and my conscience is captured by God's own word, I cannot and will not recant, since to set against one's conscience is neither safe nor honest. Here I stand. God help me, I can do no more. Amen.

By the time of his appearance before the Emperor, Luther had already produced a voluminous amount of writing. His pen did not cease for the remainder of his life. Question after question in theology came under his scrutiny, and he wrote about all of them with passion if not always with brilliance. He struck out not only against the authority claimed by Pope and bishops but also against the sacramental system of the Church and the belief in the sacrificial nature of the Mass. Like a leitmotiv, there recurred in his writings the themes of the primacy of scripture, the priesthood of the laity, and, above all, the doctrine of justification (holiness) by faith in Christ alone. Luther's writings, including a German translation of the Bible, constitute over four hundred works. They fill more than one hundred volumes.

The Reform movement spread from Wittenberg throughout Germany and beyond. It developed to an extent Luther had never dreamed possible; the reform that he had intended within the Church had become a movement outside of it. Dr. Luther, as he was now called, had married a former nun in 1525, four years after his excommunication. They had a family, and Luther's home became a center for students who came to enjoy Luther's hospitality, profit from his learning, and be regaled by his broad, oft-times crude peasant wit. Despite all of his fame and apparent success, however, the last days of the Reformer were not happy ones. Martin Luther died in 1546 at the age of sixty-three, well aware that the Reform he had started would not only remain outside the Catholic Church but that it was already suffering schism within itself.

An Attempt at Understanding

Like any controversial figure, Martin Luther is difficult to assess. Catholics have been wont to describe him as a scoundrel in league with the devil, a man with the mind of a cesspool and a mouth to match. Protestants have clothed him with the mantle of an Old Testament prophet, regarding him as the "dove of the Holy Spirit," a superhuman warrior engaged in battle with the anti-Christ. Such extremes do no justice to Luther. He was neither a giant villain nor a giant hero. As one ecumenically oriented historian put it: "He was an Augustinian Friar, of good intellect, piously bred, deeply anguished in his spiritual life, solving his personal dilemmas in a re-thought biblical theology. This theology led him to fulminate against the superficial legalistic religious practice of the time. He became the leader of the European religious break away from the Western Roman Church which became Protestantism."[1]

In fairness to Luther, certain popular misconceptions about him should be clarified:

1. Luther was not psychotic. It is true that he suffered from religious anxieties, sometimes to the point of anguish. But at no time were even his most critical contemporaries able to provide evidence that he had lost his balance. His early life, on the contrary, indicates that he was a person of exceptional sensitivity and conscientiousness.

2. Luther was not a lecher, nor was inability to cope with celibacy the motive for his break with Rome. Although Luther married, he seems to have done so, not out of any driving sexual need, but simply out of the conviction that celibacy was not of itself meritorious. He was convinced that marriage was a good and holy state instituted by God and that religious vows were worthless. There is reason, too, to believe that Luther married Catherine von Bora because she was having difficulty in finding anyone else who would have her.

3. Luther was not a gross or evil man. His language was strong and salty, it is true. Perhaps it would shock some of our more delicate sensibilities, but such was the popular parlance of his day. And if some of his descriptions of the Pope seem rife with invective, they are really no more so than some of the papal documents of the same period. By his own admission, Luther

[1] John M. Todd, *Martin Luther* (Westminster, Md.: Newman, 1964), pp. xvii, 271, 274.

was a man who enjoyed both food and drink, and we are given good reason to believe that these had their effects on his waist-line. If anything, however, such intemperance is often noted as a "Catholic vice."

Protestants today do not consider Luther a saint. They do, however, revere him as a champion of freedom against ecclesiastical authoritarianism. Catholic scholarship acknowledges Luther's brilliance and originality, regretting at the same time his radical subjectivism as a fatal flaw. Although most of his ideas were not novel, he did present a new synthesis. He emphasized the New Testament themes of the fatherhood of God, the sending of the Son, and the Son's message of forgiveness and love for all men. His positive contribution was "a new Christian vision, directly based on the Bible, with a renewed conviction of the sovereignty of God, of man's life as built on faith in him; a new face for religion, expressed in the people's language, taking them up into its practice in a more democratic fashion" (Todd, *Martin Luther,* p. 271).

It is important to note that history shows Luther never intended to establish a separate Church. He labored only for the reformation of the one Church established by Jesus Christ. He went to pains to show that his ideas in no way deviated from authentic Catholic tradition, that they have a basis in both scripture and the writings of the early Church Fathers. If this is true, then the following two points can be made.

For Protestants: "If Luther wanted a reformed Church, but not a multiplicity of sects, then a reformed Church of Rome could with justice claim at least the serious attention of Protestants, if she invited them to consider reunion" (Todd, *Martin Luther,* p. xvii).

For Catholics: "If Luther's criticism of the Roman Catholic Church and his separation from it and his foundation of a re-formed tradition provided the main impetus which led the Roman Catholic Church to undertake measures of reform which everyone had admitted necessary for the previous century and which she had failed to achieve, and if the Lutheran tradition has been fruitful in Christian lives, then the Protestant tradition can harldy be lacking some divine and Christian sanction" (Todd, *Martin Luther,* p. xvii).

John Calvin

The Historical Facts

John Chauvin—or, as he is usually known in English speaking countries, John Calvin—was a Reformer of the second generation but by no means one of second class. Already by the second half of the 16th century, Calvin's personal influence and that of his writings exceeded Luther's. Calvinism has been called "the chief force in the Protestant world today." His spirit animates broadly some one hundred million Protestants, including most of the members of the World Council of Churches.

John Calvin was born in Picardy, France, in 1509. His early training was received with an eye to the priesthood, but he later set his sights on becoming a lawyer. He distinguished himself in both legal and theological studies. At the age of twenty-four, however, there occurred an event that was to change his life and subsequently the history of Protestantism. Like Luther, Calvin experienced what he later called a "sudden conversion." He attached himself to the Reform movement and, in 1536, published a small catechism which was to develop into the monumental work both of his own life and of 16th-century Protestantism, *The Institutes of the Christian Religion.* From a catechism it grew into a copious manual of Biblical, dogmatic and pastoral theology, explaining the chief principles of the Reform and ordering them into a logical, coherent synthesis.

Through the efforts of men like Ulrich Zwingli, Switzerland had become a fertile Protestant field. When passing through Geneva, Calvin was persuaded to devote himself to the work of the Reform in that city. He felt under obligation to consent and began his career there as a Reader of Holy Scripture. Shortly thereafter he was elected a minister. In 1538 he was banished from the city because of a disagreement with the magistrates, but three years later he was called back and remained there the rest of his life. For the next twenty-three years, until his death in 1564, he worked tirelessly, making Geneva the nerve center of all Protestantism. Here Reform preachers were trained to do missionary work in England, Scotland, France, Poland, and Hungary. Because of them, the Netherlands in particular became a bastion of Calvinism.

The first major split within Protestantism occurred when Luther and Calvin parted ways over their understanding of the Eucharist. Luther maintained belief in Christ's real presence in the sacrament; Calvin followed the earlier example of Zwingli and taught that the Eucharist is simply a symbol of the Lord's body and no more. Their differences later became more acute and extended to other areas as well, e.g., the canon of scripture, the Church, the sacraments, and predestination.

An Attempt at Understanding

John Calvin has been caricatured as a frigid logician, a grim puritan with a Messianic complex, an enemy of laughter who enjoyed hurling anathemas from the pulpit. Such an image is not altogether fair. It is true that Calvin could be petty and irritable, and in controversy he could display both bitterness and wrath. But these faults resulted in great measure from his notorious bad health and an inability to sleep, and Calvin was not above admitting his failings. "I confess that I am irritable, and though this vice displeases me, I have not succeeded in curing myself as I would wish."

Closely related to his apparent intransigence was Calvin's implacable dedication to purity of doctrine; for him it was the very soul of the Church. Because of his zeal, Calvin insisted upon the execution of Michael Servetus for the heresy of denying the trinity of persons in God. But heretic burning should not single Calvin out; in the 16th century it was both a Catholic and Protestant pastime. It is to Calvin's credit that he pleaded, although unsuccessfully, for a less barbarous method of execution than burning at the stake. Although he is usually painted as the dictator of a Genevan theocracy, history shows that the greater part of Calvin's time there was spent in struggle with the civil authorities to maintain the Church's independence.

Calvin's greatest contribution to the Reformation was undoubtedly his systematization of Protestant theology. His *Institutes,* as a synthesis of his ideas, compare with the *Summa Theologica* of St. Thomas Aquinas. Some of Calvin's core ideas include the transcendent majesty of God and the utter sovereignty of his will. Calvin maintained vigorously the divinity of Christ, together with the belief that all we have received from God has come to us through Christ. It is precisely Calvin's emphasis on God's sovereignty that has led to his distorted image. He was not able to reconcile man's free will with the doctrine of God's almightiness, and so preferred to uphold God's complete sovereignty. From this arose his doctrine that God predestines some men to heaven and others to hell.

King Henry VIII of England

The Historical Facts

King Henry VIII of England is not to be put on a par with Luther or Calvin as an innovator or leader in the Reformation. Rather, he was an instrument in the transformation of England from a Catholic to a Protestant country. However, since England was to become a dominant political power in Europe and eventually throughout the world, Henry deserves consideration along with Luther and Calvin as one who helped to shape the course of the Protestant Reformation.

Henry VIII had married Catherine of Aragon, the widowed wife of his deceased brother. Since they were brother and sister-in-law, the marriage was permitted only after a dispensation from the Pope. But when Catherine was not able to produce a male heir for Henry, he began to regret the marriage. At the same time, he became infatuated with a woman of the court, Ann Boleyn. Henry knew that a divorce was out of the question, and to produce a legitimate heir Ann would have to be his lawfully wedded wife. Consequently, he sought a declaration of nullity for his marriage to Catherine on the grounds that the Pope did not have the authority to grant such a dispensation. When it became apparent that the annulment was not forthcoming, Henry grew restive. By an act of Parliament he had himself declared sovereign head of the Church in England, thereby denying that the Pope had any jurisdiction in the affairs of the Church in England.

Doctrine and ritual remained basically Catholic during Henry's reign, but after his death Protestant missionaries were imported from the Continent to introduce Protestantism into England. The nobles were interested in having England remain outside the Catholic camp, since their personal fortunes had been handsomely enriched by grants that Henry had made to them from property that had originally belonged to monasteries. When Henry's daughter Mary assumed the throne, she endeavored to return England to Catholicism, but her reign proved too short. Her zeal led her to the extreme of executing Protestant leaders, including the Protestant Archbishop of Canterbury; the only gain she made from her efforts was the inglorious title of "Bloody Mary."

With Queen Elizabeth I, any link that might have existed between Rome and the Church in England was dissolved. Elizabeth was the daughter of Henry and Ann Boleyn; and since Catholics would have some scruple concerning the legitimacy of her claim to the throne, Elizabeth saw a distinct advantage to retaining her father's claim to be head of the Church in England. Protestantism was systematically taught throughout the realm, and the *Thirty-nine Articles* became the basis for English belief. The subsequent history of the Church in England saw the rise of extreme Calvinistic influences, only to be followed by a reaction to more Catholic tendencies. To this day the Church of England maintains a middle road between Geneva and Rome.

An Attempt at Understanding

The breakaway of the Church in England from the Catholic communion did not result merely from a monarch's amorous whim. It was the culmination of a trend toward an independent national Church that had been at work for some time. The Conciliar Theory had been popular in England long before Henry's love affair with Ann Boleyn, and the exact nature and extent of Papal primacy and authority were not at all clear in the 16th century. Considering these facts together with the low ebb at which Papal prestige found itself at those times, it is not altogether surprising that only two Catholics of any note demurred from taking the oath which recognized Henry as head of the Church in England. They paid with their lives for their loyalty to Rome. These two dissenters were John Cardinal Fisher, Bishop of Rochester, and Sir Thomas More, former Chancellor of England. Both have been enrolled in the Catholic Church's canon of saints and martyrs.

It might be mentioned in fairness that it was not simply a reverence for the sacredness of the marriage bond that prevented the Papacy from giving Henry the annulment for which he asked. Granting such an annulment would have been both an insult and an embarrassment to Henry's first wife, Catherine of Aragon. Catherine was a relative of the German emperor, Charles V. Pope Clement VII, from whom Henry asked the annulment, was loath to offend the Emperor, particularly since he was then being held captive in Rome by Charles' troops. The Pope procrastinated in his decision with the hope that in time Henry's infatuation would cool and the whole matter would pass. Henry's infatuation did cool, much to the discomfort of Queen Ann Boleyn's head, but the matter did not pass until England had already progressed far along the road to becoming the political champion of Protestantism.

The Catholic Counter-Reformation

The Historical Facts

A review of the 16th-century beginnings of Protestantism would not be complete without at least some word about the reaction it engendered in the Catholic Church. For some three hundred years Popes, councils, and saints had called for a reform within the Catholic Church, but to no avail. Protestantism compelled the Church to apply the scalpel to the festering wounds and excise the corruption. Unfortunately, just as the Protestant Reform was a reaction to Catholic abuses, the Catholic Counter-Reform was a reaction against what it considered Protestant excesses. It solidified the break between Catholics and Protestants, endowing it with a permanency which no one anticipated. It was an age of debate instead of dialogue. The break which began at Wittenberg was completed at Trent.

The outstanding monument of the Catholic Counter-Reformation was the Council of Trent. Periodically it convened from 1545 to 1563, enunciating Catholic doctrine pertinent to the questions raised by the Reformers and promulgating decrees for the reform of discipline within the Catholic Church. In its dogmatic decrees, the Council of Trent defined Catholic teaching on the canon of sacred scripture, tradition, the nature of original sin and justification. It defined the number and nature of the sacraments, above all the Eucharist and the sacrificial aspects of the Mass. In its disciplinary decrees, it set down clear rules of proper conduct for bishops, religious, and diocesan clergy. One of its most significant acts was the call for the establishment of seminaries for the adequate education of priests.

Almost as important as the Council of Trent in reforming the Catholic Church was the establishment of several new religious orders with the express purpose of counteracting Protestantism. After all, councils had called for reform before, but their mandates had never been carried out. Not so with the Society of Jesus, founded in 1534 by an ex-army officer, St. Ignatius Loyola. Ignatius organized his Society like an army, imbuing it with a spirit of intellectual and moral discipline together with an unswerving loyalty to the Pope. But Ignatius was not the only reforming saint of his day. St. Teresa of Avila and St. John of the Cross reformed the Discalced Carmelites; St. Philip Neri established the Congregation of the Oratory; St. Charles Borromeo established the first diocesan seminary; and St. Pius V put the programs of the Council of Trent into action.

Another, but not so consoling, aspect of the Counter-Reformation was the Inquisition. Systematically and sometimes even ruthlessly it sought to prevent Protestantism from taking root in Italy and Spain by ferreting out unorthodoxy and crushing it in the bud. The Inquisition was based upon the assumption that the Church is bound in justice to crush out error wherever it exists; and it was not above using secrecy, torture, and the death penalty for the vigilant protection of doctrinal purity. Such methods seemed at that time and in that mentality to be in the best interests of both Church and State.

An Attempt at Understanding

The Catholic Counter-Reformation rejected unequivocally nearly every aspect of the Reformation protest. With a long series of anathemas, the Council of Trent set forth Catholic teaching in contradistinction to the doctrines of Luther and Calvin, although it never mentioned either one by name. It assumed a posture of defensiveness which characterized the Catholic Church for the next four hundred years. Whatever was attacked or ridiculed by the Reformers was deliberately upheld and even emphasized by the Counter-Reformation. Devotion to Mary and the saints, the veneration of relics, worship of Jesus as the "Infant of Prague," the rosary, novenas—all of these and similar thoroughly "Catholic" practices have flourished since the 16th century almost in defiance of Protestant feelings.

The defensiveness engendered by the Council of Trent developed into a polemical attitude among Catholic theologians. From the day Luther challenged all-comers to a debate on indulgences until the convocation of the Second Vatican Council, Protestant-Catholic relations were characterized by attack and counterattack. Catholic theological manuals formulated Catholic teaching in terms of a defense against what were considered Protestant errors. The result was a one-sided, apologetic theology:

1. Protestants emphasized the Bible as the unique foundation for faith; the Catholic Church reacted by emphasizing tradition as the basis for faith.

2. Protestants emphasized the internal, spiritual nature of the Church; Catholics reacted by emphasizing the Church's external organizational structure.

3. Protestants emphasized the priesthood of the laity; Catholics countered with an emphasis on the hierarchic, ministerial priesthood.

4. Protestants laid emphasis on the Eucharist as a meal commemorating the Lord's Supper; Catholics reacted by laying emphasis on the sacrificial nature of the Mass.

5. Protestants denied the validity and usefulness of devotion to Mary and the saints in an effort to emphasize devotion to Christ;

Catholics countered with stronger exhortations than ever to venerate Mary and the saints.

The Catholic Church reacted not only to Protestant doctrines but also to its tendency toward individualism. The Catholic Church had always tended to lay stress upon the importance of ecclesiastical unity. Now, with the disintegration of Christendom and the movement toward national Churches, a strong reaction set in not only for unity but uniformity:

1. Papal primacy was emphasized to the extent that it obstructed a full appreciation and expression of episcopal dignity. Bishops came to be considered as little more than the Pope's ambassadors. The result was a strong, centralized Vatican bureaucracy, chiefly Italian in character.

2. Latin was maintained as the language of the Church's worship, not only as a sign of unity among Catholics, but as a means of preserving it. The vernacular in the liturgy was regarded as dangerous to Catholic unity and conducive to national Churches. For a period of time even translations of the Canon of the Mass, i.e., vernacular missals, were forbidden.

3. Uniformity was demanded in all the liturgical rites of the Church. The slightest deviation was considered a rash and unlawful innovation. Even in the foreign missions, accommodation to the local culture was forbidden. Roman prelates presumed to direct the missionary apostolate of the Church in the Orient and elsewhere, even though they themselves had never left the shadow of St. Peter's Basilica.

The establishment of the seminary system proved to be one of the most far-reaching reforms effected by the Counter-Reformation. It raised the caliber of intellectual and moral formation for priests to a standard of excellence which the Church had not previously known. Unfortunately, it also served to cut off the Catholic clergy from the mainstream of contemporary intellectual life. Separated from the university, the instruction of seminarians for the priesthood tended all too often to be more of a process of indoctrination than education.

A final characteristic of the Catholic Counter-Reformation was its siege mentality. Criticizing the Church was regarded as tanta-mount to heresy or at least a grave expression of disloyalty. It was felt that calling attention to any shortcomings within the Church ran the risk of doing more harm than good. Furthermore, the Church became hypersensitive to innovation. Any new ideas, interpretations, or ways of expressing Catholic teaching immedi-ately became suspect. Catholic theologians were reduced to parroting the tried and true formulas of ages past without regard for problems, needs, or thought patterns of their own day. The 13th was canonized as the greatest of centuries, and the Catholic Church made a mighty effort to close any further advancement out of its life.

Conclusion:

Vatican Council II has been described as the "end of the Counter-Reformation." The phrase is both apt and significant. It implies that the time for polemics is done, that defensiveness is past. It connotes openness instead of argument, dialogue instead of debate. The Protestant Reformation has traditionally been regarded as a punishment visited by God upon the Church because of its sins. It is now the time to consider whether or not it was perhaps also a blessing. As Cardinal Newman pointed out, "It could never be that so large a portion of Christendom should have split off from the communion of Rome and kept up a protest for three hundred years for nothing."

The Reformation did not end with Luther and Calvin. Protes-tantism has developed since the 16th century, changed, and, in certain instances, has even come to contradict some of its original principles. Understanding Protestantism demands a knowledge not only of its 16th-century beginnings but also of its subsequent history and development.

Suggested Reading

Baum, Gregory, ed. *Ecumenical Theology Today.* Ch. 17, "The Changing Image of Luther." Paulist, 1964.
Greenspun, William B., and William A. Norgren. *Living Room*

Dialogues. Dialogue No. 5, "Reform—An Essential Element in the Church." Paulist, 1965.

Hughes, Philip. *A Popular History of the Reformation*. Doubleday, 1957.

Jedin, Hubert. *Ecumenical Councils in the Catholic Church*. Herder, 1960.

Lortz, Joseph. *The Reformation*. Newman, 1964.

Osborne, John. *Luther*. New American Library, 1963.

Todd, John M. *Martin Luther*. Newman, 1964.

5 / The History and Development of Protestantism

We must count among the worst evils of our time the fact that the Churches are separated from one another to the extent that a human society scarcely exists among us much less that holy communion of Christ, which all profess by their words, but which few sincerely seek in reality.

—JOHN CALVIN

The spark struck by Luther ignited into a movement that spread with brush-fire rapidity and a similar devastation. From Wittenberg the Reform movement exploded out into the rest of Germany and beyond its borders. The enthusiasm and passion of Luther and the first generation of Reformers gave way to the systematizing efforts of Calvin's Geneva, not only in the area of theology but also in missionary activity. The result was chaos, both personal and political. At first the onslaught between Catholics and the Reformers was only verbal, but words soon enough gave way to weapons. It was an age in which religion, despite its low ebb, was taken with great seriousness by men and was recognized as influencing all other facets of life. Almost from the beginning, opposing loyalties split Europe, individual countries, and even families. Few Catholics or Protestants proved able to approach one another with any sentiment other than enmity. Even when violence subsided, hostility remained.

Four Centuries of Conflict

Europe

Religious differences in 16th-century Europe aggravated tensions caused by political interests and ambitions. Nationalism fused with religious zeal and ignited into conflict, persecution, and even war, all in the name of God and religion. Early in the Reformation, German princes, at odds with one another over the question of religion, reached a practical political compromise with the principle that "the religion of the leader is the religion of the land." This standard was adopted throughout Europe. The civil ruler dictated the criteria of orthodoxy, and religious dissent became tantamount to treason. State Churches were the norm, and until recent times a map could be drawn separating Catholic from Protestant Europe.

In *Germany* the Thirty Years War (1618–1648) marked the struggle between the German Protestant princes and the German Catholic princes led by the Emperor. Although it was supposedly a war of religion, it had strong and even primarily political motivations. Witness the alliance of Catholic France led by Cardinal Richelieu with the Protestant princes against the Catholic Emperor of Austria. The war concluded with a treaty permitting Protestant princes to dictate the religion of their people. Since that treaty, the Peace of Augsburg, Austria and southern Germany have been traditionally Catholic, northern Germany traditionally Lutheran.

In *France* struggle ensued between the Catholics and the French Calvinists, called Huguenots. The French kings opposed the introduction of Protestantism into France and persecuted the Calvinists, but French Protestantism continued to grow both in numbers and influence. The Catholics were alarmed at the possibility of losing political control, and the ensuing civil conflict became violent and often bloody. The most notorious example is the so-called St. Bartholomew's Day massacre in which Catholics slew thousands of French Protestants out of anger, revenge, and political ambition. Eventually the French Huguenots were given almost complete religious freedom and civil rights.

In *Italy* the Inquisition was used by the Popes to ferret out heresy and prevent it from spreading. Spying, denunciation, and the use of torture were used to obtain confessions. Heresy was punishable by death at the stake, and Pope Paul IV is said to have vowed, "If my own father were found to be a heretic, we would carry the fagots to burn him."

In *Spain* the Inquisition was used by the Spanish Crown to discover and prosecute any political dissenters. This included heretics, since they were considered subversive and disruptive of good order.

In the *British Isles, England* became Protestant under Henry VIII and the subsequent reign of his son, Edward. Henry's daughter Mary, a Catholic, succeeded to the throne and tried to return Britain to the Roman Catholic fold. She was beset by political opposition, however, and her execution of several Protestant bishops led to her unpopularity and the title "Bloody Mary." She was succeeded by Elizabeth I, whose long reign saw the complete establishment of Protestantism in England. Catholics were prosecuted, fined, and executed, not on the charge of religous conviction, but on that of treason. Protestantism in England was divided, however, into two camps. There were the Calvinists—or Puritans, as they were called—who wished to abolish the system of religious rule by bishops as well as any form of worship or practice which smacked of Catholicism. The Calvinists were opposed by the traditionalist Anglicans, who preferred to retain much Catholic theology and practice, including the episcopacy. The Puritans obtained control of the government for a brief period and, with Oliver Cromwell as head of State, persecuted both the Anglicans in England and the Catholics in Ireland. When the Puritans lost control, Anglicanism became the established Church; and the Calvinist party, now a minority, was expelled from the Church of England. These "dissenters" against Anglicanism gradually developed into the Congregational, English Presbyterian, Baptist, and Quaker Churches.

In *Scotland,* Calvinist Presbyterianism became the established Church through the efforts and preaching of John Knox. In *Ireland* political and religious persecution by the English Protestants led the Irish Catholics to remain even more staunchly faithful to their Catholic traditions.

In *Poland* the aristocracy became Lutheran at the onset of the Reformation. The peasants, however, remained loyal to the Catholic Church. The missionary efforts of the Jesuits eventually brought all of Poland back into the Catholic fold.

In *Switzerland* religious conflict developed into civil war. With Geneva as a Protestant stronghold, several Swiss cantons (states) became Protestant, while others remained Catholic.

In *Scandinavia,* Norway, Sweden, and Denmark became Lutheran. The *Netherlands,* while still a Spanish colony, witnessed a persecution of Protestants. The result was a civil war which saw the separation of Catholic Belgium from Reformed (Calvinist) Holland.

The United States

Animosity between Catholics and Protestants did not remain confined to Europe. It was brought over the Atlantic to the New World, and has marked much of the history of the United States. Except for Maryland, which granted toleration to non-Protestants for a period of time, the English colonies were generally intolerant of religious dissent. Catholics were not accorded basic civil rights. In the American Revolutionary War, Canada refused to join the Revolution against Britain because French Catholics feared the anti-Catholic bias which prevailed in the colonies.

It was only with the Constitution and Bill of Rights of the newly established United States of America that religious and civil liberty were accorded to members of all faiths. The newborn nation refused to establish a State Church. In the 19th century, however, European wars, famines, and political upheavals brought waves of Catholic immigrants to the United States from Ireland, Germany, Italy, Poland, and several other heavily Catholic countries. The fear that these "foreigners" would take over political control led to a campaign of anti-Catholic propaganda. In defense of the WASP (White Anglo-Saxon Protestant) tradition, there arose the Know-Nothing movement and the Ku Klux Klan. Anti-Catholic publications disseminated hair-raising tales of Popish plots and Catholic take-overs. Only the most servile jobs were open to

Catholics, who were segregated and compelled to live in Catholic ghettos.

Anti-Catholic bias has since declined in the United States, except for a brief resurgence during the Al Smith campaign of 1928. The election of a Catholic, John F. Kennedy, to the presidency in 1960 demonstrated conclusively that the United States was no longer simply Protestant, but pluralist, in its religious traditions.

A Theological History of Protestantism

The Protestant Reformation was a movement, not a man. It established a number of basic principles which changed the lives of whole nations, their thinking and their values. And further changes came with the subsequent development of these principles, as Protestants began reacting not only toward Catholics but toward one another. The history of the Catholic Church from the Reformation to the Second Vatican Council is largely one of retrenchment, centralization, and a harkening back to medievalism. The history of Protestantism, however, during this same period, is one of dialectical development, disintegration, and a mighty tension between two opposing forces—those who wished to return to apostolic Christianity and those who wished to conform Christianity to the contemporary. Understanding Protestantism today is futile without some knowledge of its history after the deaths of Luther and Calvin.

Confessions and Orthodoxy (c.1550 to c.1650)

In making the scriptures the sole rule of faith, the Reformers were compelled to draw up Confessions, i.e., statements of their Christian beliefs as Protestants. This led to the *Augsburg Confession* for the Lutherans, the *Institutes of Religion* for Calvinists, and the *Thirty-nine Articles* for Anglicans. Once these statements of belief were formulated, they had to be defined, explained, and defended. Protestant theologians set themselves to the task of upholding them against Catholic critics. Polemical histories were written; so, too, were scholarly compendiums of Protestant theology which used philosophy to buttress Protestant dogmas. Thus 17th-century Protestantism became marked by a period of stabilization and a somewhat dry intellectualism. Protestants began to yearn for the primitive dynamism of the early Reformation.

Revivalism (c.1650 to c.1800)

The age of Confessions and Orthodoxy was followed, in turn, by a period of reaction against the intellectualization of Protestantism. Instead of dogmas and theology, an "experience of the Holy Spirit" came to be considered essential to being a Christian. A personal and fervent relationship to Christ was considered the essence of faith, not just a profession of belief. With its emphasis on experience over dogma, Protestant Revivalism led to a certain doctrinal indifferentism: "It doesn't matter what you believe, so long as you believe *on* the Lord Jesus Christ." The spiritual openness which leads to faith thus came to be considered more important than the content of that faith. Justification by faith alone was no longer regarded as the cornerstone of the Reformation. In its place, freedom of conscience was held up as the principle tenet of Protestantism. Virtue and freedom were considered superior to dogma. The Reformation was viewed not so much as an evangelical revival as the event which liberated men from a servile dependence on the dogmatic formulations of an institutional Church.

Pietism was the result of Revivalism within the Lutheran Church in Germany. Concentrated at the University of Halle, Pietism originated as a moral and spiritual reform. It sought to enflame the heart of the believer at the expense of his intellect. Faith and reason thus became estranged from one another, and believing came to be regarded as more of a feeling or a sentiment than an act of the intellect.

The *Methodist Church* resulted from Revivalism within the Church of England. John Wesley, an Anglican priest who remained loyal to his Church, had one driving desire: to bring new life to its religious devotion. Influenced by Pietism, he preached the necessity of personal conversion and developed the religious revival as a veritable technique for inspiring religious fervor. Wesley's life was marked by tireless, devoted preaching of the Word of God. After his death, his followers broke with the

Anglican Church. They found its liturgy too temperate, its parochial life too uneventful. Methodism developed into a perpetual revival aimed at obtaining and maintaining an experience of the Holy Spirit. The early history of this country is marked by religious revivals led by Methodist preachers, particularly the Circuit Riders who traveled the western planes on horseback, their Bibles under their arms.

The *Society of Friends,* or *"Quakers,"* was formed by George Fox. This group lacks statements of belief, ordained ministers, ritual or sacraments. It rejects external forms, seeking instead to rely upon the "inner light," "the seed of God within." It is perhaps the most extreme form of experiential Christianity.

Liberalism (c.1800 to c.1900)

The next notable influence on Protestantism resulted from the impact of 19th-century rationalism. Since faith was considered little more than feeling or sentiment, reason became absolute in its field. Liberalism sought to reconcile faith with the principles of the Enlightenment and the discoveries of science. Reconciliation, however, often led to a de-supernaturalization of Christianity, resulting in the caricature of a God without wrath bringing men without sin into a kingdom without judgment through the ministrations of a Christ without a cross. A faith identified with feeling was unable to withstand the onslaught of scientific discoveries which seemed to contradict it. Protestant Liberalism capitulated to the rationalism of the age and reduced Christianity to merely natural components. Jesus Christ was regarded as no more than an ethical philosopher, a religious genius. The scriptures were an outstanding example of man's religious insights, inspiring maybe but not inspired. The doctrines of traditional Christianity were expressions of religious sentiments adequate for their age but no longer relevant.

Unitarianism was founded in England and in the United States in the late 18th century. It denies both the divinity of Christ and the Trinity, along with any form of supernaturalism, whether a revelation or a relationship, such as grace. In short, it rejects all the basic dogmas of traditional Christianity; yet it claims to be

Christian simply because it seeks to profess and practice "the religion of Jesus, so simply and beautifully given in the Sermon on the Mount." It is an example of how far Liberal Protestantism can go and still call itself Christian.

Biblical Criticism and the *Quest for the Historical Jesus* both resulted from the application of science to the study of scripture. Archaeology, linguistic analysis, and comparative literature indicated that the Bible is not unique. This led some scholars to deny that it was inspired. Investigation brought to light that the authors of the scripture did not intend to write merely factual, scientifically accurate, detailed history. This led some scholars to deny that the Bible was historical at all. Since the gospels were written by men who viewed Christ with the eyes of faith, a number of scripture scholars, including Dr. Albert Schweitzer, began a "Quest for the Historical Jesus," an attempt to sift faith from history. They failed to do so, and many came to deny any historical foundation whatever for the faith. Liberal Protestant scripture scholars continue in their efforts to free the Bible from "myths," accepting some of the words of Christ but denying his miracles.

The *Social Gospel* became the substitute for a Christianity which had lost its doctrinal foundation. If the revelations and miracles of the Bible could not be accepted by Liberal Protestants, at least the ethical teachings could. Loving one's neighbor and doing good became the heart of the Liberal Protestant gospel. Outstanding commitment to the alleviation of misery and social evils, such as war, poverty, and racial hatred, characterize exponents of the Social Gospel. But their dedication often springs more from a philanthropic, humanitarian ideal than from an explicit love of God. And thus, ironically, the same Protestantism which initially expounded faith without works became, under the influence of Liberalism, a religion of works without faith.

Fundamentalism and Neo-Orthodoxy
(1900 to present)

Fundamentalism was a reaction to the dogmatic indifferentism of Liberalism. It cuts across denominational lines in its attempt to preserve orthodox Christianity from rationalism. Since the

Bible is the sole rule and basis for a Protestant's faith, Fundamentalism seeks to defend that faith with the doctrine of the Bible's utter and complete immunity from error.

Fundamentalism holds that there are certain "fundamentals" of the Christian faith. If a man denies any of these, he cannot be called a Christian. These fundamentals include, first and foremost, the infallibility or inerrancy of the Bible, then the divinity and virgin birth of Christ, his miracles, the saving power of his death, his physical resurrection, and his return in glory at the last day. There is some disagreement among Conservative Christians, as Fundamentalists prefer to be called, but all of them hold vigorously to the doctrine that the Bible contains no error whatsoever. The scripture is taken as the literal word of God. Every word in it, according to Fundamentalists, was dictated by God to the men who wrote it. Some have even gone so far as to insist that even the punctuation of the Bible was inspired and hence without error. In its tendency to consider everything in the Bible literally as the "gospel truth," Fundamentalism upholds as literal such theses as the creation of the world in seven days of twenty-four hours each, the talking serpent of Eden, and the story of Jonah in the whale's belly. It refuses to apply scientific literary criticism to the Bible.

At the heart of Fundamentalism is its concern for an individual's salvation. The one important question is, "Have you been saved?" The man who accepts Christ as his Savior is assured of heaven and receives the grace of God to enable him to overcome sin in his earthly life. Belonging to this theological family are most Pentecostal and Holiness Churches, a number of Baptist Churches, particularly the Southern Baptist and Conservative Baptist, some Presbyterians and Lutherans. With Fundamentalism, Protestantism became a "religion of the Book," a religion based upon the words of a "paper pope."

Neo-Orthodoxy is an attempt to take the Bible seriously but not literally. It is Orthodoxy, but with a difference. It upholds the great Biblical themes of sin and grace, crucifixion and resurrection. At the same time, however, it makes unhesitating use of the insights of scientific Biblical study. The dividing line between "Liberal" and "Neo-Orthodox" Protestants has become increasingly difficult to trace. Most Neo-Orthodox are converted Liberals.

For them the Bible is considered not so much as being the Word of God as containing the word of God. They repudiate emphatically the literalism of the Fundamentalists. To this theological family belong most of Protestantism's contemporary theologians.

Contemporary Trends in Protestant Theology

Karl Barth emphasizes the fact that God is utterly transcendent, that is, "wholly other." According to Barth, there is a gulf between God and man, between time and eternity, a gulf dug by man's sin. Because of this gulf, God cannot be known by us through any comparison with anything that we are or have. Barth extols faith over reason, since, according to him, man's reason is sullied by selfishness and man cannot know God unless God reveals himself. God reveals himself, according to Barth, in concrete situations as in "I" to "Thou." Barth has been attacked by Liberals because he denies that man's reason is a valid means to know God. He is also attacked by the Fundamentalists because he denies the verbal inspiration of the Bible.

Emil Brunner was once a disciple of Karl Barth, but later broke with him. Brunner admits that man can know something about God from reason, but holds that this natural knowledge of God is always blurred by the sinfulness of man. God, he maintains, cannot be known objectively, however; he is truly known only through an "I-Thou" relation. Original sin, he holds, is not inherited, but rather requires a free decision.

Reinhold Niebuhr is the leader of Neo-Orthodoxy in this country and is considered by many as the most important contemporary American theologian. He holds that God transcends the world, but is also immanent and active within it. Our earthbound logic can speak about God, but not adequately; reason must use symbols in speaking about God, symbols that point to another dimension of reality. These symbols Niebuhr calls "myths." God can be known by men only through these symbols, such as the creation and fall accounts in Genesis. These symbols are to be taken seriously; they do contain truth, but not literally. Niebuhr denies vigorously the divinity of Christ and the very possibility of an Incarnation.

Paul Tillich has been called "the last Liberal," in holding that Christianity can be understood by reason and must be subjected to it. Religion, according to Tillich, is not a matter of certain beliefs or practices, but simply an "ultimate concern" whereby a man says to someone or something, "Not my will but thy will be done." According to Tillich, the popular idea of God is not worthy of ultimate concern. God should not be sought outside of nature, but rather through nature. The world is not apart from God; it is the medium of his continuing activity. God, for Tillich, is the very "ground of our being," and we must surrender ourselves to him and to no other, whether Church, Book, or System.

The "Death of God" theologians maintain that the popular notion of God, and even that notion described by the Bible, is not adequate for our age. They deny that we can know anything positive about God. According to them, traditional Christianity, its creeds, worship, and sacraments, are totally irrelevant to our age. It would be unrealistic to presume that all—or even most—Protestants have been influenced by the thought of the aforementioned theologians. They have received mention here, however, because they are the outstanding thinkers in contemporary Protestantism.

A Brief Sketch of Major Protestant Churches

The Evangelical Churches (Lutheran)

Founded by Martin Luther in the 1520's in Germany. They are found primarily in Germany, Scandinavia, and the United States.

Doctrine consists of the Nicene Creed, the Apostles' Creed, and the principles that a man is made holy by grace alone, which comes from faith alone, which is based on scripture alone. These are found in the Book of Concord, which contains the Lutheran Confessions.

Church government is theoretically congregational, whereby a parish is governed by a council made up of elected laymen, headed by the pastor. Parishes band together into synods, however, equivalent to the Catholic dioceses. Synodal presidents are coming to function more as bishops in their authority.

Sacraments are only two, Baptism and the Lord's Supper. Confirmation and Penance are practiced, but are not considered sacraments. Christ's real presence in Holy Communion is believed, but without an explanation of how. Marriage is considered holy but not a sacrament, and remarriage after divorce is considered wrong but admissible.

Special characteristics of the Lutheran Churches include their willingness to retain many of the Catholic traditions which other more radical reformers rejected. The Missouri Synod in this country is noted for its conservatism.

The Presbyterian and Reformed Churches (*Calvinist*)

Founded by John Calvin in the 1530's in Switzerland. John Knox was an apostle of Calvinism to Scotland and founded Scotch Presbyterianism. Reformed Churches are found primarily in Holland, France, and the United States.

Doctrine is contained in the Westminster Confession (Creed), as the "system of doctrine taught in the Holy Scriptures." The Church is considered as any congregation where the scriptures are rightly taught and the sacraments rightly administered. Predestination, the doctrine that God infallibly decrees some men to heaven and others to hell, was once a focal point but is no longer emphasized.

Church government is presbyteral, hence the name "Presbyterian." A presbyter is an elder. The pastor is the teaching elder of a parish; a group of ruling elders, elected by the congregation, care for the administration of the parish; a deacon is elected to care for the poor and administer the charitable works of the congregation. A pastor is "called" by a congregation and acts as an employee. The ultimate authority within the Church, however, is held not by one person, not by a group of bishops, not by the local congregation. Rather, it is vested in a quasi-democratic organization called the Presbytery, consisting of delegates representing a number of congregations.

Sacraments are only two in number, Baptism and the Lord's Supper. Infant baptism is practiced. In the Lord's Supper, Christ is said to be only represented and not present. Any sacrificial character of the Eucharist is denied. Marriage is not considered a sacrament, and remarriage after divorce is permitted if there was reason for the divorce, e.g., infidelity, or if there is penitence for failure.

Special characteristics of Calvinist Churches include their emphasis on sacred scripture and Biblical preaching. Little deference is paid to ecclesiastical tradition. Their worship is marked by gravity and restraint, with little or no ornamentation in their churches. Calvinist morality has been traditionally puritan with a heavy emphasis on honesty, thrift, and cleanliness.

The Anglican Communion of Churches (Episcopalian)

Founded in 1563 when Queen Elizabeth conclusively severed the ties between the Church in England and the Roman Catholic Church by the promulgation of the Thirty-nine Articles of the Anglican Church. American Anglicans seceded from those in England at the time of the American Revolution, taking the name "Protestant Episcopal Church."

Doctrine is expressed in the four principles of the Lambeth Quadrilateral, namely, the sufficiency of scripture, the Apostles' and Nicene Creeds, the sacraments of Baptism and the Lord's Supper, and the historic episcopate.

Church government is episcopal, with bishops holding the ultimate authority in a diocese, assisted by priests and deacons. The bishops of a country are united to form the ruling body of a national Church, and these national Churches are members of a world association described as the "Anglican Communion." No bishop is supreme, but a position of honor is accorded the Archbishop of Canterbury.

Sacraments are Baptism and the Lord's Supper technically, although Holy Orders is considered sacramental in character; Confession and Anointing of the Sick are practiced in certain areas. The real presence of Christ in the Eucharist is affirmed, and the Lord's Supper is considered as having a sacrificial character.

Special characteristics of the Anglican Churches include their close kinship with the Roman Catholic Church. They include both

Catholic and Protestant elements, resulting at times in doctrinal and liturgical tension. So-called "High Church" Episcopalians emphasize Catholic tradition, sacramental worship, and elaborate liturgy; among them is a faction who refuse even to be called Protestants, preferring to be called Anglo-Catholics. "Low Church" Episcopalians minimize liturgy, conduct simple services, and emphasize scripture and personal religion more strongly; they tend toward the Protestant and evangelical. Added to these two groups are the "Broad Church" Episcopalians, who tend toward Liberalism in their theology, e.g., Bishop Pike. The great affinity of the Episcopal Church with Catholicism is demonstrated by the presence of religious orders of men and women and the acceptability of a belief in purgatory. Episcopalians today look upon themselves as a bridge between Protestantism and Catholicism; they have been leaders in the ecumenical movement.

THE FREE CHURCHES

The Free churches are a diverse number of Protestant denominations which broke away from an established Protestant Church from whose domination they wished to be freed. Among the larger of these Free Churches are the Methodist Churches, the Baptist Churches, the Church of Christ, and the Holiness Churches.

The Methodist Churches

Founded by John Wesley, an Anglican priest. He worked for the spiritual and moral renewal of the Church of England, and remained a member of that Church all his life. He assumed episcopal powers by ordaining priests. He is said to have preached three times a day for over fifty years, traveling over 200,000 miles on horseback. Methodists were active missionary evangelists in the early years of the United States.

Doctrine is based on the Thirty-nine Articles of the Anglican Church with some modification. Tradition is rejected as a source of revelation; scripture is regarded as sufficient. The Trinity and the divinity of Christ are upheld. Methodism emphasizes that man is made holy by faith alone. This faith, however, is a conscious feeling of the Holy Spirit working within, an "experience" of God's presence. The Church is considered primarily invisible.

Church government is highly organized and democratic. A bishop is the equivalent of a district superintendent, with the power to appoint pastors to congregations. Elders, i.e., ministers, and deacons make up the remainder of the Methodist hierarchy. Women may be ordained to either rank.

Sacraments are only two, Baptism and the Lord's Supper. Christ's presence in the Lord's Supper is accepted only "after a heavenly and spiritual manner," symbolically, without a sacramental or "Catholic" understanding. Methodism concedes the State the right to grant divorce and permits remarriage. It also permits any minister to preach in its pulpits and any believer in Christ to receive Communion.

Special characteristics include a "methodical" application to scripture study and to prayer, hence the name "Methodist." Emphasis is placed upon the "experience" of religion. Total abstinence from alcohol is part of its traditional morality. Methodists were most influential in bringing about national Prohibition.

The Baptist Churches

Founded by John Smythe, an Anglican minister, in the 1600's. It was brought to this country and established in Rhode Island in 1639 by Roger Williams. It has since developed into the largest single Protestant denomination in the United States. It divided before the Civil War over the slavery question; the cleavage along Northern-Southern lines was further fragmented after the Civil War along racial lines. Today there are some twenty-seven separate Baptist Churches in the United States.

Doctrine includes the Trinity, the divinity of Christ, original sin, our redemption by Christ, heaven and hell. The sufficiency of scripture is upheld; tradition is rejected. Justification comes by faith alone, and the "truly regenerated" are guaranteed final perseverance in grace and the attainment of heaven.

Church government is strictly congregational and democratic. The independence of the local parish, i.e., the "autonomy of the local church," is strictly upheld; this explains Baptist fragmentation. The ultimate governing power resides in the people, and majority rule prevails. A man becomes a pastor of a congregation at the will of the people.

Sacraments are only two, Baptism and the Lord's Supper. These, however, are not considered sacraments, but merely ordinances of Christ which are carried out in obedience to him. Since justification or holiness comes by faith alone, Baptism is simply an expression of faith and obedience and has no saving effect. Infant baptism is rejected, since faith in Christ is first demanded. Baptism is by total immersion and is considered valid only if performed by one of their own. The Lord's Supper is also simply the carrying out of the Lord's command. The bread and wine are considered mere symbols, and Christ's real presence is rejected; but only members baptized by immersion may receive it.

Special characteristics include emphasis on religious liberty and strict separation of Church and State. Baptist theology ranges from very Liberal, e.g., at the University of Chicago, to Fundamentalist, e.g., Billy Graham and the Southern Baptist Convention. Because of their emphasis on the independence of the local parish, Baptists fear a Christian super-Church and for the most part have remained aloof from the ecumenical movement.

The United Church of Christ
(Congregationalist; Evangelical Reformed)

Founded in June 1957, with the merger of the Congregationalist Churches and the Evangelical Reformed Church. The Congregationalists began with the merger of the Massachusetts Puritans and Pilgrims in 1629. The Evangelical Reformed Church resulted from a merger in 1934 of a German Lutheran Church with a Swiss Calvinist Church.

Doctrine in the United Church of Christ has been affected by its unionism. It has been very compromising. Belief is not required in any set creed, and doctrines are considered simply intellectual statements of religious experiences. The Bible is considered a natural, but sublime, record of religious sentiments. The Trinity and the divinity of Christ are not given traditional interpretations. Hell is implicitly denied.

Church government is congregational, with the local church determining not only its personnel but also its own doctrine and ritual.

Sacraments are considered only sacred ceremonies, and these are Baptism and the Lord's Supper. Baptism is not considered essential for either salvation or Church membership. The Lord's Supper is considered simply a symbol.

Special characteristics include an openness to cooperation and union to the extent that the United Church of Christ has been called the "interdenominational denomination." Congregationalists were pioneers in education in this country and were responsible for the founding of both Yale and Harvard Universities. Once intolerant of other religions, they have become very Liberal and anti-Fundamentalist.

The Churches of Christ (Disciples of Christ)

Founded in the United States by Thomas Campbell in the 1800's.

Doctrine is very flexible and anticredal, with the Bible alone as the only rule of faith. Some Churches are very Liberal, while others are Fundamentalist.

Church government is strictly congregational.

Sacraments are Baptism, which is by immersion and only for believers, and the Lord's Supper, which is only a symbolic memorial. Both are simply ordinances.

Special characteristics include the active involvement of the Liberal elements of the Disciples of Christ in the ecumenical movement. American Protestant ecumenism has greatly taken on the noncredal aspect of the Disciples of Christ. They are responsible for the publication of the *Christian Century,* the outstanding Liberal Protestant periodical.

The Holiness, Pentecostal, and Missionary Churches

Founded, and continue to spring up, in reaction to intellectualization and structuralization of the gospel.

Doctrine is Fundamentalist and rigidly Biblical, with heavy emphasis on "feeling" the presence of God. Among the Pentecostals this experience of the Holy Spirit expresses itself in an

emotional ecstasy. Christ's Second Coming is considered imminent.
Church government is strictly congregational.

Sacraments are considered simply ordinances, and these are
Baptism and the Lord's Supper. Services are consistently re-
vivalist in character.

Special characteristics include the proliferation of such Churches
in storefronts and among the poor.

Conclusion:

It is obvious from this brief study of the history and development of Protestantism that it is not a single Church. Neither is it
a single set of doctrines. Not only are there differences between
Churches, but often there are differences within single denominations. Protestantism is not a monolith, and while it might be
convenient to refer to all non-Catholic, non-Orthodox Christians
as "Protestant," the designation perhaps conceals more than it
reveals. This fragmentation of Protestantism, however, does not
mean that there is not a unifying principle or spirit among Protestant Churches. There is such a spirit and such a principle, and it
is one that explains the vitality, faith, and genuine holiness which
can be perceived within Protestantism.

Suggested Reading

Bouyer, Louis. *The Spirit and Forms of Protestantism*. A. V. Littledale,
    tr. Newman, 1956.
Brown, Robert McAfee. *The Spirit of Protestantism*. Part I, Ch. 3,
    "The Varieties of Protestantism." Oxford University Press, 1961.
Hardon, John A. *The Protestant Churches of America*. Newman,
    1958.
Neill, Stephen C., ed. *Twentieth Century Christianity*. Doubleday,
    1963.
Norwood, Frederick A. *The Development of Modern Christianity since
    1500*. Abingdon, 1956.
Pelikan, Jaroslav. *From Luther to Kierkegaard*. Concordia, 1963.
Rosten, Leo, ed. *Religions in America*. Simon and Schuster, 1963.
Tavard, George H. *Understanding Protestantism*. Paulist, 1964.

6 / The Spirit and Central Idea of Protestantism

> *The Catholic Church looks with due reverence at the common heritage which its separated brethren have preserved and which some of them have developed.*
>
> —POPE PAUL VI

In the light of its divergent history and the broad variety of Churches which claim adherence to its tradition, Protestantism is easier to describe than to define. Despite apparent contradictions, there is a logic to Protestantism; there are principles and patterns. Concentrating on the differences among Protestants does far less justice to their faith and religious practices than studying the principles which they hold in common. Protestantism is a spirit. Like any spirit, it might best be approached by first stating what it is not. Only then can some success be expected in trying to understand just what it is.

What Protestantism Is Not

Not a Single Church

A study of the history and development of Protestantism shows that it is not a single Church, such as the Catholic Church. Nor does the term "Protestant" refer to a number of sister Churches unified by the same faith and practice, such as the Eastern Orthodox Churches. Protestantism, rather, is the principle to which Protestant Churches subscribe. It is a common spirit, an idea. Much to the confusion of outsiders, Protestant Churches often differ radically from one another. Not only do they seem to lack common beliefs and worship; they also mutually contradict and often disown each other. Lutherans, with their emphasis on creeds, are Protestant; so too are Unitarians, who refuse to accept any form of creed. Episcopalians in mammoth gothic structures are Protestant; so too are Pentecostals in their storefront churches. Presbyterians are Protestant, and they worship with somber gravity; Southern Baptists are Protestant, and they worship with heated enthusiasm.

Not a Belief in Certain Doctrines

Although there are several convictions which most Protestant Churches share, Protestantism cannot be considered simply as believing in certain doctrines. For some Protestants, the Bible was handed down word for word from on high and is to be understood literally; for others, the Bible is simply a good book comparable to the Moslem Koran or the sayings of Confucius. Some Protestants believe that Jonah actually spent three days in the belly of a whale; others do not believe that Jesus Christ is God. Some Protestants baptize infants with a few drops of water on the head; others would not think of baptizing anyone but adults, and this perhaps in a lake or hired swimming pool. Some Protestant Churches hold that bishops are necessary; some say that they are only useful; others claim that they are a human corruption of the gospel. This wide variety of beliefs is found not only among individual Protestant Churches but even within them.

Not Simply a Protest against Catholicism

To many Catholics—and, indeed, to many Protestants themselves—Protestantism is simply a protest against Catholicism. A Christian who is neither Catholic nor Orthodox feels that automatically he must be a Protestant. Consequently, Protestants have often been encumbered with the negative image of being against, in principle, whatever the Catholic Church is for. Protestants seem to be against the Blessed Virgin Mary, against the saints, against the Pope, against confession, against purgatory, against indulgences, against parochial schools and bingo. This negative image of Protestantism is really quite unfair. To *stand against* something means to *stand for* its opposite. No faith lives by its denials. Neither does Protestantism. Traditional Protestantism embodies several basic, positive, Christian principles. Catholics do a severe injustice to Protestantism when they concentrate *only* on the "protest" aspect, and Protestants do a severe injustice to themselves and to their own faith when they neglect the positive principles of Protestantism and emphasize instead their negative denials of Catholicism.

The Spirit of Protestantism: Four Positive Christian Principles

Grace Alone

It has been said that the fundamental principle of Protestantism is the gratuity of salvation, the fact that God draws us and unites us to himself freely, without our deserving it in any way. It is not by our worthiness, our deservingness, our good works, that we are made holy and are united to God. It is by grace alone. The word "grace" means *gift,* and our union with Christ here on earth (our justification) and our future eternal union with Christ in heaven (our salvation) are both distinct gifts of God, gifts pure and simple, to which we have no claim. God can never be in our debt. To imagine ourselves as God's creditors would be to reverse the roles of creature and Creator. Union with God through Christ is supernatural, that is, entirely beyond any right of human nature. We enter into this union solely on the basis of God's love and generosity. This is the clear teaching of sacred scripture, particularly that of St. Paul:

But God, who is rich in mercy, out of the great love with which he loved us, even when we were dead through our trespasses, made us alive together with Christ (by grace you have been saved), and raised us up with him, and made us sit with him in the heavenly places in Christ Jesus, that in the coming ages he might show the immeasurable riches of his grace in kindness toward us in Christ Jesus. For by grace you have been saved through faith; and this is not your own doing, it is the gift of God—not because of works, lest any man should boast.

For we are his workmanship, created in Christ Jesus for good works, which God prepared beforehand, that we should walk in them. (Eph. 2:4–10)

. . . God shows his love for us in that while we were yet sinners Christ died for us. Since, therefore, we are now justified by his blood, much more shall we be saved by him from the wrath of God. For if while we were enemies we were reconciled to God by the death of his Son, much more, now that we are reconciled, shall we be saved by his life. (Rom. 5:8–10)

For the wages of sin is death, but the free gift of God is eternal life in Christ Jesus our Lord. (Rom. 6:23)

Catholic tradition affirms emphatically the doctrine of the gratuity of grace. It teaches that we are saved by God's grace alone. In the fifth century the Church condemned the doctrine of Pelagius, a priest who held that a man could get to heaven by virtue of his own natural powers without any special help from God. Pelagianism taught that a man could perform by himself good works worthy of the reward of union with God, that a man could, as it were, pull himself up to heaven by his own boot-straps. St. Augustine assailed this doctrine and won for himself the title "Doctor of Grace." Pelagianism was condemned as a heresy by several councils of bishops in Africa. Their condemnation of Pelagianism was solemnly approved by Pope Boniface II. To this day a man cannot remain a Catholic unless he holds that we are united to Christ, not by our natural good works, but by God's grace alone, that this grace is a gift which we cannot merit, that not only our initial union with God is a gift but also our perseverence in that union.

Martin Luther lived at a time when Catholicism, especially in Germany, was characterized by a heavy emphasis on externals. The great majority of Catholics acted as if their salvation depended upon the performance of a variety of pious practices. These external good works presumed the belief that God's grace unites us to Christ, but neither grace nor faith were sufficiently explained or emphasized. They were taken for granted and, hence, often forgotten. As a consequence, a man like Martin Luther, religiously sensitive and troubled at times by scruples, wrestled with the problem of how many pious practices he must perform to be holy. Luther was burdened with anxiety about his salvation. He was haunted by the question, "Have I done enough?" Nothing ever seemed enough; and Luther despaired of ever becoming convinced of his salvation, something for which he wanted absolute assurance. In this critical, anxiety-ridden state of mind, Luther obtained an insight from his reading of St. Paul's epistles to the Galatians and Romans concerning man's salvation by God's grace alone. He had heard this doctrine before and had read these words of St. Paul before, but suddenly they acquired a new relevance to him. They had a new meaning for him now, and he began to find in them the peace and assurance he was aching for. At last he *experienced* his own salvation: he became personally convinced that God's love and mercy, expressed in Christ's death on the cross, were infinitely greater than his weak sinfulness. Luther realized that salvation was not a reward; he did not have to try to earn it, because he could not possibly earn it.

From the Catholic viewpoint, justification by grace alone is a thoroughly Catholic principle. Without God's grace, man can do nothing. But Luther seems to have taught that, even *with* God's grace, man can do nothing. So taken up was Luther with man's weakness, sinfulness, and nothingness that he despaired of man's doing anything really pleasing to God, even after he had been united to Christ by grace. Luther implies in his writings that grace changes nothing in us, that we remain no less sinners after receiving grace than before. He describes grace as enveloping us like a cloak. Because man, even after union with Christ in grace, is not changed, neither are his works; therefore, they cannot in any way please God or bring a man closer to God. They cannot merit. Catholic teaching takes exception to this interpretation.

Luther wrote at a time when he, and almost all Catholic theologians with him, was unfortunately influenced by a decadent "hardly Catholic" philosophy which taught that there could be no real relationship between any two individuals, let alone between God and man. This philosophy, that of the Franciscan William of Occam, prevented Luther from seeing how God could make a man truly holy. Luther not only denied that man was good and could do anything good; he also seemed to deny that God could make man truly good and his actions truly pleasing. This attitude has sometimes led to pessimism, the attitude that man is simply vile and, even after receiving God's grace, can do no good. A reaction to this attitude has subsequently taken place within some Protestant Churches, one emphasizing man's initiative—"God helps those who help themselves"; "It really doesn't matter what you believe, or even if you believe, so long as you do the best you can, so long as your works are good." In essence, this is the very contradiction of Luther's primary principle.

Faith Alone

Both our justification, i.e., our union with God here on earth, and our ultimate salvation, i.e., our eternal union with God in heaven, are free gifts of God. We receive them by grace alone. But God has created us free human beings, and he respects that freedom. He does not thrust himself or his gifts upon us against our wills. We must be open to receive his gifts, and this openness is faith. We are justified and made holy by grace alone, on God's part, and by faith alone, on our part. Faith is man's response to God's revealing word, preeminently God's Word-made-Flesh, Jesus Christ. Sacred scripture testifies that God gives us his free gift of himself only if we believe; faith, in other words, is necessary both for our justification and our ultimate salvation:

And he said to them, "Go into all the world and preach the gospel to the whole creation. He who believes and is baptized will be saved; but he who does not believe will be condemned." (Mark 16:15–16)

And without faith it is impossible to please [God]. For whoever would draw near to God must believe that he exists and that he rewards those who seek him. (Heb. 11:6)

For I am not ashamed of the gospel: it is the power of God for salvation to every one who has faith, to the Jew first and also to the Greek. For in it the righteousness of God is revealed through faith for faith; as it is written, "He who through faith is righteous shall live." (Rom. 1:16–17)

. . . if you confess with your lips that Jesus is Lord and believe in your heart that God raised him from the dead, you will be saved. For man believes with his heart and so is justified, and he confesses with his lips and so is saved. (Rom. 10:9–10)

Catholic tradition affirms the teaching that faith is absolutely necessary for salvation. As stated by the Council of Trent: "We may be said to be justified through faith in the sense that faith is the beginning of man's salvation, the foundation and source of all justification, without which it is impossible to please God." Catholic theologians, however, with their penchant for precision, have analyzed the Biblical notion of faith into various components. The word "faith," when used in the Bible, refers to a reality which comprises *belief* in God's revelation (intellectual faith), *hope* in God's mercy, *love* for God, and *repentance* for past sins. The Church has traditionally taught that mere intellectual faith is not enough; for, in this sense, "even the demons believe" (James 2:19). Biblical faith, a living faith conjoined to love for God, opens a man to God's freely offered gift of himself. It is in this wider sense that a man is justified by faith alone. But this faith, made up of belief, trust, love, and repentance, is not an act which a man performs by himself and thereby wins God's grace; such faith is itself a free gift of God. Grace leads to faith, and faith leads to further grace. In other words, it is not because we believe that God loves us; it is because God loves us that we believe, and this belief expresses itself in acts of confidence, love, and repentance.

In living his faith, a Christian not only expresses his union with Christ; he grows in it. This increase of grace, that is, this greater intensification of a man's union with God, is likewise a gift of God. But it is a gift which demands our openness, our willingness, our faith filled with love; God does not make us holy contrary to our desires. Thus, acts of faith and love, already made holy by God's grace, not only express faith and love but also increase our capacity for faith and love and make us more open to receive God's grace, to become more intimately united to Christ. The preeminent acts of faith and love, whereby God unites us to himself, are the sacraments, above all, Baptism and the Eucharist.

Martin Luther rightly understood that justification by faith alone was a co-principle with justification by grace alone. Rather than being two distinct principles, they are two aspects of one and the same principle, namely, justification by Christ alone. We are made holy, not by ourselves, but by Jesus Christ. In coming to this validly Christian and thoroughly Catholic realization, Luther experienced the peace of mind he was looking for. He could allay his anxiety because, although by himself he could do nothing, he now understood with St. Paul that God "justifies him who has faith in Jesus" (Rom. 3:26). Luther defined faith not so much as belief but, rather, as a "lively, reckless confidence in the grace of God." He was a scripture scholar rather than an analytical philosopher-theologian, and his understanding of faith was the broader, Biblical-orientated one which included hope, love, and repentance as well as intellectual belief. Faith, for Luther, was an intensely personal act, an internal commitment, involving a man totally with all his powers and faculties. So intense was this act that it became for Luther a veritable "experience."

Since the time of Luther, Protestantism has laid extraordinary emphasis upon the internal, vitally personal nature of faith as a commitment to Christ. It has studiously refrained from any externals or formalities which might distract from the practice of personal religion or substitute for it. Thus, statues and images are conspicuously absent from most Protestant Churches. Worship ordinarily is simple and unadorned, bereft of ceremony or symbolism. Formulas of prayer are avoided in favor of spontaneous, informal prayer; and there is a minimum of legislation—and, sometimes, none at all—regarding requirements of worship, prayer, and penance.

Although a certain amount of misunderstanding arose between the early Reformers and Catholic theologians over the precise meaning of the phrase "justification by faith alone," there is no essential disagreement between the traditional Protestant approach to man's justification and the traditional Catholic approach. The narrower notion of mere intellectual assent, belief, was at that time confused with the broader Biblical understanding of a faith infused with trust, love, and repentance. Recent theological study, disengaged from the passion of heated controversy, has come to the conclusion that the two approaches complement rather than contradict one another. Protestantism tends to emphasize God's free generosity, while Catholicism tends to emphasize man's openness to that generosity. Both emphases are compatible, and any Catholic can stand shoulder to shoulder with any Protestant in singing the battle hymn of the Reformation, "A mighty fortress is our God, a bulwark never failing."

From the Catholic viewpoint, however, the principle of justification by faith alone has sometimes suffered from misunderstanding within Protestantism. Faith, for the Reformers, meant an internal, personal commitment to Jesus Christ. An intensely personal religion, one which springs from the very core of a man's personality, was the reaction of Luther and Calvin to the legalism, ritualism, and externalism which infected the Church of their day. This personal faith, for Luther, resulted in his veritable religious experience. But, for some Protestants, so closely has faith come to be associated with a sensible experience of salvation that the association of the two actually became an equation. Faith and the feeling of faith became identified. Particularly for John Wesley and such Protestantism as was influenced by Revivalism, faith consisted essentially of a personal conviction of "having been washed in the blood of Jesus Christ." Unfortunately, this kind of experience of salvation can too often emanate as the product of human effort on a psychological plane, a form of mere emotionalism. For some Protestants, emotional or mystical experience has become not only the essence of faith but the sole purpose of prayer. Likewise, the subjective experience of faith becomes so important that the object of that faith loses its significance. "It doesn't matter what you believe, so long as you have faith," seems a not altogether unfair caricature of this kind of Protestantism. It has logically led to the doctrinal indifferentism of several Protestant Churches.

Scripture Alone

Sacred scripture holds a place of sovereign authority in the Church. The Christian faith rests entirely upon the self-revelation made by God to the apostles, and, before them, to the prophets and inspired writers of the Old Testament. Within the text of the Bible is the witness of the prophets and apostles, handed down to us with the direct authority of God. It follows that sacred scripture has a unique authority for the Church, because the Church is subject to God's revelation and scripture alone was inspired directly by God. Unlike the words of any Pope, council, or saint, the Bible alone can claim God as its author. All other writers, including the greatest of theologians, can provide only probable arguments for a particular doctrine; the arguments drawn from scripture are conclusive. The proper attitude of the Church toward the Bible is one of listening. The Church also has the distinct mission of preserving the revelation of God as it is found in scripture, keeping it free from error and human corruption, preaching it to all nations, and making it relevant to every age. To this mission given to the Church, the Bible itself gives witness:

If any one is preaching to you a gospel contrary to that which you received, let him be accursed. (Gal. 1:9)

And we have the prophetic word made more sure. You will do well to pay attention to this as to a lamp shining in a dark place, until the day dawns and the morning star rises in your hearts. First of all you must understand this, that no prophecy of scripture is a matter of one's own interpretation, because no prophecy ever came by the impulse of man, but men moved by the Holy Spirit spoke from God. (2 Peter 1:19–21)

Catholic tradition upholds the sovereign authority of sacred scripture. For its two-thousand-year history the Catholic Church has derived its teaching from the Bible. The Church has taught with St. Jerome that "ignorance of the scriptures is ignorance of Christ." Popes, councils, and theologians have consistently resorted to the scriptural argument as the fundamental one. The most important aspect of the rule of piety which St. Benedict laid down for his followers, the rule which has influenced religious orders ever since, was the *lectio divina,* the reading of sacred scripture. Before the invention of the printing press, monks would laboriously copy down the scriptures by hand in order to preserve the inspired word. The First Vatican Council proclaimed explicitly that "the Church holds [the books of the Bible] as sacred and canonical, not because, composed by unaided human effort, they have been approved by her authority; nor solely because they contain revelation unmixed with error; but because, being written under the inspiration of the Holy Spirit, they have God for their author and, as such, have been delivered to the Church."

Martin Luther embraced, as a third principle for the Reform, scripture alone. Grace alone, faith alone, and scripture alone became the three watchwords of the Lutheran Reformation. It was in the scriptures that Luther found the answer to his personal problem concerning his own salvation. Consequently, it was to the scriptures that he turned to find the answers for all of his questions. His solution was quite valid. But, in turning to the Bible, he set up not only a distinction but an opposition between the authority of the Word of God in scripture and the authority of the Church in its tradition. Luther denied the infallibility of the teaching Church, whether that of the Pope or the councils. Whatever he found in the Church that he could not substantiate in the Bible he rejected. He thus reduced Christianity in principle to the explicit teachings of sacred scripture. No longer was there room for the development of dogma, for progressive unfolding of the initial faith of the apostolic Church.

From the Catholic viewpoint, there is no opposition between the authority of scripture and that of the Church, since both are based upon the authority of God. The scripture was not handed down from on high by some extraordinary or magical process; it was the inspired record of a living tradition, of Israel in the Old Testament and of the apostolic Church in the New. The Church, under the inspiration of God, not only recorded the apostolic teaching in the writings of the New Testament, but it recognized them as inspired, collected them, and placed them beside the Old Testament. Protestantism, however, almost from its very outset, tended not only to distinguish the authority of scripture from the authority of the teaching Church, but to set them in opposition to one another. The Protestant tendency has been to equate the authority of scripture with a denial of the authority of the Church.

When Protestantism divorced the authority of scripture from

the authority of the Church, it opened the possibility for two extremes, illuminism and literalism. Since the Church's interpretation of the Bible was no longer considered authoritative, a Protestant became faced with two choices: to interpret the Bible for himself, or to permit only the scripture to interpret itself. In the first instance, a man with a Bible in his hand became his own pope; in the second instance, the Bible became a "paper pope." *Illuminism* permits a man to read the Bible and become illuminated or inspired directly by the Holy Spirit. He interprets the scripture according to his own sincere understanding, and his understanding is no less valid than that of anybody else. *Literalism* permits only the Bible to interpret itself. The Bible came to be considered as dictated from on high with every word to be taken literally, from the creation of the world in seven days of twenty-four hours each to Jonah's ride in the belly of the whale. When the divine authorship of scripture is overemphasized in this way, a reaction inevitably sets in. Biblicism leads to Liberalism, and the divine authorship, which is not perceivable, is rejected in favor of the more discernible human hand which has gone into the origin of the scripture. Thus, the Bible eventually comes to be considered simply as a written record of the natural religious genius of the Hebrews and the apostolic Church, inspiring but not inspired.

All for the Glory of God Alone

No word, no image, no sign can adequately express God. That which is finite cannot contain the Infinite. Nothing compares to God or adequately describes him. He is the sovereign Lord of all creation, enjoying unlimited power, superior to all others. He is independent of everyone and everything, subject to no one, least of all to us. But God has expressed his holiness, his sovereignty, in creating the universe and, above all, in redeeming man, that is, in drawing us to himself. And mankind expresses its recognition of God's holiness and sovereignty by worship. Since God alone is holy, then God alone deserves glory, God alone deserves worship.

The Old Testament consistently emphasized God's holiness and glory. The first commandment forbade any attempt to represent God with a picture or statue; it also forbade worship to be given to anyone but God alone. For Isaiah the prophet, "Holy, holy, holy is the Lord of hosts, the whole earth is full of his glory" (Isaiah 6:3). All things are not only from him but for him; he is the Alpha and Omega, the beginning and the end. We can neither completely know God, nor understand God, nor explain God, and it goes without saying that we have no right to judge God. The only proper attitude we can have toward God is one of reverence and worship, an expression of our creaturehood and his Lordship.

Catholic tradition upholds the fact that God alone is holy, God alone deserves glory, God alone may be worshiped. It maintains that our knowledge of him is necessarily limited. Jesus Christ did not destroy the Old Testament and its commandments; he fulfilled and perfected them. The early martyrs of the Church shed their blood rather than give the slightest semblance of worship to pagan idols. The Church in its teaching has traditionally made a very sharp distinction between worship, which is reserved for God alone, and respect, which may be shown to Mary and the saints. The great mystics of the Church, such as St. John of the Cross, the "Doctor of Christian Mysticism," have taught that union with God requires "complete submission of the will and absolute detachment from all for the sake of God alone" (*Ascent of Mt. Carmel,* II, Ch. 4). The hallmark of St. Ignatius' rule for the Society of Jesus is *Ad majorem Dei gloriam,* "All for the greater glory of God."

John Calvin emphasized the principle of "all for the glory of God alone." It was his contribution to the spirit of Protestantism. Calvin felt that the first three principles of grace, faith, and scripture alone were too heavily man-centered. Calvin had an Old Testament prophet's consuming concern for the acknowledgment of God's sovereignty. So horrified was he by the sin of idolatry that Calvinism forbids any token of religious reverence or respect to be paid to anything or anyone other than God. Because wood and stone and paint cannot adequately describe God, images are absent from Calvinist churches. Because merely human words cannot worthily speak of God or to God, Calvinist worship rarely allows in its liturgy any prayer other than the inspired Psalms of scripture. Because God is all and man is nothing, Calvin taught that a man is saved or damned solely because of God's sovereign will, which predestines some men to heaven and others to hell. Calvin was not able to reconcile God's almighty sovereignty with man's free will; he chose to side with God's sovereignty.

From the Catholic viewpoint, Protestantism has sometimes so overemphasized the aspect of God's sovereignty that it has gone to the extreme of crushing down man and demeaning both his intelligence and his endeavors. Some Protestants have considered the gulf between God and man so great that not only does it become impossible for man to know God by his unaided reason but it also becomes impossible for man to know God's self-revelation. This leads to agnosticism. And agnosticism leads to secularism and the Social Gospel. If God is in heaven and heaven is so far away, there is a great temptation to say, "Let God stay in his heaven; the earth is good enough for me." Such championing of the sovereignty of God results in the annihilation of man. The eventual outcome is, paradoxically, a limiting of God's power, for he is denied the capacity of communicating to men any part of his knowledge, goodness, or holiness.

Summary

The spirit, vitality, piety, and genius of Protestantism are based on the four positive Christian principles of grace alone, faith alone, scripture alone, and God's sovereignty alone. Because of these valid, positive principles, Protestantism lives by, and has handed down through the centuries, an authentic Christian existence. A Catholic has no quarrel with these principles, which are deeply rooted in both scripture and Catholic tradition. From the Catholic viewpoint, however, these four principles have sometimes suffered within Protestantism from improper interpretation, a dangerous exclusivism, and extremism. An unbalanced philosophy of individualism, especially in the early and formative years of Protestantism, vitiated in several ways the understanding and practice of these principles. As a result, varying interpretations of these principles have led to extreme differences within Protestantism, resulting in conflict, contradiction, and confusion. "Grace alone" has led in some instances to "God helps those who help themselves," a clear example of works alone. "Faith alone" has led to "it doesn't matter what you believe" and "doctrine divides, service unites," both clear examples of doctrinal indifferentism. "Scripture alone" has led to a liberalism which denies to the Bible divine authorship. "All for God's glory alone" has led to a secularism which denies God any access or importance to our lives in the here and now.

Not all Protestant Churches, of course, have been affected the same way; neither have all the members of a single Church been affected the same way. Many Protestants, the Lutherans in particular, have adhered strongly to the original religious convictions of the 16th-century Reformers. Others have been affected by the emotionalism of the 18th-century Revivalists, the skepticism of the 19th-century Liberals, or the Biblical literalism of the 20th-century Fundamentalists. Yet the word "Protestant" is applied to each, and perhaps rightly so. The most characteristic quality of contemporary Protestantism is precisely its tolerance of dogmatic differences and its insistence upon total freedom of conscience in choosing between those differences.

The Central Idea of Protestantism: An Attempt at Understanding

Almost from the very beginning of the Reformation, attempts have been made by theologians to single out in some way one central idea or principle which sums up and explains all of Protestantism. Arriving at such a central idea proved to be a problem from the first, since almost immediately Protestants experienced disagreement and disunity among themselves. One early Lutheran theologian, Philip Melanchthon, maintained that the sufficiency of scripture alone and justification by faith alone were the two central ideas of Protestantism. This thesis is difficult to defend today, since the history of Protestantism has witnessed the development of conflicting and even contradictory interpretations of those two ideas. Is there any one central idea which serves as a common denominator for the orthodox Lutheran and the "un-orthodox" Unitarian, for the staid Presbyterian and the hand-clapping Pentecostal? One prominent Catholic ecumenist, Gustav Weigel, suggested that there is such a central idea and proposed that it is to be found in Protestantism's emphasis upon personal religious experience. The following is a brief consideration of Father Weigel's theory, as he presented it in the book he co-authored with a renowned Protestant ecumenist, Robert McAfee Brown, *An American Dialogue*.

For the Protestant, God is *experienced immediately*. Whereas Catholics tend to find God within a community, Jews through solidarity with a tradition, and Hindus through a culture, Protes-tants tend to find God through an "experience." This experience, caused within a man by God himself, is labeled in various ways— faith, conversion, a decision for Christ, "getting religion," "getting the Spirit," a movement of religious sentiment, or "finding Jesus Christ." Whatever it is called, it is an "encounter" with God, a psychological moment in a man's life, an event which can be dated, remembered and relished. It need not be a flamboyant or hysterical experience. It may be a deep, inner, and calm awareness of divinity. But, like an ecstasy, it is felt, and it pro-ceeds to make a difference in a man's life. Luther experienced God's saving action when reading the epistles of St. Paul; this God-encounter helped to resolve his anguish over his salvation. Calvin likewise gives testimony to a religious experience, and his Puritan American follower Jonathan Edwards demanded it as a condition for Church membership. John Wesley devised a "method" for attaining it, and Billy Graham crusades so that people will get it. This experience of encounter with God is primary and central to Protestantism; and all else, whether service or sacrament, is meant to recall or revive it.

This experience of God can be *interpreted with freedom*. This experiential encounter with God is decisive for the Protestant. All else is subsequent, including membership in the Church, since the fellowship of the Church consists of those who have had this encounter. Subsequent, too, is the interpretation and explanation of this God-encounter. To express this experience in concepts and words, the Protestant is free from the domination of either Church or congregation. He enjoys the freedom to reject traditional interpretations, just as Luther and Calvin did those of the Catholic Church in the 16th century and as the 19th-century Liberals did those of the original Reformers. Because of the Protestant's freedom to interpret his personal and immediate experience of God, Protestants of every age claim the right to formulate new creeds and confessions. And these creeds do not have to correspond with those of their Protestant forebears. The religious encounter with God is considered infallible, but not the formula expressing or explaining it. If a man's interpretation of of his religious experience is considered unorthodox, he may be rejected from the fellowship of his Protestant coreligionists, but not from that mystical union made up of all believers; he justly retains his right to the title of Protestant. Such a rejection is less common today than formerly, however, and contemporary Protestantism is marked by a generous toleration of diversity, the inevitable result of the Protestant exercise of doctrinal freedom.

This experience of God and its interpretation, however, must be *founded upon scripture,* at least in its claim. The Protestant's freedom to formulate his experience of God is not absolute; if it were, complete chaos and dissolution would result. The scriptures provide the test of genuine Protestantism. To be considered truly Protestant, a man's belief must be at least related to the Bible, either in fact or in claim, and it is most frequently expressed in Biblical terms.

Conclusion:

The central idea of Protestantism, then, seems to be the personal experience of encounter with God, interpreted and expressed in freedom but based, at least in claim, upon the Bible. This idea serves to explain the pluralism within Protestantism; its toleration even within single Churches of doctrinal diversity; its characteristic dislike of authoritarianism; its tendency toward revivalism; its emphasis on scripture and distrust of tradition. The realization of these principles may well help to explain the primary differences between the spirit of Protestantism and the spirit of Catholicism.

Suggested Reading

Bouyer, Louis. *The Spirit and Forms of Protestantism.* A. V. Littledale, tr. Newman, 1956.

Brown, Robert McAfee. *The Spirit of Protestantism.* Oxford University Press, 1961.

Brown, Robert McAfee, and Gustave Weigel. *An American Dialogue.* Part II, "A Catholic Looks at Protestantism." Doubleday, 1960.

First Steps in Grass-roots Ecumenism. "Protestant Communions in America." National Council of Catholic Men (Washington, D.C.), 1966.

7 / Post-Protestant Christianity

. . . other religions to be found everywhere strive variously to answer the restless searchings of the human heart by proposing "ways" which consist of teachings, rules of life, and sacred ceremonies. The Catholic Church rejects nothing which is true and holy in these religions.

—DECREE ON ECUMENISM, NO. 2

A Christian is ordinarily labeled as Catholic, Orthodox, or Protestant. Catholics are united to the Bishop of Rome and accept the teachings of scripture as they are officially interpreted by ecumenical councils and Popes. The Orthodox adhere to the traditions of the Eastern Fathers of the Church and accept the teachings of scripture as they are interpreted by the first seven ecumenical councils. Protestants are regarded usually, though not always accurately, as anyone else who cares to claim he is a Christian.

The term "Protestant" arose in the 16th century as a reference to those Christians in Europe and America who separated themselves from the Catholic Church and claimed that the Bible needed no interpreter other than the reader or the Bible itself. To this classification rightfully belong Martin Luther, John Calvin, John Wesley, and those who follow in their traditions. Subdivided as they are into Lutherans, Presbyterians, Methodists, Baptists, etc., these traditional Protestants share a common spirit if not always a common doctrine.

Besides these major Churches, however, the name Protestant is also accorded to other religious bodies, associations ranging from the Seventh-Day Adventists, with some 330,000 members, to the United Holy Church of America, Inc., with some 30,000 members. There are, in the middle alphabet of Protestantism, some

250 separate religious bodies reported in the *Yearbook of American Churches*. Among them are such small groups as the 2,500 members of the Schwenkfelder Church and the 213 members of the Pentecostal Evangelical Church of God, National and International. Many of these religious bodies disclaim the title of Protestant. Some even disclaim the title of Church. Popular opinion will probably continue to accord them both titles, but in fairness to them and their distinctive characteristics, they should be considered separate from the mainstream of Protestants. Perhaps a fair description of these religious bodies would be Post-Protestant Christian Churches.

Of these many Post-Protestant Christian Churches, three have been selected for special examination: the Church of Latter-Day Saints (Mormons); the Church of Christ, Scientist; and the Jehovah's Witnesses. These three have been chosen for several reasons. First, all three have the unique distinction of being successful native American religions. They share little in common theologically, except perhaps their extreme divergence, in different directions, from traditional Protestantism. But all claim adherence to the written word of the scriptures. Futhermore, because of the size of the Mormon Church, the image and influence of Christian Science, and the rapid and almost phenomenal growth in recent years of the Jehovah's Witnesses, they merit more than cursory notice. No official attempts at ecumenical dialogue have been made between the Catholic Church and these Post-Protestant Christian Churches: perhaps none will be attempted in the very near future. But they deserve consideration here nevertheless, if only for a more complete appreciation of the contemporary American religious scene, dotted, as that scene is, with Mormon temples, Christian Science reading rooms, and Jehovah's Witnesses' kingdom halls.

Church of Jesus Christ of Latter-Day Saints (Mormons)

History

Joseph Smith, the founder of Mormonism, was born at Sharon, Vermont, in 1805, the son of a farmer. He moved with his family to Manchester, New York, where in 1820, at the age of fifteen, he received the first of "a series of divine communications" as he was praying for light to recognize the true Church. He later wrote:

I saw two personages whose brightness and glory defy all description, standing above me in the air. One of them spake unto me, calling me by name, and said, pointing to the other—This is my beloved Son, hear Him. Then I asked the personages who stood above me in the light, which of all the sects was right—and which I should join. I was answered that I must join none of them, for they were all wrong.

Three years later another revelation occurred, the "celestial beginnings" of Mormon faith. While in prayer on the night of September 21, 1823, an angel clothed in white appeared to Joseph Smith, identifying himself as Moroni, a messenger from God. The angel told Smith that his name "should be for good and evil among all nations," and explained how he must go about establishing a new religion. In Smith's own words:

He said there was a book deposited, written upon gold plates, giving an account of the former inhabitants of this continent, and the source from whence they sprang. He also said that the fulness of the ever-lasting Gospel was contained in it, as delivered by the Savior to the ancient inhabitants; also that there were two stones in silver bows—and these stones, fastened to a breastplate, constituted what is called the Urim and Thummim—deposited with the plates; and the pos-session and use of these stones were what constituted seers in ancient or former times; and that God had prepared them for the purpose of translating the book.[1]

After three more revelations, Smith finally went to Hill Cumorah, near Palmyra, New York, the place designated by the angel Moroni. Here, it is said, he found the golden plates. They were engraved with an unknown language, Reformed Egyptian, but with the help of miraculous spectacles he was able to decipher the inscriptions. Unable to write himself, the 22-year-old Smith dictated the translation to a secretary, the original *Book of Mor-*

[1] Joseph F. Smith, *Essentials in Church History* (Salt Lake City: Desert News Press, 1950), pp. 51–52.

mon. It told of how North and South America were populated by exiled Israelites some six hundred years before Christ, how Jesus later appeared to a group of them after his ascension, how Jesus then chose another twelve apostles and set up another Church. The history of these early Americans from 600 B.C. to 421 A.D. was recorded on the golden tablets by a prophet named Mormon and his son Moroni, shortly before the entire race was vanquished by enemies and destroyed. After translating the tablets, Smith claimed, he returned them to the angel; they have not been seen since. Smith's translation, the *Book of Mormon,* believed to have been originally written before 421 A.D., abounds in Bible idioms also found in the King James version and even contains a line from Shakespeare.

The subsequent history of Mormonism tells of further revelations to the prophet and, ultimately, of his violent death. Joseph Smith acquired a following of believers in his revelation, and in April of 1830 they were formally organized into the Church of Jesus Christ of Latter-Day Saints. Constantly harassed because of their ideas of faith and their practice of polygamy, Joseph Smith and his followers moved from New York to Ohio to Missouri to Illinois. Their membership continued to grow. Finally, charged with treason, the 39-year-old prophet was awaiting trial in a prison in Carthage, Illinois, when a mob of some two hundred men stormed the building, shot Joseph Smith, and killed him.

After Smith's death, the Mormons split into several factions; they have not been reunited since. The largest segment, known as the Church of Jesus Christ of Latter-Day Saints, was led by Brigham Young to Utah, where they founded Salt Lake City in 1847. Here, through thirty years of uncompromising rule, Young developed the Mormons of Utah and Idaho into a well-organized, self-sustaining religious body which today numbers some 2,500,000 members. Its missionaries are all over the globe and add 90,000 converts to their membership each year.

A smaller group of Mormons protested Brigham Young's assumption of authority, claiming that Joseph Smith's son had sole title to leadership. Led by Joseph Smith III, the Reorganized Church of Jesus Christ of Latter-Day Saints settled in Independence, Missouri. Here the "gathering of Zion" is expected to take place before the second coming of Christ. Present membership is about 150,000. Four other splinter groups were organized in protest to Young and to Smith's son.

Beliefs and Practices

Mormons believed that Joseph Smith was commissioned by God to restore the gospel of Jesus Christ and to open a new dispensation. Mormonism claims authority, not from the Bible alone, but from a direct divine revelation. Mormons believe that Joseph Smith and his successors, from Brigham Young to the present president of the Church, are prophets no less inspired than those of the Old and New Testaments.

God. Mormons accept God as three literal, distinct personalities —Father, Son, and Holy Ghost. God, for the Latter-Day Saints, is a loving and understanding Father, with Jesus Christ as the image of his person, the Son of God in the flesh. Mormons believe in both Christ's atoning sacrifice and his literal resurrection. They accept Christ as the Savior and Redeemer of mankind, and look to him as the unique mediator between God and men. They pray to the Father in his name and believe that he will come again and reign on earth.

The Bible and the Book of Mormon. The Bible is basic to Mormon belief. The King James version is the official text, and is believed to be the Word of God. The *Book of Mormon* is not the "Mormon Bible" but one of the complementary works that the Mormons accept as inspired scripture. Mormons do not believe that the revelations of God were confined to ancient Israel, since a loving Father would not restrict his communication to one part of his family, to one time of history, or to one land. They believe that God will yet reveal in the future many great and important things pertaining to the kingdom of God.

Man. According to Mormon belief, God created a multitude of spirits or souls. When united to material bodies, these spirits forget about their pre-mortal existence; they become men. Of these billions of people who have inhabited the earth, only apostates and murderers go to hell. All others enjoy the happiness of the afterlife in one of the three grades of heaven. The highest live with God; it is a place reserved for those Mormons who marry in the mystic temple rites. The middle group lives with Christ, while all others must be satisfied with living with the angels. Heaven is considered a place of endless association with family and friends, perhaps more akin to the Moslem idea of paradise than the Christian concept of the Beatific Vision.

Sacraments. Baptism is practiced by Mormons, but only for those eight years of age or older. The rite consists of total immersion, but since Mormons do not believe in original sin, it is considered simply an initiation. Peculiar to Mormonism is the practice of proxy baptism, whereby a Mormon may be baptized in a Mormon temple on behalf of those who have died without the opportunity of receiving it for themselves. Mormons observe the Lord's Supper with bread and water, blessed and eaten by the congregation in memory of Christ and as a sign that they are willing to keep his commandments.

The sacrament which receives the most emphasis in Mormon practice and belief is marriage. Celibacy is regarded as an inferior state, contrary to the Word of God. The unmarried have no chance of entering into the highest plane of heaven. Large families are encouraged; birth control is condemned. Family solidarity is fostered by regular recreational Home Evenings. Mormons believe that a marriage contracted by their members in a Mormon temple lasts not only until death but for eternity. Only marriages between two Mormons are performed in temples; marriages with non-Mormons are discouraged. Divorce is permitted, but only for serious cause, such as infidelity.

To remove the stigma of virginity from their women, polygamy was formerly practiced by Mormons. They believe that Jesus Christ himself was a polygamist, that Mary and Martha were his two wives. When in 1890 the Supreme Court upheld the constitutionality of federal laws prohibiting polygamy, Wilford Woodruff, then president of the Mormon Church, issued a manifesto prohibiting the practice any further. The present penalty for any Mormon entering a plural marriage is excommunication.

Church Organization. The Church of Latter-Day Saints maintains a strong central organization, including a First Presidency, a Council of Twelve Apostles, a Patriarch, and a Council of Seventy. There is no professional clergy, since nine out of ten male members hold some office of priesthood. Negroes are not permitted to enter the priesthood, and, as a result, they are not attracted to the Latter-Day Saints. Geographically the Church is divided into stakes (dioceses), and these stakes are in turn divided into wards (parishes). Although their chapels are open to the public, Mormon temples are not considered places of public worship and are closed to non-Mormons. There are thirteen such temples in the world.

Members of the Latter-Day Saints deserve special note for their generosity to the Church and their missionary activity. In order to remain a member in good standing, a member is expected not only to attend church regularly but to donate one-tenth of his earnings to the Church. All young men are expected to spend a year or two as unpaid missionaries, and each year some six thousand missionaries leave Utah in pairs to spread the Mormon gospel.

The Mormon Church today is not only a religion but a close-knit society. A Mormon family in good standing is likely to spend three or four evenings a week working for the Church. It is expected that a Mormon family fast for two meals each month, donating the money saved to the Church's vast welfare program. This program reaches some 100,000 Mormons at an estimated annual cost of $10,000,000. Besides this high ideal of community welfare, Mormons are also noted for hard work, respect for law, individual responsibility, and a high regard for education. Brigham Young University is the largest Church-operated school in the country.

The Church of Jesus Christ of Latter-Day Saints consists today of 2,500,000 members in 6,000 congregations. It employs 12,000 full-time missionaries in 51 countries and operates three universities and colleges, 190 religious institutes that serve Mormon students in colleges, 2,000 seminaries for public school students, and 15 hospitals. It regards itself, not as a Protestant denomination, but as the one true Church, the restored Church of Jesus Christ.

Church of Christ, Scientist
History

In this age of miracle drugs, revolutionary surgical techniques, and X ray, it is difficult for most Americans to understand how some 350,000 well-educated and socially prominent people could believe that sickness can be healed by faith healing alone. Yet this precisely is the faith of the followers of Mary Baker Eddy, the founder of Christian Science.

Mary Baker was born in 1821 in Bow, New Hampshire. A high-strung child with nervous temperament, she joined the Congregational Church when she was seventeen, but objected to the stern Calvinism it practiced. She lost her first husband, George Glover, a few months after their marriage, and later divorced her second husband, Daniel Patterson, on the grounds of desertion. Throughout this time she suffered various mental and nervous ailments, seeking relief from a multitude of sources, but always in vain. Finally, after trying mesmerism and spiritualism, Mrs. Patterson discovered a faith healer in Portland, Maine, Phineas P. Quimby. She became a student of his and claimed to obtain some relief from her illnesses.

Quimby died in 1866. A month after his death, Mrs. Patterson slipped on some ice and suffered injuries which she pronounced incurable. During her third day in bed, she opened her Bible to the Gospel of Matthew and there read of Jesus' cure of the man sick with palsy. "Arise, take up thy bed," she read, and with that she became convinced that sickness and death were illusions. Within a few days Mrs. Patterson was walking about, believing that she had rediscovered the principles of healing which Christ had demonstrated in the New Testament, principles which, according to Christian Science, the early Church had lost through apostasy.

Mrs. Patterson set out to devote her energies to developing and propagating her discovery. For the next four years she worked on her book, *Science and Health,* the textbook of the Christian Science movement. She added a section entitled "With Key to the Scriptures" which metaphysically interpreted the books of Genesis and Revelation. Finally, in 1875, *Science and Health* was published under the authorship of Mary Baker Glover, Mary having now resumed the name of her first husband. In that same year a group of her students rented a hall and employed Mrs. Glover as their "pastor." One of her most devoted pupils was a mild-mannered, former sewing-machine salesman, Asa Gilbert Eddy. In 1877 he became her third husband. On August 23, 1879, the Church of Christ, Scientist received its state charter.

Mrs. Mary Baker Glover Patterson Eddy spent the remainder of her life organizing and consolidating the Church which she had founded. She established the Mother Church of Christian Science in Boston, where all of Christian Science came to center totally upon her. The Mother Church in Boston was to be the only church; all other churches were only branches, affiliated with the Mother Church and totally dependent upon its jurisdiction. The office of pastor in her movement was abolished; she substituted instead the office of reader, and only graduates with degrees from the Mother Church could be readers. No conference of churches was permitted; and all officers, from the board of directors to local branch managers, were selected only with Mrs. Eddy's approval. She must have been held in the highest esteem by her followers, since the pastors of Christian Science were deposed without their slightest demur.

Mrs. Eddy received a goodly share of opposition in her lifetime, but her greatest fear was that of MAM, Malicious Animal Magnetism. She reasoned that if mental methods could be used to overcome disease and death even at a distance, then these same psychic powers could be misused to create an illusion of sickness and death. When her husband Asa Eddy died in 1882 of a heart ailment, Mrs. Eddy wrote in a letter to the *Boston Post,* "My husband's death was caused by malicious mesmerism . . . I know it was poison that killed him, not material poison but mesmeric poison . . ."

Death finally claimed Mrs. Eddy herself in 1910. Her followers decided at that time that "there will be no Leader named to take the place of Mrs. Eddy. There is no need for any leader." The magnetism of Mrs. Eddy's personality seemed enough to influence and guide members of Christian Science. It continues today, holding sway in the five periodicals published by Christian Science. Of these publications the highest ranking is the *Christian Science Monitor,* a daily newspaper which since 1915 has won over sixty awards for journalistic excellence. The *Monitor* is noted for its assiduous avoidance of sensationalism in reporting news of tragedy and death.

Since an article of the *Church Manual* asserts that nothing will be amended or annulled without the written consent of the Leader, change in the Church has been impossible since 1910. Another tenet of Christian Science forbids tabulation of membership, so the present strength of the movement can only be ventured. There are more than 3,100 branches of the Mother Church, however, with each branch averaging 150 members. Approximately three out of four of its members are women.

God. For Christian Science, God is the Divine Mind, and the Mind is all that exists. He is "the great I AM; the all-knowing, all-seeing, all-acting, all-wise, all-loving, and eternal; Principle; Mind; Soul; Life; Truth; Love; all substance; intelligence." God is the conceiver of the universe, above all, of man. The Divine Mind expresses itself, and its expression is man. Christian Science's belief in God has at times been described as pantheistic, a charge which Mrs. Eddy denied indignantly.

Spirit and Matter. Spirit, according to Christian Science, is "Divine Substance, Mind; divine Principle; all that is good; God; that only which is perfect, everlasting, omnipresent, omnipotent, infinite." Matter, on the other hand, is "Mythology; mortality; another name for mortal mind . . . the opposite of Truth; the opposite of Spirit; the opposite of God . . ." Spirit is eternal and real; matter is an unreal illusion subject to decay and dissolution. Since evil is involved with matter, it is therefore also unreal, an illusion. Death is likewise an illusion; the individual continues to live in the reality of spirit, even though unseen by persons and unrecognized on the plane of mortal existence.

Man. Both man and the universe were made in the image of God. Therefore, according to Christian Science, like God, they are wholly good, immortal, and perfect. Like God, too, man is spirit, soul, life, truth, and love. Health is a spiritual reality and, therefore, is likewise eternal. Disease is a delusion of the human mind, a falsehood which can be destroyed by prayer and spiritual understanding. The "divinely mental" can and does replace the "materially mental." Salvation consists in being freed from the illusions of mortal sense, from the mistaken belief of being susceptible to sickness or death. Thus, man, for Christian Science, is really sinless, since sin is nothing else than the belief in the real existence of any mind other than the Divine Mind.

Jesus. "Christian Science accepts the divinity of Christ, but it does not deify him." In other words, Jesus is considered the Son of God, but not God himself. His mission was to redeem mankind from the mistaken belief of mortality by showing that man's real nature is spiritual and not material. The healings he performed, as recorded by the scriptures, were not miracles, according to Christian Science, but rather the result of the application of the same natural spiritual law as Mrs. Eddy formulated. Christian Science accepts the virgin birth of Jesus and makes reference to the Trinity. Its understanding of the Trinity, however, is not that of three persons in one divine nature but, rather, of Life, Truth, and Love as aspects of the triune Principle called God. Much to the confusion of someone unfamiliar with it, Christian Science employs traditional terms of Christian theology, but gives them totally different meanings. As these doctrines are traditionally understood, Christian Science rejects a personal God, the Trinity, the divinity of Christ, the devil, sin, atonement, resurrection, heaven and hell.

Devotional Practices. For Christian Science, the understanding of God is reached through praying, the application of one's thought upon God. Both devotion and experience are needed to pray perfectly, and the efficacy of his prayer reflects the degree of a Christian Scientist's spiritual understanding. Christian Science demands faith from its adherents, that is, acceptance before proof. Through this faith, degrees of evidence are said to appear, serving to lift faith into spiritual understanding; and through such understanding, healing is attained. Since Christian Science believes that illness is an illusion, it necessarily rejects medical treatment. Christian Scientists are encouraged to treat themselves, but in difficult cases the assistance of professional practitioners may be sought. These healers, who hold regular office hours and charge their clients for their services, attempt to convince the sufferer that sickness and death are an illusion. The *Christian Science Journal* lists about 7,000 such practitioners, mostly women.

The order of service in a Christian Science church is prescribed to the least detail by the *Church Manual;* it is the same the world over on any one Sunday. After an organ prelude and hymn, there is a reading from the King James version of the Bible and a recitation of the Lord's Prayer, with a paraphrase written by Mrs. Eddy inserted after each clause. The heart of the service is the sermon-lesson, an alternate reading by the First and Second Readers from the Bible and from Mrs. Eddy's book, *Science and Health.* There is no sermon in the usual sense; no reader may interject his own thought into the service. After a final hymn the service is closed with the recitation of the Scientists' statement of being. Daily readings of the Bible and *Science and Health* are also advised and formulated by the Mother Church. To make such reading convenient, Christian Science maintains a host of reading rooms in all the major cities of the United States. They provide no other literature but the Bible, Christian Science publications, and the writings of Mary Baker Eddy. Christian Scientists claim to accept the authority of the Bible, but also regard Mrs. Eddy's book, *Science and Health,* as being inspired. Mrs. Eddy herself declared, "No Human pen nor tongue taught me the Science contained in this book. . . . I was only a scribe echoing the harmonies of heaven in divine metaphysics."

The Church does not baptize members. It observes two spiritual communions a year; there is no bread and wine, but the worshipers spend a few moments in silent prayer. Mrs. Eddy prepared no ritual for marriages or funerals in her Church, and Christian Scientists seek the services of Protestant ministers or civil officials when they wish to be married. Marriage is only tolerated by Christian Science (Mrs. Eddy regarded marriage as "legalized lust"), and childless marriages are encouraged. She likewise urged her followers to overcome any depraved appetite for alcohol, tobacco, coffee, tea, and opium.

Jehovah's Witnesses

History

Few are the homes in this country that have not been visited by a representative of the Jehovah's Witnesses. Sunday mornings will see the Witnesses methodically canvassing neighborhoods, carrying their Bibles and copies of the *Watchtower,* giving testimony of faith in the God Jehovah. Because of their remarkable missionary zeal, the Jehovah's Witnesses have grown from 115,000 members in 1942 to almost 1,000,000 today. Their missionary activities extend to some 158 countries. They are the fastest growing Church in the world.

The Jehovah's Witnesses were founded in Pittsburgh in 1872 by a former Congregationalist haberdasher, Charles Taze Russell. Russell had been distressed in his early years at the thought of damnation, and his Bible study convinced him that the Hebrew word *sheol* should be translated, not as "hell," but as "grave." He had been further influenced by the Adventist movement, which taught that the Last Days and the second coming of Christ were imminent. Russell began an extensive preaching campaign and acquired a sizable following.

Russell died in 1916, and was succeeded by a lawyer who had defended him in several conflicts with the civil authorities, Joseph F. Rutherford. Rutherford organized the Russellites into a highly centralized machine and began a massive publishing effort. He gained the nation's attention with a slogan that blossomed on road signs, posters, and handbills, "Millions Now Living Will Never Die." The Russellites had come to be called Rutherfordites and Millennial Dawnists. In 1931 a new name was announced, one that would supplant all others, Jehovah's Witnesses. It was a happy choice, since any mention of the word "witness" in the Old or New Testaments could be considered as evidence for the antiquity of the cult.

When Rutherford died in 1942, he was succeeded by Nathan Knorr. Knorr set about giving the Witnesses a new image. Prior to his time, Witnesses had evangelized by going from door to door with a portable phonograph and a recording of Judge Rutherford; their approach at times tended to be quite belligerent. Now, however, Witnesses are trained in public speaking and missionary techniques. They present their message in person and tactfully, and are schooled to answer any questions posed by unbelieving skeptics. Knorr has also directed a massive foreign mission endeavor, particularly in Latin America. The Witnesses' appeal is primarily to the intellectually, socially, and economically disinherited. Only one Witness out of a hundred is a college graduate. About twenty percent are Negroes.

Beliefs and Practices

The Jehovah's Witnesses are commonly regarded as a Protestant Church. They themselves, however, disclaim the title of Protestant as well as that of Church, although they do believe that they are the heirs of the Reformation. They claim the Bible as their one and only infallible guide, but the writings of Russell and Rutherford interpreting the scripture must be accepted by Witnesses without question. As a result, Witness doctrine has been able to maintain a relative consistency. Basing themselves upon these interpretations of the Bible, the Jehovah's Witnesses oppose blood transfusions, business, Catholicism, Christmas trees, evolution, flag saluting, movies, the Trinity, tobacco, the United Nations, voting, and the YMCA.

God. There is but one God, the Witnesses proclaim, and his name is Jehovah. In the Old Testament, when Moses is said to have asked God what his name was, the answer was YHWH. Since Hebrew had no vowel signs at that time, we are not entirely sure what the exact pronunciation of the word was. The King James version of the Bible followed common practice, substituting a German J for Y and V for W, and printed the name as Jehovah. Recent scholarship in ancient Semitic languages has since indicated that the word should probably be pronounced *Yahweh.* The Witnesses have been adamant in maintaining, however, that the proper pronunciation is *Jehovah.*

The Witnesses explicitly deny the doctrines of the Trinity and the divinity of Christ, objecting that they have been "fraudulently imposed upon men to destroy their faith in Jehovah." Jesus, according to the Witnesses, was originally Michael the Archangel; he lived and died a man and lives now as an exalted being. The Holy Spirit is not considered to be either God or a person.

Theocracy. Theocracy, or the Rule of God, is the foundation of Witness belief. According to Rutherford, when Lucifer rebelled, he became ruler of the world. As master of the earth, he organized his empire, founding Churches, businesses, and governments as tools for working his evil designs. The great tragedy of history, according to the Witnesses, is that Satan has compelled men to practice religion through an unholy alliance of ecclesiastical, commercial, and political power. But in 1914 Satan, who up to that time had remained in heaven, was driven out by Christ. This celestial struggle was reflected on earth by World War I. Since that time Christ has struggled with Satan here on earth. This conflict will reach its climax very soon at the Battle of Armageddon, when Christ and his angels will vanquish Satan and his army; and this will usher in the millennium, a thousand years of earthly happiness.

Life after death does not come automatically along with human nature. According to the Witnesses, it is a gift from God, a reward for virtue. God alone is immortal by nature. The wicked are annihilated at death; as a result, there is no hell. The godly alone enjoy resurrection. Of these virtuous people, only 144,000 faithful followers of Jesus will be with him in heaven; all the others will enjoy an earthly paradise.

Organization. The Jehovah's Witnesses consider themselves a "society of ministers." They practice mass baptisms by immersion in swimming pools or lakes. This ceremony renders one a minister of Jehovah, expected from that time to devote ten to twelve hours a week to studying, selling pamphlets at street corners, and canvassing from door to door. The Witnesses tolerate no inactive or associate members; only the blind and lame are excused.

Although the Witnesses profess to have no clergy, they do have Pioneers, full-time laborers who devote at least 150 hours a month to the Witness apostolate. These Pioneers already number some 7,000 and work by supervising local congregations and handling administrative details. About 16,000 such congregations or "companies" exist in this country. They meet on Sunday and Thursday evenings in their kingdom halls for meetings which resemble discussion groups more than worship services.

Regular members of the Witnesses normally maintain full-time jobs, while devoting their free time and weekends to their apostolic activities. Witnesses are encouraged to provide a decent living for themselves from their own income, but are invited to turn over all their surplus income to the Society. Full-time Pioneer workers live in the homes of regular members. At headquarters in Brooklyn, New York, some seven hundred Witnesses live a community life in a nine-story apartment building called Bethel House. The salary of all these full-time members, from the president to the janitor, is the same—room, board, and $14 a month.

Practices. The Witnesses claim that every member is a minister, and their literal interpretations of obscure Biblical passages have resulted in their involvement in more legal suits than any other denomination in America. The Witnesses believe that the government of this country, along with every other government, is an instrument of the devil; hence, they refuse to vote, hold public office, salute the flag, or serve in the armed forces. Witnesses claim draft exemption on the grounds that every member is a minister. Because commerce is likewise considered evil, Witnesses may not be salesmen or shopkeepers. The Old Testament proscription against the ritual drinking of blood is interpreted by Witnesses as forbidding blood transfusions. The Biblical warning against carving and decorating wooden idols makes it taboo for a Witness to have a Christmas tree. Motion pictures, the theater, dances, liquor, and tobacco are likewise forbidden. The Jehovah's Witnesses have also been known for their vituperative attacks against organized religions, especially the Catholic Church. These characteristics, together with their oft-times aggressive missionary techniques, have aroused both hostility and harassment for the Jehovah's Witnesses. They view such opposition, however, as a sign of divine approval, since, according to St. Paul, "all who desire to live a godly life in Christ Jesus will be persecuted" (2 Tim. 3:12).

Conclusion:

A Catholic, Lutheran, or Presbyterian may be sorely tempted to look upon these Post-Protestant Christian Churches as little more than distortions of the gospel. After all, what do Urim and Thummim, Malicious Animal Magnetism, and the impending Armageddon have to do with traditional Christianity? They may easily seem at worst grotesque, at best bizarre. This is not, however, an altogether fair judgment. The doctrines of one God in three persons, God made man, and a virgin birth can be easily taken for granted by a person born and raised in a traditional Christian cultural milieu; to an agnostic, a Buddhist, or a Jew, however, these beliefs might well appear equally extravagant and incredible. The Catholic prohibition against direct therapeutic abortion may seem just as unreasonable to an unbeliever as the Jehovah's Witnesses' prohibition against blood transfusions.

The sincerity of the Mormons, Christian Scientists, and Jehovah's Witnesses is difficult to question. The genuineness of their faith is demonstrated emphatically by their uncompromising dedication. It is an easy thing to dismiss their apostolic zeal as fanaticism; it is more difficult to equal some of their ardor. God speaks to the Church not only through the scriptures but also through human events, through movements in history. It could be that God is speaking to the Church today through these Post-Protestant Christian Churches. Such, at least, is the opinion of Vatican Council II:

The Catholic Church rejects nothing which is true and holy in these religions. She looks with sincere respect upon those ways of conduct and of life, those rules and teachings which, though differing in many particulars from what she holds and sets forth, nevertheless often reflect a ray of that Truth which enlightens all men. Indeed, she proclaims and must ever proclaim Christ, "the way, the truth, and the life" (John 14:6), in whom men find the fullness of religious life, and in whom God has reconciled all things to Himself (cf. 2 Cor. 5:18–19).

The Church therefore has this exhortation for her sons: prudently and lovingly, through dialogue and collaboration with the followers of other religions, and in witness of Christian faith and life, acknowledge, preserve, and promote the spiritual and moral goods found among these men, as well as the values in their society and culture. (Declaration on Non-Christian Religions, No. 2)

Suggested Reading

Braden, Charles S. *These Also Believe*. A study of modern cults and minority religious movements in America. Macmillan.

Hardon, John A. *The Protestant Churches of America*. Newman, 1958.

Rosten, Leo, ed. *Religions in America*. Simon and Schuster, 1963.

8 / Atheistic Humanism

I questioned myself about the meaning of this life. It did not seem logical that being endowed with a capacity for thinking and loving could be thrown into an absurd universe, where there was nothing to think, nothing to love, nothing to hope for. It was with these psychological dispositions that I encountered the Christian message.

—IGNACE LEPP, *Atheism in Our Time*

The Second Vatican Council described atheistic humanism as "among the most serious problems of this age" and "deserving of closer examination." But it is not its gravity alone that entitles atheism to consideration within an ecumenical framework. At first glance, in fact, it does not seem to fit into ecumenical concern at all: What does atheism have to do with Christian unity or inter-religious dialogue? It explicitly rejects religion of any sort, and Christianity in particular. Yet atheistic humanism does deserve ecumenical consideration, for no longer is it simply a negative rejection of Christian claims. Atheistic humanism has taken on a positive, all-encompassing, and even religion-like character in that it has come to provide a world view, a life goal, and a methodical system for achieving that goal. Atheism today seeks not only to dislodge God from his throne but to put man there in his place. It has assumed the slogan made famous by Karl Marx, "To make of man the supreme being for man."

Atheism is nothing new to human history. Its extent and influence in contemporary society, however, certainly is, especially in traditionally Christian countries. Atheism is no longer the stance of "an enlightened few." It has become the lot of a very high proportion of our contemporaries, and it portends to become the

norm for human society. Intellectuals were the first to
.....om religious ties; the middle class followed; and today
great masses of men are joining in their denial of all religion.
Furthermore, it is not for base selfish reasons that many modern
atheists reject belief in God, but often in the name of high and
noble ideals, in the name of a humanism for which many are
willing to serve without stint and even give their lives.

In the United States the great majority of men profess a belief
in some sort of Supreme Being and shun the description of atheist.
A very creative and influential minority, however, does not deny
the appellation. Physical and social scientists, philosophers and
educators, can say of God, "I have no need for that hypothesis" to
construct their systems. Modern playwrights create a drama of
the absurd, expounding the meaninglessness of human existence.
Artists reflect on their canvases the chaotic turmoil of men's minds
and lives today. Even theologians, without necessarily agreeing
with each other about what they mean, make headlines with
affirmations that "God is dead."

Related to the atheistic humanism of so many people today is
the secularism of those who profess to believe in God and to
accept Jesus Christ as Savior. Masses of churchgoing Christians
today conduct their lives, for all practical purposes, as if God did
not exist. Religion for them is a one-hour-on-Sunday affair which
makes no serious impact upon their lives or decisions. On the great
controversial issues of our day, such as the morality of war and
the need for racial integration, surveys indicate that churchgoers
are in the mainstream of popular thinking; they differ in no
appreciable way from those who do not align themselves with
the Church. In other words, for the first time in the history of mankind, men today, both believers and unbelievers, are building a
radically secular civilization, having little reference of any kind to
a Supreme Being. The God of Abraham, Isaac, and Jacob, the
Father of Jesus Christ, has become for countless contemporaries
no more than a historical curiosity with little more relevance to
their lives than Zeus, King Neptune, or Thor.

In the light of these facts, committed Christians cannot help but
become distressed. Mature faith, however, should prevent panic.

Atheistic humanism has acquired grave importance in our time and Christians need to confront it with earnest, calm, and ecumenical openness, for the sake of their own faith and for the sake of those who reject that faith. To initiate their own Christian renewal, as well as to cooperate in the attainment of humanitarian ideals, ecumenical communication is required between those who believe in God and those who do not:

While rejecting atheism, root and branch, the Church sincerely professes that all men, believers and unbelievers alike, ought to work for the rightful betterment of this world in which all alike live. Such an ideal, however, cannot be realized apart from sincere and prudent dialogue. (Pastoral Constitution on the Church in the Modern World, No. 21)

Historical Roots

Rationalism

Disbelief is not a new phenomenon in the history of mankind. And if in prior generations there appeared to be many more religious men than today, some of the difference is due to the earlier failure to distinguish between genuine religion and superstition. In every generation there are probably far fewer truly religious men than appear on the surface. Nevertheless, the historical roots of modern atheism, its influence, and its extent can be traced to the beginnings of our modern age.

Shortly after the Catholic Church ceased being the mistress of nations, theology ceased being the mistress of sciences. Wars in the name of religion and the Spanish and Roman Inquisitions attempted to crush innovations and preserve doctrinal unity by force; it was to no avail. The 17th century became the Age of Reason. Advances in the natural sciences—and, above all, in mathematics—led men to discredit medieval philosophy in favor of the scientific method. The trial of Galileo and the Index of Forbidden Books proved desperate attempts to preserve what seemed orthodox Christianity; they served only to alienate thinking men from Christianity. There appeared to be an insoluble conflict between science and religion, and the age opted on the side of science.

Scientism

When Sir Isaac Newton performed the unprecedented task of explaining the material world by means of a few fundamental principles, philosophers became so enamored of the scientific method that they tried to prove that everything in the world moved according to predictable, unchangeable physical laws. They saw the universe as a vast machine, fabricated by some Supreme Being. Deism believed in God, but one who had created the world and then left it to its own devices. This God did not interfere with the petty trifles of men, and it was no great step from a God who did not enter into the lives of men to a God who did not exist at all. In the meantime, so successful had been the scientific method of measuring, weighing, and observing that ideas which could not be proved experimentally came to be considered as unscientific, unproven, and unacceptable. Science not only did without the necessity of God; it took his place. Optimism ran high that, given enough time for scientific research, men could solve all the riddles of the universe and explain away all the mysteries of life.

Religious faith had suffered a shock when Copernicus demonstrated that the earth was not the center of the universe. Even though it had never been a dogma of faith, a geocentric universe somehow made divine revelation seem more plausible. The stature of mankind suffered even greater decline in the 19th century, however, when Charles Darwin produced ample evidence for the hypothesis that most living species on the earth today, including man, were the products of an evolution from lower forms of animal life. Homo sapiens suddenly appeared to be the descendant of little more than an ape. On top of that, the Biblical accounts of creation came to be regarded by many as little more than mythology. When, in the last century, scientific methods of literary criticism established that much in scripture could not be taken literally, great numbers of people lost faith in the Bible altogether.

Sigmund Freud inflicted another devastating blow when he reduced God to an infantile wish for a father, and man to a complex bundle of unconscious animal instincts.

Humanism

The 19th century was a time of revolt against political tyranny. Monarchy and aristocracy trembled alike as the disinherited masses rose up to strip them of their privileges in the name of liberty, equality, and fraternity. But if human dignity and freedom warranted revolution against the authority of autocrats, it called even more so for revolution against the claims of a Supreme Being. The very idea of a Supreme Being seemed oppressive to the dignity of man; and in the name of human values, men set out to liberate mankind from divine tyranny. God, according to Ludwig Feuerbach, was the product of man's imagination, a projection of all that makes up the greatness of man. Much the same theme was taken up by Friedrich Nietzsche, for whom God was nothing more than the mirror of man. He became an apostle of atheism, a militant antitheist. Faith in God had served to tame man, to emasculate him of his greatness; it had to be rooted out. Only then could humanity be raised up into a race of supermen. "God is dead," Nietzsche cried; "it is we who have killed him."

Feuerbach the philosopher is all but forgotten today. His influence lives on, however, in the movement inaugurated by one of his chief admirers, Karl Marx. "Religion is the opium of the people," Marx declared; by promising pie in the sky, by providing illusory consolations amid the miseries of life, it renders men servile. "The social principles of Christianity remove to heaven the compensation for infamies and thus justify their perpetuation on earth," Marx wrote. The revolution he set off has ever since made war against any God who would assume what Marx believed to be the rightful place of man alone. Nietzsche's dream of a race of supermen materialized into the Third Reich and its Nazi terror. Marx's promise of a classless society, free from the yoke of capitalists and their God, resulted in a series of communist revolutions. It still serves to inflame men with a hope for a better world, a world which would suffice for many of our contemporaries as heaven enough.

Philosophy of the Absurd

For another segment of this generation, however, fulfillment of Nietzsche's dreams and Marx's promises has proved too long in coming. The twin shocks of Adolf Hitler and Hiroshima destroyed for them any faith in the omniscience of science or the meaning of life. Disillusionment, despair, and acceptance of the absurdity of life characterize the existentialism of modern philosophers and writers such as Jean Paul Sartre and Albert Camus. For them the individual and his subjective experience is all that matters. A man's personal freedom in a meaningless universe is both his burden and his prize possession. Life has no purpose, no principles, no laws. For Sartre, "Every existing being is born without reason, prolongs itself out of weakness, and dies by chance." For Camus, "There is but one truly serious philosophical problem, and that is suicide. Judging whether life is or is not worth living amounts to answering the fundamental question of philosophy." Why men, after acquiring some vision of the reality of things, do not commit suicide, Camus could not explain. He concludes that it is man's destiny to struggle and rebel against the absurdity of life, struggling without hope, convinced that it is better to die on one's feet than to live on one's knees.

Varieties of Modern Unbelief

Modern unbelief is not a simple rejection of the existence of God. It is a complex attitude, taking a variety of forms, resulting from a variety of causes. As the bishops of Vatican Council II recognized: "The word atheism is applied to phenomena which are quite distinct from one another" (Pastoral Constitution on the Church in the Modern World, No. 19).

Atheism

Atheism is a form of unbelief which implies a positive act of disbelief, a formal rejection of all belief in the existence of God. Although nearly all forms of unbelief have come to be considered as atheism, the word in its strict sense refers to a dogmatic disbelief. It is a firm conviction that God does not exist, that for such a Being to exist would be impossible. So dogmatic and radical a denial of God usually arises as a retaliation against an environment professing belief. Atheism is a reaction of veritable antitheism, an aggressive counter-assault against faith in God.

Agnosticism

Agnosticism is a radical form of skepticism. It does not reject the possibility of God, but rather withholds belief on the grounds of insufficient evidence. An agnostic is usually antidogmatic; he claims to be purely rational. He refuses to believe in God, not because of any particular human value, but because the indications for God's existence are inconclusive. For him, seeing is believing—seeing, or weighing, or measuring. The traditional proofs for the existence of God do not serve to convince him because, for him, scientific proof alone merits acceptance.

Scientific agnostics were once optimistic in their belief that they could give an adequate account of the genesis and evolution of the universe. They have since become less sanguine. Few claim any longer that science will someday provide all the solutions and explanations. Agnosticism does not propose that science has discovered irrefutable proofs for the falseness of religion. It simply holds that nothing within the positive, physical sciences confirms the teaching of religions; therefore, religious teaching is no more than a gratuitous hypothesis.

Agnosticism is the most prevalent form of intellectual unbelief today. It asks no ultimate questions, seeks no basic meanings, requires no intelligible explanation for the beginnings or purpose of the universe. It accepts the universe simply as being there—and shrugs its shoulders.

Marxism

Marxism is a form of atheism which seeks actively to suppress belief in God in order to elevate man to the highest possible degree of his self-realization. It wages a positive battle against religion because it looks on religion as an obstacle to human progress. It demands an act of faith in man and in the ultimate victory of the socialist revolution. This act of faith which Marxism demands renders it something of an ersatz religion. It has its own prophet, Karl Marx; its own canon of sacred books; a priesthood by way of the International Communist Party; and a missionary zeal comparable to that of the early Christians. It aspires to transform human nature as well as society, and offers as a reward for self-sacrifice to the Marxist cause the satisfaction of helping to "build a new world."

Marxism regards religion as having performed an important and even necessary function in the evolution of human progress, but a function that is now obsolete. It considers its own variety of humanism as the inevitable successor to religious belief, one that gives men a new view of life, a new pattern for behavior, a new purpose for existence. Its primary attitude toward religion in general, and Christianity in particular, is one of indictment. According to the Marxist, Christianity has existed for almost two thousand years, and has failed in that time to do away with poverty, servitude, social disorder, or war. The chief criticism of Marxism against religion is, not that it is not true, but that it does not work.

Atheistic Existentialism

Atheistic existentialism rejects belief in God, not for the sake of society, but for the individual. It is obsessed with the physical and moral evil in the world, and regards as absurd a universe in which the innocent suffer along with the guilty. A philosophy born of despair, it rejects the existence of God because it first rejects the existence of the universe as we find it today. For Jean Paul Sartre, the individual is all there is, and the individual's only value is the assertion of his own freedom. Nothing else matters: "To become drunk or to be a leader of men is all the same thing."

Reasons for Modern Unbelief

The varieties of unbelief found in contemporary society spring from a complex of motives. Pope Paul VI, in his first encyclical letter *Ecclesiam Suam* ("The Paths of the Church"), addressed himself to the problem of modern atheism and examined its various motives:

> Though we must speak firmly and clearly in declaring and defending religion and the human values it proclaims and upholds, we are moved by our pastoral office to seek in the heart of the modern atheist the motives of his turmoil and denial. His motives are many and complex, so that we must examine them with care if we are to answer them effectively.

Insufficiency of the Traditional "Proofs" for God's Existence

From the time of Plato, some 400 years B.C., men have attempted to prove the existence of God through purely rational means. These rational "proofs" for the existence of God have taken a number of different directions.

Some philosophers, such as St. Anselm and Descartes, attempted to prove God's existence by pure deduction. We are capable, they say, of conceiving in our minds an idea of the most perfect Being which could exist; therefore, such a Being must necessarily exist. Philosophers like St. Thomas Aquinas and Immanuel Kant have refuted this line of reasoning with the argument that the mind is quite capable of creating concepts which do not exist in reality.

St. Thomas, in his celebrated Five Ways, attempted to demonstrate God's existence from the existence of motion and causes and beings about us. Rejecting as impossible the idea of an infinite series of causes, St. Thomas argued for the necessity of a Prime Mover, an Uncaused Cause, an Absolutely Necessary Being ultimately responsible for all of us unnecessary beings. He based his argument on the principle that every effect must have an adequate cause; otherwise, the world is ultimately unintelligible. Modern critics reject St. Thomas' theistic argument precisely because of its presumption that the world is intelligible. They say his argument begs the question, that it rests upon a fundamental act of faith in the ultimate rationality of existence. Modern atheists are not willing to make that act of faith in the ultimate reasonableness of existence. For them the universe just is—and that's all. It is devoid of ultimate purpose, they say; and the question as to why there is anything at all has no meaning and, therefore, no answer.

Other forms of theistic argument do not attempt to prove conclusively the existence of God, but simply offer strong persuasion for the likelihood of his being. Most notable among these is the argument from design or order in the universe. According to this argument, the laws of nature imply that there is a supreme lawgiver; the cosmic and microcosmic order of the universe imply that there is a supreme intelligence responsible for it. Critics of this form of reasoning answer that there is a great deal of chance and disorder in the universe. They point to the existence of physical evils, of suffering, war, injustice, and depravity of every sort, as strong indications that there exists neither order nor design in this world of ours. The Nazi concentration camps, the very real danger of atomic annihilation, the tragic and unnecessary deaths of innocent children, the births of physically defective and mentally retarded children—all speak to the unbeliever of absurdity in the universe rather than intelligence. The relative insignificance of the earth as one planet in one solar system in one galaxy among countless such planets and stars further convinces him that he has no special role in any divine plan and that no such divine plan exists.

The debate continues among philosophers as to just what and how much the traditional arguments for God's existence prove. St. Thomas referred to his so-called proofs as "ways" of knowing rather than as proofs. For a man who doubts being, significance in life, or the reliability of human knowledge, the "proofs" prove nothing. For a man who accepts being, significance, and the reliability of human knowledge, they are personally convincing. There are reasons for accepting the existence of a Supreme Being, and there are reasons for rejecting it. Weighing the probability of the one against the other is impossible. In practice, however, there are few atheists who reject belief in God for rigorously rational motives, just as there are few believers who adhere to their faith in God for logical, historical, or scientific reasons. The motives for belief and for disbelief are almost always of an existential nature.

Rejection of Popular, Mistaken Notions of God

In writing of the reasons why so many modern men reject the idea of God, Pope Paul pointed out the "demand that divine things be presented in a worthier and purer way than is, perhaps, the case in certain imperfect forms of language and worship . . ." It cannot be denied that in many instances the God preached from Christian pulpits or worshiped in Christian sanctuaries is hardly the God revealed "of old to our fathers by the prophets" and "in these last days . . . to us by a Son" (Heb. 1:1). Origen, the first great theologian of the post-apostolic Church, began the history of theological reflection realizing that "it is always dangerous to speak about God." St. Thomas Aquinas reechoed that sentiment and emphasized the fact that what we know about God is what he is not rather than what he is.

Together with the great thinkers of Jewish and Orthodox Christian tradition, Catholic and Protestant theologians have recognized, in their better moments, that everything we say about God requires essential qualification. We are more capable of awareness of God's attitudes toward us than of his attributes. Yet popular concepts of God, often acquired in childhood, have a knack of assuming for many Christians more than symbolic value. These naïve, unreflected notions about God are in many instances little better than caricatures. They may characterize God as a cosmic policeman, a Big Brother always watching and waiting to catch one in a moment of weakness, or a Grand Old Man smiling down benignly upon his little children. He may be Mr. Fix-It, who makes all things well when they go awry; the Answer Man, who manages matters beyond our control; the Heavenly Bosom, always ready to provide consolation when it is needed. He may even be a security blanket, a teddy bear, a parental hangover, a crutch.

Every one of us, along with St. Paul, once "spoke as a child, felt as a child, thought as a child." Not all believers, however, "have put away the things of a child." Immature, mistaken, and even harmful ideas about the nature of God have come to be identified with Christian faith. In all too many instances our "world come of age," rightfully rejecting these notions of God, is also rejecting all that religious faith has to offer. The Reality has become confused with the symbol—a very distorted symbol at that.

Desire for a Scientific Explanation of the Universe

The phenomenal advance in modern times of science and technology has led our society to make a veritable act of faith in science. Many moderns believe that the human mind is quite capable of eventually solving all the problems and answering all the questions that life poses. Some of these scientific humanists, especially those who did not personally experience the ravages of World War II, still maintain a certain naïve faith that "every day in every way, things are getting better and better." Others may not be quite so optimistic as to the future of the human race in an atomic era, but they nevertheless believe that if it does not first destroy itself, mankind will find a scientific explanation for the beginnings of the universe, of life, and of man. They are confident that mankind can scientifically manage life on earth without any reference to a divine hypothesis.

Ours is an age enamored of science, technology, results, and action. It is not overly fond of meditative reflection upon large questions as to meaning, purpose, and ultimate causes. The proper domain of the physical sciences is the immediate, adequate causes of perceptible phenomena. The outstanding success of science inclines many people in our day to remain within that scientific domain and to go no further. As one university professor put it, "Whenever I think about the meaning of life, I get a headache." Rather than suffer the headache, a great many people in our age have ceased to think about it altogether.

Rejection of Christian Passivity and the Desire to Build a Better World

Christianity has always had to contend with those who considered its demands too exacting and difficult. It is only in more recent times that it has had to face the charge that it is not exacting and difficult enough. A cultural Christianity which went no further than practicing ritual and giving lip service to dogma deserved the contempt it received from Feuerbach, Nietzsche, and

Marx. They saw it as a terrible weight upon the shoulders of humanity, a burden to be dropped, for the sake of freedom, human progress, and personal dignity. They have their followers today, not only those affiliated with communist and socialist causes, but countless men of good will who are disheartened by a Christianity which seems dedicated to little else than maintaining the status quo for the sake of preserving its structure and privileged position.

Religion is being rejected today, in the name of mature human values, by men who are dedicated to building a better world not only for an elite but for all mankind. They disdain religion as a distraction from this vital task and as a tool of the bourgeois for keeping the masses resigned to oppression. They point with contempt to the teaching of St. Thomas Aquinas that "slavery among men is natural." They remind Catholics that in 1903 Pope Pius X wrote that "it is in conformity with the order of human society as established by God that there be rulers and ruled, employers and employed, learned and ignorant, nobles and plebeians." They reject the resignation urged as late as 1931 by Pope Pius XI when he encouraged workers to "accept without rancor the place which Divine Providence has assigned to them." Christian complacency toward, and often complicity in, the social evils of our day are regarded by many as adequate demonstration of the malignancy of religion. Slavery, colonialism, exploitation of backward nations, and, in our own day, racial segregation and war—long is the list of crimes committed and social evils countenanced, all too often in the name of religion.

Not for the sake of truth but for the good of mankind, for the sake of a higher humanism, do many of today's atheists reject God. They answer with Nicolai Lenin: "It is taken for granted that for us Communists, there is no God. But even if God did exist, that would be but one more reason for us to fight him, so evil do we find the works attributed to him."

Meeting the Challenge

Gilbert K. Chesterton once observed that Christianity has not been tried and found wanting; it just has not been tried. In any case, a man who believes in God and considers religion an important aspect of his life cannot help but doubt that radical atheism is capable of building a better world and answering all the important questions. The attempted "escape" of so many of our contemporaries by way of alcohol, drugs, material striving, and the pursuit of pleasure offers proof to believing men that there is need for some sort of faith, some sort of meaning, some sort of purpose. Until recent times religion has always been regarded as the most effective foundation for morality. To a man who believes in God, simple expediency does not seem to offer an adequate basis for law and order. Faith in man as "the supreme being for man" also seems to lack an adequate basis, since within the atheistic context itself, man is simply an advanced form of animal life, an accidental quirk of a blind evolutionary force.

To one who believes in God, the existential atheist seems to be the most honest and ruthlessly logical of all unbelievers. He alone seems to take the implications of his negation to their utmost conclusions. He accepts the universe as meaningless and his life as absurd, "a tale told by an idiot." In refusing to make an act of faith in God, he likewise refuses to make an act of faith in life, in himself, or in anyone else. Perhaps the destruction, human degradation, and disorder in today's world are not so much a cause of modern unbelief as a symptom of it, a result of it. If so, it is the unbelief not only of atheists that is responsible; it is also—and perhaps far more culpably—the unbelief of believers.

Meeting the problem of modern atheism is one of the most serious challenges confronting the Church today. Like the problem itself, its causes, and its results, the challenge posed by atheism is many faceted, one which demands a concentrated response from every area of the Church's life. It demands clarification of much of the Church's doctrine, greater involvement in working for a better world, and dialogue. In short, it demands total Christian renewal.

Clarification of the Church's Doctrine

In addressing itself to the problem of modern atheism and the solutions which should be attempted, Vatican Council II gave first place to the "proper presentation of the Church's teaching."

There is a great deal within Catholic doctrine which demands clarification and emphasis, for the sake of those both within and outside the Church. To make religion relevant to this "world come of age," some very fundamental ideas must first penetrate the Christian consciousness, ideas about the nature of faith, about God, man, and the world.

According to the Council, it is the function of the Church

to make God the Father and His Incarnate Son present and in a sense visible. This result is achieved chiefly by the witness of a living and mature faith, namely, one trained to see difficulties clearly and to master them. (Constitution on the Church in the Modern World, No. 21)

A mature faith is one prompted by a free choice, a desire to believe. Too many Christians are under the erroneous impressions that a man can reason himself to faith, that doubt is incompatible with faith, that the proofs for believing are intellectually compelling to all who look at them with a clear eye and an unbiased mind. Faith is a gift, a gift from God, a gift accepted freely by choice. The motives for believing can make faith reasonable, but they cannot compel. And they do not necessarily dispel doubts. A free, mature choice requires the real possibility of an alternative. Mature belief requires the real possibility of disbelief. Furthermore, besides being a response, freely chosen, to God's revelation, faith is a response which brings with it responsibilities. Faith without works is dead; it demands expression in acts of unselfishness, love, generosity. It calls for such expressions to a heroic degree. The clarification of these essential aspects of faith—its freedom, its compatibility with doubt, its responsibilities—can serve to bury forever a merely cultural Christianity which makes no serious demands on either men's minds or their lives.

The mistaken, crude, and often unhealthy notions of many Christians about God demand dispelling. For too long have infantile images served as the object of Christian belief—a God who is doddering, irascible, or even ludicrous. The same is true of the image many Christians have of Christ—weak, saccharine, feminine.

Catholics and Protestants both would do well to return to the healthy sense of awe which ages past had for divine mystery, a reverential agnosticism concerning what God is really like. The Church should dare not ask the world to worship a God or to accept a Christ who never outgrew a child's imagination.

Christian theology, in the light of its faith in God, needs to give serious consideration to the dignity and vocation of man. Proof is required to show that belief in God does not denigrate man but exalts him, that it gives his life meaning, his work purpose. Belief that God is a Father does not imply that men must be children— sons, yes, but not children. Maturity, both as men and as believers, means a willingness and ability to imitate God as Creator. The Biblical mandate to "take the earth and make it yours" has not been abrogated. Christians need to realize more fully their responsibility to work for the building up of the earth and not to wait for God to function as a *deus ex machina* in performing the task assigned to an inept steward.

For too long have Christians been fleeing the world, condemning its sins, suspecting its pleasures, and resigning themselves to its evils. For too long has the world been considered a "vale of tears," an "exile from the heavenly homeland." According to Christian belief, the Incarnation has meant a radical reversal for all creation, a transformation which Christ began and which Christians are called to carry through. Not only does man have a central place in the divine plan, but, according to Christian theology, so too does his work, his research, his inventions, his scientific discoveries. As so magnificently expounded by Teilhard de Chardin, Christians are to be men *of* the world as well as *in* the world—building the earth, bringing men together into a community which transcends racial, national, and cultural barriers. "Behold, I make all things new," is not an empty promise but a mission; the Christ whom Christians profess to follow is not only the Lamb of God but also the Lion of Judah. There has been entirely too much sweetness about Christianity and not enough strength, too much of the lamb and not enough of the lion. Christianity was meant to be not a conservative but a revolutionary force in the world, an innovation. Vatican II's Constitution on the Church in the Modern World is a revolutionary document, setting forth a very solid foundation for the theology of the dignity of man, his right to freedom, and his mission to make this world a better place. That foundation laid by the Council must be built up until all Christians realize that the City of God is not at variance with the City of Man, but rather, one with it.

Involvement in Making the World a Better Place

Clarification of the essential Christian doctrine on man and his role in the world will be just so much empty verbiage until it results in effective action. Ours is a pragmatic age; it wants to see results. It must be made as true of Christians today as it was two thousand years ago that "by their fruits you will know them." The seed must not only be retained; it must take root, it must bring forth fruit a hundredfold. In speaking of the results which mature faith implies, the Council stated:

This faith needs to prove its fruitfulness by penetrating the believer's entire life, including its worldly dimensions, and by activating him toward justice and love, especially regarding the needy. (Constitution on the Church in the Modern World, No. 21)

Christian action in the world is required to make Christianity meaningful to its own adherents as well as to unbelievers. In the laboratory, in the union hall, at the international conference table; upholding the basic rights of man; working for peace, equality, brotherhood; fighting poverty, hunger, injustice—in all these must the Christian community take its calling seriously. Faith requires involvement in the world, not escape from it. If it does not result in service, it is counterfeit.

Dialogue between Believers and Unbelievers

Nearly one-third of the human race professes faith in Jesus Christ; another third pays homage to the teachings of Karl Marx. Christians cannot afford to keep their eyes closed to the communistic beliefs of these countless millions or to the utter *non*belief of many millions more. Confrontation is necessary, not only for the betterment of the human race, but for its very preservation. For too long have the anathemas been hurled from one side to another. For too long have both sides stereotyped one another as total opposites. Catholic philosophy has traditionally maintained that error cannot exist except within a larger truth. Christian morality has traditionally distinguished between error, which has no rights, and persons, who despite their error do have rights. The human rights of unbelievers, with their devotion in many instances to truth and humanitarian ideals, deserve recognition and respect from Christians. They call for a willingness to enter into serious deliberations with unbelievers and to cooperate with them in answering the needs of today's world. In the spirit of Pope John XXIII and his encyclical *Peace on Earth,* Vatican Council II encouraged just such meetings and activity: "Such an ideal [that of all men working together for the betterment of the world] cannot be realized, however, apart from sincere and prudent dialogue."

Would it be too bold to hope that dialogue between unbelievers and believers and possible cooperation between them for the betterment and progress of mankind could lead to some sort of synthesis? Teilhard de Chardin did not think that this was out of the question. He went so far as to say: "The synthesis of the [Christian] God of the Above and the [Marxist] God of the Ahead is the only God whom we shall in the future be able to adore in spirit and in truth." Perhaps these words written in a poetic vein may also be words of prophecy.

Christian Renewal

In speaking of the schisms which divide Christianity today, Vatican Council II admitted the share which Catholics have in the blame for the origins of the schisms and their perpetuation. Forgiveness was sought at the same time it was extended. The same honesty and courage could well be shown by all Christians in admitting their share in the responsibility for the advance of atheism. After nearly two thousand years of preaching about love, brotherhood, and human solidarity, much of the world has responded to the Church with a thundering indictment: What you are speaks so loudly, I cannot hear what you are saying!

The Council has declared that ecumenism, for Catholics, primarily means Christian renewal, the clearer demonstration within the life of the Church of the presence of Jesus Christ. Such renewal is necessary for rapprochement not only among divisions within Christianity but also among believers and unbelievers. It was not its convincing arguments that attracted pagan antiquity to the early Church; it was its charity. Those outside the Christian community today do not always have reason to say, as they once said of old, "See how these Christians love one another." It is Christ-like charity, above all, which will make Christianity relevant to unbelievers. If they are to find God in the Risen Christ, they must first find Christ in the lives of those who profess to follow him:

What does the most to reveal God's presence . . . is the brotherly charity of the faithful who are united in spirit as they work together for the faith of the gospel and who prove themselves a sign of unity. (Constitution on the Church in the Modern World, No. 21)

Conclusion:

Atheistic humanism today poses to Christians what is perhaps the most demanding challenge the Church has ever been asked to face. It is a challenge we dare not refuse. It requires disentangling the message of Christ from the historical and social context of the past and translating it into the historical and social context of the present. It requires the transformation of Christianity from a cultural pattern to a vibrant and challenging way of life. Today's unbelievers ask for effectiveness. Let Christians show us the fruits of their love, they say; let them show us that they are capable of creating a superior humanity. Then we will want to believe in their Christ, we will want to join their numbers; then we will listen to their words, and their Word.

Suggested Reading

De Lubac, Henri. *The Drama of Atheistic Humanism*. Edith Riley, tr. World Publishing Co., 1967.

Hebblethwaite, Peter. *The Council Fathers and Atheism*. Paulist, 1967.

Hick, John, ed. *The Existence of God*. Macmillan, 1964.

Lepp, Ignace. *Atheism in Our Time*. Macmillan, 1963.

Padovano, Anthony. *The Estranged God: Modern Man's Search for Belief*. Sheed and Ward, 1966.

Rahner, Karl, ed. *The Pastoral Approach to Atheism*. Paulist, 1967.

9 / The Catholic Church—
From the Outside Looking In

Christ summons the Church, as she goes her pilgrim way, to that continual reformation of which she always has need, insofar as she is an institution of men here on earth. . . . There can be no ecumenism worthy of the name without a change of heart.

—DECREE ON ECUMENISM, NO. 6

Successful ecumenical encounter requires insight not only into others but also into ourselves. We need to see ourselves as others see us. Critical self-examination from an outsider's viewpoint can be painful as well as revealing. But the pain can be quite salutary. It would be well for Catholics to realize that much within the Church which for them is natural, familiar, and easy to take for granted is, for non-Catholics, confusing, objectionable, and even fearsome. This fear, often enough, arises from fables. The confusion, however, arises primarily from Catholicism's many apparent contradictions.

Fables concerning the Catholic Church have instilled suspicion and even dread in many people who have had little or no contact with Catholicism.

The Church has long been considered by some Protestants as being the "Whore of Babylon." St. John in his Apocalypse refers to the Roman Empire of his day as a harlot because of its moral decay and its persecution of Christians:

. . . and I saw a woman sitting on a scarlet beast which was full of blasphemous names, and it had seven heads and ten horns. The woman was arrayed in purple and scarlet, and bedecked with gold and

jewels and pearls, holding in her hand a golden cup full of abominations and the impurities of her fornication; and on her forehead was
written a name of mystery: "Babylon the great, mother of harlots
and of earth's abominations." (Rev. 17:3–5)

According to one traditional Protestant interpretation, however,
the harlot depicts the Catholic Church seated upon the seven hills
of Rome. The purple and scarlet are said to refer to ecclesiastical
vestments, the gold and precious stones to the Pope's regalia; and
the golden cup is supposedly none other than the chalice used at
Mass.

The Pope has been regarded for centuries by many Protestants
as the anti-Christ foretold by scripture. Two years after the beginning of the Reformation, Luther wrote in a letter, "I whisper it
in your ear, I am not sure if the Pope is anti-Christ or his apostle."
Any doubts Luther had were eventually dispelled. He discon-
tinued whispering his opinions; instead, he proclaimed loudly and
with considerable animus:

The Pope is the real anti-Christ who has raised himself over and set
himself against Christ . . . Accordingly, just as we cannot adore the
devil himself as our Lord or God, so we cannot suffer his apostle, the
Pope or anti-Christ, to govern us as our head or Lord, for deception,
murder and the eternal destruction of body and soul are characteristic
of his papal government. (Smalcald Articles, II, No. 3)

Priests and nuns have fared no better from fables than the Pope.
Priests were considered to be scoundrels ever busy subverting the
peace and well-being of Protestants. Convents were believed to be
little better than brothels, at which all kinds of dreadful and out-
landish horrors took place. One of the best-selling exposés of
nunneries, *The Awful Disclosures of Maria Monk,* told blood-
curdling tales of how Catholic nuns kept children in dungeons and
murdered infants in their basements.

Catholic laymen were commonly suspected of gathering an army
to invade the United States. The Knights of Columbus were
viewed as the leaders of the insurgents, with the local Catholic
rectory and convent serving as likely arsenals. Such stories about
the Church often bordered on the ludicrous, but they seemed

credible to Protestants fed on chilling tales of Spanish Catholic cruelty in the *Black Legend* and the martyrdom of English Protestants by Bloody Queen Mary in Foxe's *Book of Martyrs*. Fortunately, time, togetherness, and education have dispelled many of the fables concerning Catholicism.

More confusing to Protestants of our own time are the *apparent contradictions* in the Catholic Church. Among those most commonly noted are the following:

1. Catholics will kiss the Bible and surround it with clouds of incense at Mass, reverencing it to an extent Protestants would never think of doing. Yet Catholics don't seem to read the Bible or care if what they believe is found in the Bible.

2. Catholics vigorously defend the divinity of Christ in opposition to Liberal Protestants who consider Jesus simply a religious genius. Yet Catholics seem to almost lose sight of Christ in crowds of saints and choirs of angels, preferring the intercession of some favorite patron.

3. Catholics hold that the marriage of baptized Christians, even of two Protestants, is a sacrament; most Protestants do not. Yet the Catholic Church seems to favor celibacy and virginity over marriage, to consider dedicated virginity a more perfect way of life.

4. The same Catholic Church is able to give rise to such apparently mutual contradictions as Holland and Italy, Augustin Cardinal Bea and Alfredo Cardinal Ottaviani, St. John's Abbey at Collegeville and the National Shrine of the Immaculate Conception.

The negative reactions of those outside Catholicism are not all without foundation. Catholics, as naturally sensitive and resentful as anyone else of criticism, should not presume that every critic is a bigot. Instead of becoming angry, emotional, or hurt because of feelings of persecution, Catholics need to look at themselves to see if correcting the Catholic image might not mean effecting a Catholic reform. Least of all should criticism lead to defensiveness. The Second Vatican Council has indicated as much in its call to reform certain Catholic institutions and practices. Both the Vatican Council and the ecumenical movement ask of every

Catholic an attitude of honest seeking for truth, a humble admission of guilt where necessary, and a firm decision, with the grace of God, of conversion and reform.

Objections to Roman Catholicism

The following are several broad categories of the more common objections to aspects of Catholicism that have held sway since the Council of Trent. Unfair exaggerations and outright fallacies are not discussed in any detail; it is felt that there are numerous other books offering pertinent explanations, so that no apologetic is needed here. Given in far greater detail are those facts which often lead the Church's critics to misunderstand its teachings or misconstrue its motives. Each category is concluded with a brief note on the reforms required and, often enough, already inaugurated by the Church.

Catholics are credulous and superstitious.

Fallacies, Facts, and Clarifications. It is believed by many that Catholics practice idolatry, because they pray before pictures; that they use medals, scapulars, and plastic statues as charms to ward off accidents and bad luck; that they believe in numerology, assigning magical powers to certain numbers, such as 3 and 9. Such accusations against genuine Catholic piety and practice may be understandable, but they are nevertheless false. Catholic theology teaches that images are simply aids for prayer. Medals and scapulars are signs of faith and tokens of honor. While there is no intrinsic power to the number 3, human psychology finds in it a certain satisfaction and completeness. It has no special value or power, but is simply as likely a time as any to stop when repeating a particular prayer or act. It is also symbolic of the Holy Trinity.

Despite the fact that Catholics do not worship statues, use scapulars as magic charms, or believe in magic numbers, there is some foundation for this false image. Repetition is a natural means of emphasis in prayer. It is also a psychologically beneficial way to establish a habit of devotion. But there is the danger of attributing magical powers to such practices as saying certain prayers for nine days in a row or receiving Holy Communion on nine First Fridays or five First Saturdays. Undue emphasis can too easily be placed upon establishing an unbroken series rather than on the internal dispositions which the repeated prayers or acts are meant to express.

Medals, scapulars, and statues on one's automobile dashboard or in one's home are distinguishing marks of a Catholic. They are signs of faith and, as such, are a laudable public profession of Catholic loyalty. But there is a very real and human tendency to transform such marks of faith into magical charms little better than a rabbit's foot or a four-leaf clover. The devotion which these tokens are meant to represent can thus be forgotten. Occult powers can too easily be attributed to these scraps of metal, cloth, plastic, or wood, simply because they bear a sacred image.

Other areas of similar—and, again, often justified—criticism concern Catholic attitudes toward the sacraments, indulgences, and relics. According to Catholic teaching, the sacraments are signs of faith and encounters with Christ. They are channels of grace, means by which we are drawn closer to God. But Christ does not unite us to himself against our will; we must be open to this greater nearness to God. Some Catholics have the erroneous idea that the sacraments cause grace in us no matter what our openness, no matter what our dispositions. Such an attitude demeans the sacraments to the level of being little better than magical rites. And it is just such an attitude that leads to the justified criticism by those outside the Church.

Regarding indulgences, the Church teaches that they are the remission of the temporal punishment due to sins. Even when a person, after having sinned, returns to God with sincere conversion, certain vestiges of sin remain. They require acts of faith, patience, or unselfishness to be removed. In the early Church, penitents practiced long, arduous penances to be cleansed of these vestiges of sin. Aware of its "supernatural solidarity," however, the Church realized that just as the sinfulness of one harms all the others and the holiness of one benefits all the others, so too can the penances of one profit all the others. The inexhaustible merits of Christ and all those united to him were seen as constituting a kind of "treasury" from which all could draw. In the place of the long, difficult penances practiced in its early centuries, the Church began the practice of indulgences, dispensing from its treasury the satisfaction for sins merited by Christ himself and through his saints. An indulgenced prayer or act is thus a prayer or act, not of an individual, but of the entire Church, which, as a body, prays for sinners and cooperates in bringing men into perfect union with God.

The doctrine and practice of indulgences have a long history in the Church. They are an extension of the sacrament of Penance, the expression of the contrition which alone permits the forgiveness of sin. As such, they have their roots in divine revelation and represent a development of the doctrine and practice of the early Church. Unfortunately, however, indulgences are open to much misunderstanding and even abuse. There is the all-too-human tendency to become lost in externals and to forget the internal dispositions which those externals are meant to express. In the area of indulgences, this becomes a tendency to emphasize the act performed or the prayer recited rather than the disposition of contrition which is supposed to inspire it. Indulgences can thus become mechanistic devices for warding off divine punishment. It is easy to become lost in trivial technicalities to obtain indulgences rather than concentrate on the faith, love, and contrition which they presume.

A similar problem arises with relics. Honoring relics can be a legitimate means for expressing devotion to a particular saint and, thereby, indirectly to God by whose grace that person became a saint. In the earliest days of the Church, Christians began expressing devotion to the martyrs by visiting and honoring their tombs. This veneration spread to other saints as well as martyrs, and to their relics as well as their tombs. Possessing and honoring the relic of a saint became an external expression of an internal bond with a saint and, through that saint, with Christ.

In an era quite different from our own, venerating relics became an immensely popular devotion. Their popularity, however, led to their rarity, and their rarity led to their manufacture. Spurious relics abounded to such an extent that it was often difficult to discern the genuine from the counterfeit. Theologians dissipated any qualms about authenticity by proposing that it did not really matter if a relic was authentic or not. The devotion shown to a relic, whether genuine or not, is shown to the saint it means to represent and, therefore, ultimately to Christ. Such subtlety in making distinctions is not well understood or appreciated in our own culture. Neither for that matter is the practice of collecting relics as if they were trophies or stamps. The devotion to relics was never meant to become a casual hobby. Such deviations are neither inevitable nor common; they are, however, an ever-present danger.

Room for Reform. There is certainly room for improved religious instruction in the area of the use of sacraments and sacramentals. Fortunately, it has begun. A theologically well-founded understanding of the sacraments and prayer must continue to be emphasized both from the pulpit and in the classroom. And greater emphasis must continue to be placed on sacred scripture as the core of Christian life. Private revelations and the practices associated with them need to be seen as pertaining to the periphery and not the essense of Christianity.

Two areas that require a great deal of clarification are indulgences and devotion to relics. Both are valid religious practices. Both are capable of being reconciled with sacred scripture and human nature. Yet it cannot be denied that both practices have led to misunderstanding and abuse. Deviations can easily arise to pervert the real purposes of indulgences and devotion to relics, endangering Christian orthodoxy and exposing the Catholic Church to misunderstanding and mockery. Since the benefits derived from indulgences and devotion to relics can be obtained through means less easily misunderstood and abused, there is ground to believe that both practices could be prudently de-emphasized without any danger of diminution to Catholic faith or Christian piety.

In an effort to eliminate the more flagrant misunderstandings and abuses regarding indulgences, in January 1967 Pope Paul VI issued a constitution which revised the Church's practice of indulgences. Indulgences attached to the use of certain objects, e.g., a crucifix or rosary, were rescinded; and the list of indulgenced works was revised and greatly reduced. The designation "300 days indulgence" or "seven years indulgence" was revoked in favor of the more general description of "partial indulgence," emphasizing that remission is always proportionate to contrition.

Catholics ignore Christ in favor of Mary and the saints.

Fallacies, Facts, and Clarifications. The accusation that Catholic theology puts Mary on a par with God or with Christ hardly deserves consideration, let alone refutation. Catholic theology has been scrupulously careful to distinguish between devotion offered to Mary and the saints and adoration offered to God alone. The two simply cannot be compared. The homage paid to Mary and the saints is purely relative, more in the vein of congratulations paid to them for the wonderful works that God has accomplished in and through them. It must be conceded, however, that devotion to Mary, at least in certain Catholic milieus, has sometimes been exaggerated to the extent of verging on the unorthodox. The Vatican Council's Dogmatic Constitution on the Church rightly warned against such extremism in Marian devotion.

Even aside from the emotionalism and flamboyance that sometimes accompany Marian devotion, the Church in its liturgical year has tended to emphasize Mary's role to an extent that she might seem to be more central to Catholicism than Christ. Thus, for example, in addition to the Sunday liturgy, Christ has received nine calendar feasts, plus one Friday a month; Mary is honored with twenty-four calendar feasts and every Saturday which does not have its own feast. The Holy Spirit is honored with one novena a year, the nine days before Pentecost; Mary, in many churches, is honored with a perpetual novena, one day out of every week. The promises supposed to have been made by Christ to those who receive Communion for nine First Fridays are matched in a patently "better bargain" to those who make only five First Saturdays.

Catholic piety has been marked in not-too-distant times with the untheological attitude that Mary will protect us from Christ. Besides being both our brother and mediator, Christ is also the Son of God and someday will be our judge. Mary, the Mother of Christ, is also the spiritual mother of all Christians. These two concepts are both valid Catholic belief, but emphasizing Christ's divinity and judgeship together with Mary's maternity has led to the almost heretical attitude on the part of some Catholics that they will find an understanding and mercy in Mary that they won't find in Christ. This attitude was unwittingly fostered by a popular version of the devotion to Mary as "Mother of Perpetual Help," in which she was implored to "save us from Jesus, our judge."

Some Catholics also seem to have a congenital weakness for visions and the shrines which mark such visions, as Lourdes and Fatima. Private revelations by Christ, Mary, or the saints clearly are possible. The Church permits them to be believed so long as they are not deemed harmful to faith or piety. But Catholics are not required to believe in them, and certainly they are not central to Christian faith and practice. Yet how often Catholics are better informed on the history of Lourdes and Fatima than they are on the history of salvation. They seem to have far more interest in the letter of Fatima, which supposedly contains the words of the Virgin Mary, than the Bible, which certainly contains the word of God.

The Church's year of liturgical worship is also filled with the feasts of saints. From this multiplicity of saints are found patrons and intercessors for every task or need. Thus, St. Dymphna is the patron saint of neurotics, and St. Catherine is the one to turn to when the difficulty is a toothache. Prayer to the saints is well-founded in the most ancient Christian tradition and is based on sound human psychology. There is, however, a real danger of losing sight of central issues amid the crowd of distractions, the danger of losing sight of Christ amid the multitude of angels, archangels, patriarchs, prophets, martyrs, virgins, and confessors.

Room for Reform. Reforms have already begun within the Catholic Church to place proper emphasis on Christ, both in religious instruction and worship. A reform has already begun on the Missal and Breviary, properly emphasizing the liturgy of Sunday and eliminating some of the calendar feasts. Mary's role as the first of Christ's imitators and followers is being given equal emphasis with her maternal relationship to all Christians. Thus, there was no separate decree on Mary at Vatican Council II, but consideration of her role was incorporated as one chapter within the Dogmatic Constitution on the Church. The position of Mary and the saints within Christianity will not be properly understood except within the context of Christ and the Church. It is gratifying that emphasis on Christ and the Church is more strongly than ever the core of contemporary Catholic theology and religious instruction. This will in no way detract from the devotion paid to Mary and our appreciation of her role in bringing men to God. Rather, it will render both our devotion to Mary and our appreciation of her role more Christ-centered, which is certainly the attitude displayed by Mary in her own life.

Catholics are not free to think or make judgments for themselves.

Fallacies, Facts, and Clarifications. Many of the Church's critics are under the impression that Catholics must agree with every statement that a Pope or a bishop happens to make. They think that Catholics must obey Church authorities in every matter. Both of these notions are untrue. Since the Church is a community of faith, a person, in order to be part of the Catholic community, must believe what the Church officially, authoritatively, and infallibly teaches that God has revealed in matters of faith and morals. As any Catholic theologian can tell you, the teachings so defined by the Church are really relatively few. In other matters on which Church authorities speak, a Catholic owes serious, thoughtful, and respectful consideration; in these matters he is entitled—indeed, even obliged—to follow his personal conscience and its convictions, presuming of course that it is a conscience informed by the Church's teaching. However, if and when a Catholic, whether priest or layman, is called upon to represent the Church's doctrine on a particular issue, honesty requires that he accurately reflect, not his own personal inclinations, but the understanding and authoritative teaching of the total community.

In the past, and particularly since the Protestant Reformation, Catholicism has been woefully dominated by the self-image of "Holy Mother Church." This view of the Church has led to an exaggerated emphasis upon unquestioning obedience as the most basic and important of all virtues. From the Pope and his Curia down to the lowliest pastor and his curate, the chain of command within the Church has been clearly defined. The result, in many instances, has been the pervasive atmosphere within the Church of an army camp rather than a community of charity.

Then too, for more than a few centuries, bishops and priests have tended to view themselves as fulfilling a parental function within the Church. This self-image and assessment of their role caused them to become more than somewhat paternal and protective in their attitude toward laymen. Since they were "Fathers" in the Church, they have tended to regard those whom they serve as children; they were the "shepherds," laymen the "sheep."

A consequence of these attitudes has been a misguided attempt to "protect" Catholics from what were deemed unhealthy or harmful influences. Censorship sought to protect Catholics from dangerous ideas; and there arose in the 16th century the Index of Forbidden Books and, in our own day, the National Office for Decent Literature. Priests were forbidden to publish without prior examination and an imprimatur of their bishops. The most formidable agency of the Vatican Curia, the Holy Office, was charged with the protection of Catholic faith and morals. It took its policing role most seriously. Through its influence, priests who were suspected of harboring dangerous ideas were dismissed from their teaching positions, given "safe" assignments where they could do no harm, and instructed not to publish. The most notorious example of this protectiveness in recent times was the restriction placed upon Pierre Teilhard de Chardin. In our own country the Legion of Decency attempted to protect Catholics from dangerous, immorally suggestive movies; it not only published a guide distinguishing between acceptable and objectionable films, but also placed pressure on film producers and used the threat of Catholic boycott as a means of keeping motion pictures safe for public consumption.

In their role as "Fathers," bishops have often extended their authority to authoritarianism, particularly in dealing with their brother-priests. It should be presumed, in all fairness, that bishops, in their protective guardianship of the Church, are inspired by sincere motives. Their aims are the welfare and well-being of the Church. Their zealous dedication to achieving these aims, however, has sometimes led them to justify in their consciences any means whatever for accomplishing them. Such zeal has led to silencing critics through political and economic pressure, removing troublesome "new breed" priests to safer areas of work, and preventing publication of any news which might hurt the Church's image. It is only in very recent times that Catholic criticism of the hierarchy, whether from priests or laymen, has not been taken as a form of outright disloyalty and disrespect.

Because of the exaggeration of the role of priests as "Fathers," many Catholics have not been able to reach a stage of moral maturity. Catholics have often been taught, in order to be safe and sure, to seek the judgment and solutions of a priest on moral questions. As a result, many Catholics now find it difficult to apply moral principles to their particular situations and arrive at their own judgments. They are ordinarily uncomfortable in making their own decisions on moral questions and expect to be told, for example, how many children they should have, what kind of penance they should do, how much they should pray. The result is a moral retardation hardly worthy of adults.

Christianity consists essentially of internal, personal acts of faith, love, and worship. In order to be truly human, however, these acts need to be expressed externally; and these external actions need to be guided for the sake of harmony and good order by certain norms. The Catholic Church, therefore, like any other human society, requires a certain amount of legislative guidance, of specific rules and regulations. An exaggerated emphasis on rules, however, leads to legalism with all its pharisaical concern for technicalities, details, and loopholes. Particularly in their approach to the performance of penance and the keeping of the Eucharistic fast, Catholics, until recent changes in legislation, have too often been infected by a legalism which weighed ounces and counted minutes.

Room for Reform. Vatican Council II has initiated a very real and needed reform of structures and attitudes in order to dispel autocracy and legalism. The Dogmatic Constitution on the Church emphasized the nature and role of the Church as "pilgrim" and "servant." Bishops and priests were described as being not only "Father" but also "brother" to the Catholic layman. The Council called for the establishment of senates of priests to work with bishops, and Pope Paul established a Synod of Bishops to implement the doctrine of episcopal collegiality. Whether concerning bishops within the universal Church or priests within a diocese, the principle of collegiality counteracts the danger of arbitrary autocracy.

The Holy Office has been renamed the Congregation for the Doctrine of the Faith; it has been reorganized and is establishing more democratic policies and procedures. Another indication of the demise of authoritarianism within the Church is the abolition of the Index of Forbidden Books. The Legion of Decency in this country has also been renamed. Now called the National Catholic Office for Motion Pictures, it has developed over recent years a more positive policy toward the reviewing of motion pictures; it judges films now from not only a moral but also an aesthetic viewpoint, recommending films as well as condemning them. The movement to give the layman his proper place in the Church is already resulting in the formation of democratically elected councils of laymen assisting pastors in the administration of parish affairs and advising bishops in the administration of diocesan affairs. Contemporary moral theology has begun to provide principles rather than solutions, encouraging laymen to exercise their own mature judgments on moral questions. By emphasizing the primacy of love, contemporary theology has placed law in its proper perspective. It might be encouraging to many of our readers to learn that American canon lawyers are among the most articulate and avant-garde exponents of renewal and reform in the Church today.

This change of direction from autocracy and legalism to personal responsibility is perhaps best exemplified in the way the Church has expressed itself on penance and mortification. The modifications in the laws of fast and abstinence for Fridays and Lent were notable not only for the freedom they afforded in choosing ways of practicing penance; the documents which made these changes were remarkable too for the emphasis they placed on interior attitudes and the spirit of penance. These new statements of law were evangelical and even beautiful in their simplicity. There is good reason to believe that they indicate the tone and spirit which will pervade the total body of Church law, which is now being completely revised in accordance with the principles of Vatican Council II.

Catholics belong to a Church that is
foreign and feudal.

Fallacies, Facts, and Clarifications. The Catholic Church is often accused of being a foreign political power. Many moderns regard it as a medieval relic, totally irrelevant to contemporary society. In reality, however, the Church is both supranational and supra-temporal. It is not bound to any one age, country, or culture; by its very name, it is meant to be "catholic," that is, universal, for all men of all ages. The Church has the obligation of being both conservative and contemporary—conservative, in maintaining the revelation entrusted to its keeping; contemporary, in trans-lating that revelation into forms and symbols relevant and mean-ingful to every nation in every age.

The forms, symbols, and structures employed by the Church in its mission of bringing men to God are human in origin. They can and should change with time, although the meaning they convey and the function they serve remains the same. There is a very real danger, however, that the Church will become too conservative of these external, unessential trappings along with the faith entrusted to it. There does exist within the Church an abundance of paraphernalia which smacks of medievalism—priests' cassocks; nuns' wimples, scapulars, and veils; monks' cowls and sandals. Papal and episcopal regalia often suggest the pomp and splendor of a Byzantine court or a medieval pageant rather than the simplicity of the apostolic Church. Many bishops still live in "episcopal palaces" which they have inherited from their forebears, together with elaborately wrought rings, miters, and pectoral crosses. The gold chair in which the Pope is carried at public functions provides crowds of tourists an opportunity to get a good view of the Pontiff, but it also smacks of the retinue of a Roman emperor or an Oriental potentate. The huge Egyptian fans, formerly used by the Pharaohs, have been relegated only recently from a place in Papal processions to a corner in the Vatican Museum.

The feudal caste system which once bound together a lord and his vassals cannot be found to any extent today *except* within the Church. These vestiges of an era long gone survive in a complex and often colorful maze of ecclesiastical offices, titles, and rules of etiquette. The hierarchical ladder bears a similarity to a chromatic scale, ranging from black, purple, and red for priests, monsignors, and bishops respectively, to scarlet and white for cardinals and the Pope. Titles range from Reverend Father to Most Reverend Bishop, with a Very Reverend and Right Reverend thrown in between to distinguish the monsignors. Every bishop, no matter how undistinguished his origins, acquires at his consecration a coat of arms. Etiquette upon meeting one's bishop calls for genuflecting the left knee and kissing his ring. This token of reverence, while disturbing to most men of egalitarian persuasion, is at least not nearly as servile as the former practice of a cardinal's kissing the pope's velvet slipper when he received his red hat.

Triumphalism, for the last several hundred years, has marked Catholic churches in both their art and architecture. Imposing structures elaborately decorated, rich in mosaics, heavy with gold leaf, typify the gathering places for Catholic worship. The rationale for such extravagance has been that "nothing is too good for God," but often enough lavish display in ecclesiastical architecture has also witnessed the neglect of the social and economic needs of people in its very shadow. There is a real temptation for a bishop or pastor to erect a massive church building less for the glory of God than as a monument to his own memory. Furthermore, maintaining such churches—along with rectories, schools, convents, assembly halls, hospitals, and other edifices of social service—requires a considerable amount of financial support. Since depending solely upon the good will and generosity of the Catholic faithful does not seem to provide adequate income, devices such as bingos and lotteries have been used to supplement the Sunday collection. And it is not unknown that bishops have sometimes maintained diocesan solvency by shrewd investments in the stock market. While it is unfair to blanketly accuse the Church of trying to serve both God and mammon, it would be difficult to prove that the Church has been given singlemindedly to imitating the lilies of the field.

Room for Reform. One of the primary purposes of Vatican Council II was an *aggiornamento,* an updating, which would disencumber the Church from outmoded structures and trappings. The bishops at Vatican II went on record for the abolition of triumphalism within the Church and a radical return to the simplicity and poverty which marked the apostolic era. Liturgical reform has already begun the simplification of ceremonies and rites, as well as of architecture, art, and vestments. Garb for nuns is being modernized; priests are not required to wear cassocks on the street, as they once were in some countries. Popes John and Paul have already eliminated much of the traditional regalia of pontifical pageantry, and many bishops are divesting themselves of the trappings and image of the episcopal prince in order to identify more closely with the poor. Dissatisfaction with medieval pomp and the movement toward simplification should see before too long the demise of such quaint but unnecessary ecclesiastical institutions as the scarlet-breasted cardinal or the purple-feathered monsignor.

Catholics do not know the Bible and believe in doctrines which are not scriptural.

Fallacies, Facts, and Clarifications. The Catholic Church has long suffered the accusation of chaining the Bible and not permitting it to be read by ordinary laymen. The truth of the matter is that the Church was responsible for the transmission of the scriptures down the course of fifteen centuries, long before Protestantism even saw the light of day. Bibles were handwritten, rare, and valuable; they *were* literally chained in cathedrals and monasteries, but only to prevent their theft. The Bible was being translated from Latin into the languages of the people many years before Luther began his celebrated German version. Prior to this time, however, there was little use for vernacular translations of the entire Bible, since most of the people were illiterate. Furthermore, there was an obvious physical limitation to the number of handwritten books, even in Latin, that could be available. After the

Reformation and the invention of the printing press, Catholics were forbidden to read *unauthorized* versions of the scriptures out of fear of biased translation. It is true that there were some instances in which Catholics were forbidden to read the Bible altogether, but these were undue and relatively rare overreactions to Protestantism.

Despite the foregoing, it is an unfortunate but incontrovertible fact that most Catholics, even those well educated in their faith, are not as familiar with sacred scripture as they should be. In reaction to the Protestant battle cry of "scripture alone" and the Reformers' denigration of the value of the living teaching tradition of the Church, Catholicism emphasized tradition to the neglect of the Bible. Scripture was often approached as little more than a wellspring of proof texts to buttress Catholic doctrines. It was considered safer for the faith of the people if they received their exposure to the Bible, together with doctrinal explanations, at Sunday Mass.

It is also true that some tenets of Catholic teaching, such as Papal primacy, infallibility, purgatory, and the Marian dogma of the Immaculate Conception, are not explicit in scripture. For that matter, however, neither are the Trinity, the Incarnation, or infant baptism clearly defined in scripture. They are, rather, interpretations of the Church's understanding of Christ's revelation. These interpretations have their source in the apostolic preaching of the early Church, and are more or less discernibly implicit in that preaching as it is recorded in the New Testament. A development of doctrine can be seen within the New Testament itself, even after Christ's ascension; and there is no basic ecumenical problem in this regard. A question of the gravest importance to Christian unity, however, is the possibility of further elaboration of basic Christian belief, i.e., beyond that implicitly recorded in the New Testament.

Room for Reform. Both the liturgical and catechetical movements within the Church have joined with the scriptural movement to make Catholic worship, education, life, and piety more Biblically orientated. Liturgical reform has seen a concentrated emphasis placed upon the celebration of the Word as an essential aspect of the Eucharistic encounter. Bible vigils, Bible study seminars on the parish level, Biblical institutes for Catholic educators, revised textbooks in Catholic schools from the primary to the university levels—all are serving to encourage in Catholics a deeper knowledge and love of the Bible.

The Vatican Council's Dogmatic Constitution on Divine Revelation urged both that scripture scholars "continue energetically with the work they have so well begun," and that "easy access to sacred Scripture should be provided for all the Christian faithful" so that "they might learn by faithful reading of the divine Scriptures the 'excelling knowledge of Jesus Christ.'" Catholic theology has perhaps no more important task facing it today than the dual study of the Biblical roots of Catholic teaching and the subject of the development of doctrine within the Church.

Fears concerning Roman Catholicism

It is embarrassingly easy to document the suspicions which a great many people harbor against the Catholic Church. Some critics are inclined to impute crass motives of gain and self-interest to everything the Church says and does, even the most innocent. Particularly in the United States, the Church's size, wealth, and power appear so formidable that many see therein a threat to American civil and religious liberties. Catholics are often surprised to learn that the Church is so resented and feared by people outside its sphere. Practical aspects of ecumenical relations, however, require that Catholics understand the *reasons* for this fear of the Church on the part of many non-Catholics. Only on the basis of such understanding can we hope that it might be eliminated.

Historical Reasons

Among the foremost of the historical reasons for fear of the Catholic Church are the many and varied instances in which Catholics have employed political influence to obtain their purposes. The Church of the Middle Ages did not hesitate to place an entire nation under interdict, i.e., deny its people the supernatural benefit of worship and the sacraments, in order to put pressure upon its ruler and bring him to the Church's terms. At the time of the Roman Inquisition, the effectiveness of ferreting out heretics depended upon their punishment by the political ruler of a territory; the rack and stake were used to assure the peace and security of both Church and State. In several decrees, some as late as the last one hundred years, the Popes have taught that the ideal relationship between the Catholic Church and an individual State was not one of separation but of official establishment and privilege; they have taught this ideal as something all Catholics should work for, with anything less only to be tolerated.

Historically, and even to our own day, Catholicism has been marked by a certain militancy capable (albeit not so calculated) of instilling fear into the hearts of those outside the Church, even of the most stouthearted. The Knights of Columbus, the Knights of Malta, the Blue Army, the Legion of Mary, the Legion of Decency, joined to all the "soldiers of Christ" and led by the Mother General of every religious order, constitute a formidable "army" ready, willing, and eager to "conquer souls for Christ." What non-Catholic in the face of such an onslaught wouldn't become just a bit nervous?

Unfortunately, too, contemporary examples of the Catholic Church's willingness to use political influence to its own advantage are not lacking, particularly outside the United States. Italy, Spain, and several Latin-American countries do not permit divorce by agreement with the Church. Birth control information is also restricted by law. A number of national constitutions forbid a Protestant to become president; and in some traditionally Catholic countries, although Protestants are permitted to worship freely according to their own conscience, any attempt to evangelize Catholics is interpreted as a grave disturbance to the peace.

In the United States

In areas of this country where Catholics form a considerable percentage of the local population, members of the Catholic hierarchy have been known to join Catholic laymen in putting pressure on local politicians, and they have sometimes used the social and economic resources of the Church to influence the attainment of goals considered in its best interests. Catholic sources in various states have attempted to obstruct the liberalizing of divorce and abortion laws and the dissemination of birth control information and assistance. Picketing and boycotting have been used by Catholic institutions and agencies against theaters, bookstores, and drugstores which offered to viewers or buyers matter that was considered dangerous to Catholic morals. Catholics working for State aid to Church-affiliated schools are a special cause of fear for many non-Catholics, who see this as an attempt to establish government support for religious indoctrination. Apart from the question of the validity of aims and means, it is just such "Catholic action" and "Catholic blocs" that build up attitudes of fear and suspicion toward American Catholicism.

Protestant losses and Catholic gains also explain, to some extent, the discomfort and nervous annoyance of many outside the Church. The United States was once a Protestant country, in fact if not by law. Protestantism dominated its ethics, culture, educational institutions, and national character. Although Protestants still comprise the vast majority of the American population, they are fragmented into various Churches. The Catholic Church constitutes the largest single Church in the United States, about 23% of the total population. Those outside the Church are made painfully aware of its strength, wealth, and resources by the image of bigness conveyed by American Catholicism in its churches, schools, hospitals, and institutions.

Religious Liberty: Church and State

The problem of the relationship of the Church to the civil government has vexed Christianity ever since Constantine recognized it as an official religion of the Empire. Both the Church and the State claim independence and autonomy. Since Catholics are both members of the Church and citizens of the State, Church and State are indirectly related in providing for the welfare of their members. This relationship has not always been a happy and peaceful one.

Different theories have been formulated in order to define

clearly the relationship between the Church and the State. In the Middle Ages a theory championed by several Popes claimed that spiritual authority is superior to civil authority, that the Church is sovereign in civil as well as spiritual matters. This claim has since been rejected by history as well as by the Church. In recent years, however, the question arose as to the union of Church and State. Does a State have the obligation of establishing the Catholic Church as the official religion of its people, giving it privileged protection and promotion, and suppressing anti-Catholic theories and propaganda? Until recently a bitter controversy had been waged concerning this question. The traditional, European answer to this question was yes. The newer, American answer was no. The Second Vatican Council opted in favor of the second theory.

The *traditionalist theory* maintained that the State does have the obligation of protecting the Catholic Church, promoting it, and endowing it with privilege over other Churches. The rationale behind this thesis was that society, no less than the individual, is bound to worship God; that the Catholic Church is divinely instituted; that, therefore, the Catholic Church should be the official religion of the State. Furthermore, truth must be promoted and error has no rights; the Catholic Church is the true religion; therefore, all heresies ought to be suppressed by the State. According to this thesis, there ought to exist a bond of union between the Church and the State. This ideal situation of union between a State and the Catholic Church is not attainable, of course, when Catholics constitute a minority of a particular nation's population. In such a situation, the Catholic Church tolerates the less ideal arrangement of equality before the civil law with all other Churches. If Catholics should become the majority, however, efforts should then be made to establish Catholicism as the official religion of the State. This theory claimed the support of several Papal pronouncements, as previously mentioned, within the last one hundred years, the most recent being that of Pope Leo XIII.

The *American theory* denied the position held by the traditionalists concerning the union of Church and State. It maintained that the State, at least in modern society, is not a person, but a structure; because it is impersonal, it is incapable of worshiping God. Furthermore, although error has no rights, neither does truth; only persons have rights, and the fact that people may be in error does not deprive them of those rights. Led by Father John Courtney Murray, the exponents of the American theory of religious freedom maintained that the Papal pronouncements of one thousand years ago or of one hundred years ago were conditioned by the historical circumstances of their time. Those pronouncements addressed themselves to a particular situation of a particular era with its own particular understanding of the function of government. Those Papal statements, according to the American theory, did not intend to be infallible for every nation and every age.

The Second Vatican Council's *Decree on Religious Freedom* gave the solemn endorsement of the Catholic Church to recognition of the principle that religious freedom is an inalienable human right. It must be admitted that the Church was among the last institutions to officially recognize the validity of that principle. But it must also be noted that the Decree on Religious Freedom has cleared up, finally and emphatically, the long-standing ambiguity of a double standard. It seemed that the Church had claimed freedom for itself when Catholics were a minority, but, when Catholics constituted the majority, privilege for itself and intolerance for others. The Church has now rejected this claim, together with the traditionalist concept of the ideal union of Church and State.

The Council defined religious liberty in the following terms:

. . . the human person has a right to religious freedom. This freedom means that all men are to be immune from coercion on the part of individuals or of social groups and of any human power, in such wise that in matters religious no one is to be forced to act in a manner contrary to his own beliefs. Nor is anyone to be restrained from acting in accordance with his own beliefs, whether privately or publicly, whether alone or in association with others, within due limits. (Declaration on Religious Freedom, No. 2)

It declared that religious liberty is not a benefit given by the State, but a right inherent in human nature:

. . . the right to religious freedom has its foundation in the very dignity of the human person . . . not in the subjective disposition of the person, but in his very nature. In consequence, the right to this immunity [from external coercion in religious matters] continues to exist even in those who do not live up to their obligation of seeking the truth and adhering to it. (Declaration on Religious Freedom, No. 2)

The conciliar statement likewise recognized the rights of men to form religious associations, and, as members of such religious bodies or Churches, to worship publicly, solicit funds, erect buildings, establish schools, teach and give public witness to their faith. All this is to be without external coercion, but with respect for the religious freedom of others. Governments have the duty of protecting and promoting the religious freedom of all their citizens and of maintaining their equality before the law.

Pope Paul VI called the Declaration on Religious Freedom "one of the major texts of the Council." Certainly it was a credit to the American bishops and theologians who worked for its adoption. It has served to calm the justifiable fears of those outside the Catholic Church; and it has opened the road to greater confidence and honesty, without which serious ecumenical encounters could hardly have been possible.

Conclusion:

The foregoing was in no way an attempt to draw a profile of the Catholic Church. No attempt was made to "balance" the image of the Church "from the outside looking in" with all that is true and good and beautiful in the Church. The love and loyalty of Catholics for the Church was presumed, along with the many reasons for that love and loyalty. Apologetics was taken for granted rather than dismissed.

It is important, however, for Catholics to recognize the image which non-Catholics sometimes have of the Church. Although that image may at times be extreme, unfair, or based on singular situations, it is frequently not without some justification. Even though Catholics may be convinced that there is much more right with the Church than there is wrong, this does not give us an excuse to ignore the faults, let alone defend them. The Church is human as well as divine. It has human failings and weaknesses, and it is certainly valid to raise objections against them.

"The Church must ever be reformed" was once understood to be a purely Protestant principle. This is no longer so. In the light of Vatican II, every Catholic can make that principle his own, even as we rejoice that not only has the principle been enunciated by the Church but that it is already being applied— broadly and deeply.

Suggested Reading

Berkower, G. C. *The Second Vatican Council and the New Catholicism*. Eerdmans, 1965.

Brown, Robert McAfee, and Gustave Weigel. *An American Dialogue*. Part I., Ch. 3, "A Protestant Looks at Catholicism"; Part II, Ch. 5, "Protestant Fears." Doubleday, 1960.

Lindbeck, George. *Dialogue on the Way*. Augsburg, 1965.

Pelikan, Jaroslav. *The Riddle of Roman Catholicism*. Abingdon, 1959.

10 / Religion in America

> On my arrival in the United States the religious aspect of
> the country was the first thing that struck my attention;
> and the longer I stayed there, the more I perceived the
> great political consequences resulting from this new state
> of things. In France I had almost always seen the spirit of
> religion and the spirit of freedom marching in opposite
> directions. But in America I found they were intimately
> united and that they reigned in common over the same
> country.
>
> —ALEXIS DE TOCQUEVILLE (1835),
> *Democracy in America*

In its strict sense, ecumenism refers to the movement for unity
among Christians. More broadly, it implies openness, dialogue,
and collaboration with men of all religious beliefs and even with
those who profess no religious beliefs. The primary aim of ecumenism, however, is not so much a union of Christian faiths, but
of Christians. It implies relationships, not between ideas or theological systems, but between people. The previous chapters of this
book have concentrated upon the inner principles of the major
religions found in America today, their history, beliefs, and
practices. But it is people who make up religious bodies, not
principles. Ecumenical awareness, therefore, requires some knowledge of sociology as well as of history and theology.

The contemporary religious scene in the United States is in
many ways unique, primarily because our sociology and history
are also unique. Historical and sociological evidence prove the
formative influence which religion, especially Protestantism, has
had on the origins and development of the "American way of

life," of its politics and culture. The American life, in turn, has had considerable influence on religion, influence which will undoubtedly affect the future of the ecumenical movement in this country.

Background

Protestantism: The Story of a Movement

The story of Protestantism in America is that of a religious movement, facing up to the challenge of the frontier and meeting it creatively. The Protestants who came to the New World from Europe found that they had to live their faith as well as their lives in a radically different environment. It was one which changed not only their religious structures but also their spirit.

Anglicanism was for a time the established Church in Virginia and the Southern colonies, but virtually all the other Churches that came to the American shores in the 17th century were dissidents. They were nonconformist groups, opposed to the established institutions of their European homelands—Puritans and Pilgrims, Baptists and Quakers. They came to the colonies in order to practice their religion freely, although they did not always permit this freedom to others. Their negative attitudes toward religious authority resulted in strong efforts to prevent the establishment of the Anglican episcopate. Men who had to struggle for survival in a wilderness were not overly submissive to any form of authority, political or ecclesiastical. A rigorously congregational form of church government took root in America, one which resisted any attempts to subordinate local groups to larger units of control.

Throughout these early days of Protestantism in America, there grew a sense of mission. The dissidents had become disillusioned with the unfulfilled promises of the Reformation in Europe. In America they began looking upon themselves as a "new Israel," destined by God to provide the world with a working model of a God-centered society. New England was to be "the place where the Lord will create a new heaven and a new earth, new churches and a new commonwealth together." It was to be a "holy experiment."

In 1734 there began a religious phenomenon which was to color the history of American Protestantism for the next two hundred years, the Great Awakening. It was the first of the momentous revival movements to affect Protestantism in America. By the beginning of the 18th century the initial fervor characteristic of Puritanism had declined; men had become totally absorbed in worldly enterprises, and morality was at a low ebb. In 1734 Jonathan Edwards, a scholar and theologian, initiated a series of sermons aimed at reviving the old fervor. He endeavored to bring the people of New England to repentance and conversion, to an "experience" of their salvation. He succeeded beyond all expectations.

George Whitefield, a Methodist preacher, furthered the revival movement begun by Edwards. He toured the colonies three times between 1740 and 1770, earning for himself the title of "Grand Itinerant." He consolidated individual revivals into a national movement, one which extended from Nova Scotia to Georgia. All classes of people were caught up by its excitement. In New England alone nearly fifty thousand people were converted. The national revival rose above denominational boundaries, and the differences between Churches came to be regarded as insignificant. A personal religious experience and a "warm heart" were all that counted. The Great Awakening served to cast diverse Protestant denominations into a common pattern, but not without a reaction. The established religions in Europe had emphasized respectability, sobriety, and reason; revivalism became the "religion of the proletariat," of the pioneer and the poor. An outgrowth of the Great Awakening was a national consciousness among the colonists. They severed their previous ties with Europe and developed a sense of cohesiveness, one which was to mature into a revolution and eventually the United States of America.

Shortly after the Revolutionary War there took place a Second Great Awakening, or the Great Revival. From 1800 to 1820 it spread, taking religion beyond the Appalachian frontier. In the East it succeeded in supplanting the deism of the colleges, the attitude that God was remote and disinterested in the affairs of men. In Kentucky and Tennessee it developed into a veritable conversion technique, making religion a vital concern for the

frontiersman and his family. It was a fervent, emotional, personalist religion, employing with great effectiveness the camp meeting,
an outdoor service which would last for several days and bring
throngs of people together from miles around. The chief heirs
of revivalism in America were the Baptist and Methodist Churches,
the so-called "religions of the disinherited." The Baptist preachers
and Methodist circuit riders were of the same social and cultural
class as the people they evangelized, and their zeal compared
favorably with St. Paul and St. Francis Xavier. Baptist missionaries carried their message of sin and salvation to the South and
Southwest. Methodists moved with the pioneers into the Midwest
and Northwest. Together the Methodists and Baptists transformed
the face of American Protestantism, and soon became its largest
and most characteristic bodies.

The Puritans had insisted on religion as a corporate, communal
activity. Revivalism, engendered by the rugged individualism of
the frontier, had little use for institutional forms, creeds, or liturgy.
Emotion was taken to be the most authentic working of faith, and
religion was considered an individual relationship with God. Man-
made dogmas were unimportant; religion consisted of the Bible
and "right living," an insistence on strict moral rectitude. When
the passion of the revivals was spent, the inevitable institution-
alizers moved in to conserve the numerical gains made by the
movement. The need for ministers to preach to the swelling
congregations stimulated education and the building of colleges.
The quickening of the public conscience awakened a sense of
guilt concerning the condition of slaves in the United States, and
the Abolitionist movement arose to begin agitating for Negro
emancipation.

In the meantime the frontier grew in stability and prosperity,
and the footloose pioneer became a respectable farmer or mer-
chant. Protestantism changed with the Protestants; loosely struc-
tured groups became established rural Churches. Revivalism
followed the frontier to the Pacific, but it left in its wake settled
Churches, concerned for their denominational standing, prestige,
and power. Sectional, ethnic, and cultural differences began again
to loom large. Eventually the schism between the states over the
question of slavery resulted in a similar schism within the ranks

of Protestants. The Civil War sundered Baptists, Methodists Presbyterians, and other Protestant bodies into separate divisions, North and South, divisions which only in recent times have begun to be healed.

Up to the time of the Civil War the character of America was predominantly rural. By 1900 nearly half of the nation lived in cities. The United States became urbanized and industrialized, and Protestantism suddenly found itself facing a new challenge, one that somehow it was not equipped to meet. Its success in evangelizing and growing up with the frontier had transformed Protestantism into a middle-class Church, self-satisfied and pre-occupied with maintaining itself as an institution. When waves of Catholic immigrants began streaming into the United States from Ireland, Germany, Italy, and Poland, the Catholic Church assumed the stature of an alien menace, a threat both to Protestantism and Americanism. The two had become equated. Originating on the frontier and developing a strongly individualistic piety, Protestantism had exhausted itself in campaigns to improve individual morality. The problems of the times were not individual, however, but social; a gulf began to appear between rural Protestantism and the urban, industrial masses.

Old solutions to the new problems were attempted, but they did not meet with great success. Dwight L. Moody inaugurated a revival movement tailored to cities. Beginning in Brooklyn in 1874 and then moving to Chicago, he employed the business techniques of planning, publicity, and promotion to convince his hearers of the "Three R's": Ruin by sin, Redemption by Christ, and Regeneration by the Holy Ghost. But, for the most part, urban revivalism did not attract the masses. City missions were tried, but these too proved insufficient. The YMCA and YWCA, however, flourished as centers for evangelization and religious education, and settlement houses were founded. Walter Rauschenbusch wrote *A Theology for the Social Gospel* in 1917, attempting to adapt the evangelical message to urban America. He preached a gospel of redeeming not only individuals but also institutions and social systems. Social action agencies were established by most major Protestant denominations as a result of the Social Gospel, and faith came to be increasingly equated by many with little more than social and economic considerations. Despite all these efforts, however, Protestantism had little effect upon the cities. It succeeded on the frontier in large part because its missionaries were indistinguishable from the people: the poor were evangelized by the poor. When Protestantism had to face the factory worker and the city poor, however, its approach was that of a morally sensitive middle class institution striving to do something for the "underprivileged." It didn't work.

At the same time that Protestants were confronted with the challenge of the new industrial frontier, they also found themselves threatened by the rapidly accumulating evidence of an apparent conflict between science and the Bible. Darwin's theory of evolution seemed to contradict the creation accounts of Genesis; and Biblical criticism attacked what had been the very foundation of the Protestant faith, the literal interpretation of scripture. Horace Bushnell, a Congregationalist pastor in Hartford, Connecticut, had already attempted to prepare American Protestants to make a transition from a dogmatic to a liberal faith. Earlier in the century, Bushnell encouraged believers to find assurance for their faith, not in rational logic, but in the inward testimony of the heart. Henry Ward Beecher, a Brooklyn Congregationalist and the most prominent preacher of his time, is another important name among those who molded the New Theology of the 1870's and 1880's. Its fundamental principle was that the Bible was a record of experience, rather than dogma, a source of inspiration rather than authority. According to the Liberal Protestants, "the foundation of spiritual faith is neither in the Church nor in the Bible, but in the spiritual consciousness of man." Liberal Protestantism did not go unchallenged. Lutherans preserved their orthodoxy by emphasizing their creeds, and the Presbyterians held heresy trials. The New England Congregationalists, however, as well as the Northern Baptists and Methodists, offered an open field for the growth of Liberal Protestantism. In the South a placid orthodoxy prevailed, while in the North a Conservative Protestantism found its champion in the Moody Bible Institute in Chicago. Other Bible institutes were also established to train preachers who would not become contaminated with the Liberal heresies rampant at many of the established Protestant seminaries.

Divided into numerous denominations and challenged by the new urban frontier, Protestantism was further threatened by a loss of its previously unquestioned domination of the American religious scene. The "holy experiment" was being marred by hordes of foreign immigrants, most of them bearing allegiance to a religion Protestants had been taught to regard with abhorrence. No longer could Americanism be identified with Protestantism. The United States was becoming Catholic as well.

Catholicism: A Church of Immigrants

Catholicism in America, unlike Protestantism, was never a religious movement. It was a foreign Church, arising out of successive waves of immigration and emerging finally as one of the three major American religions. Catholics, of course, were no more foreign to the North American colonies than Protestants, but except for such centers of Catholic settlement as Maryland, New Orleans, and New Mexico, they had always been a small and suspect minority.

In most of the American colonies the Catholic Church was proscribed, and in some it was actively persecuted. Only in Pennsylvania, Rhode Island, and New York were Catholics allowed any amount of toleration. Relief came, however, with the War of Revolution, the Constitution, and the Bill of Rights, when Catholics were assured of equal status under the law. At the time of the Revolution there were some twenty-five thousand Catholics in the colonies, sixteen thousand of them in Maryland; in 1789 the Holy See, with some hesitation, established John Carroll as Bishop of Baltimore with all of the Catholics of the United States under his jurisdiction.

Bishop Carroll's Catholic Church numbered forty thousand Americans out of the country's total population of four million. It should have numbered far more, since through the 17th and 18th centuries a heavy immigration had entered the colonies from Ireland. They had gone unattended by clergy, however, and lacked even the most rudimentary religious organization. As a result, some 250 thousand immigrants lost their identity as Catholics. A number became Protestant; many more simply lapsed and remained unchurched. Eager to put off their "foreignness" and become fully American, they left their Catholic faith in Europe.

Toward the end of the 18th century, the French Revolution brought to the United States an influx of priests fleeing persecution in France. They rose to positions of influence, and by 1817 nearly all of the bishops of the United States were French. They did not always get along well with the "old Catholics" of colonial stock, but this was a minor problem in contrast to their constant strife with the new group of immigrants who were coming to America from Ireland. The cultured, aristocratic French hierarchy spoke contemptuously of the "Irish mob" and complained to the Vatican for sending Irish priests as missionaries. The Irish on their part, having few priests of their own, became restive and rebellious. Observing the independent, congregational form of church government enjoyed by Protestants, the Irish Catholic immigrants took up the cause of lay autonomy. Rumblings of an independent national Church grew increasingly pronounced, and a number of minor schisms took place; but the crisis eased as the French bishops and pastors came to be replaced by priests of Irish background. This attempt to set up autonomous Catholic Churches— or Trusteeism, as it was called—was the most serious crisis the Catholic Church had to face in the course of its history in America. Its defeat meant preservation of the communion of Catholics in America with the Holy See. At the same time, however, it resulted in the virtual Irish hegemony of American Catholicism and a clerical reaction which impaired the original American Catholic spirit of clerical-lay cooperation.

Between 1790 and 1850 no fewer than one million Roman Catholic immigrants came to the United States, most of them from Ireland. Had it not been for extensive help from abroad in the form of funds and personnel, the task of ministering to this multitude would have been impossible. But preserving the faith of the Irish immigrants was not all that the American hierarchy had to contend with. Precisely because the Irish were so alike and yet so different in their language, manners, and culture, native Protestant Americans regarded them as a threat. The Irish settled in ghetto-like quarters in New York, Boston, and Philadelphia, and thus became particularly visible. Protestant apprehension grew into alarm. On the other hand, Catholics became increasingly embittered that the public schools and institutions were avowedly Protestant. Tension mounted, and in the 1830's violence erupted. Rioting broke out; Catholic churches went up in flames. In 1844 Philadelphia witnessed three days of chaos. In 1854 at Louisville, Kentucky, nearly a hundred Catholics were slain by rioters and scores of houses were burned to the ground. The anti-Catholic rancor which punctuated the three decades before the Civil War culminated in the Know-Nothing movement. It was a nativist movement, bent upon preserving the "American" religion, culture, livelihood, and way of life against "the foreigners." The Know-Nothing movement dissolved with the onslaught of the Civil War; but it succeeded, through persecution, in cementing immigrant loyalty to the American Catholic Church and in reinforcing and assuring its Irish character.

After the Civil War there continued the waves of immigrants to America's shores; but now, besides the Irish, considerable numbers came from Germany as well. Yet the Irish Catholics in this country, now somewhat established, became just as nativist in their attitude toward the new German immigrants as the Protestants had earlier been toward them. The diocesan Catholic weekly, the *Boston Pilot,* went so far as to suggest that if the Know-Nothings succeeded in obstructing German immigration, posterity might overlook their crimes of bigotry. The earliest German Catholics had little difficulty in establishing their own parishes. Those who came later, however, settled in localities where the Irish already predominated, and they found themselves in churches alien to their particular Catholic background. The result was struggle, parish by parish, between old Catholics and new. Inter-Catholic conflicts entailed such matters as language to be used at services, saints' days to be observed, and even the name of the church. Since virtually all of the American bishops were of Irish descent, German priests began addressing appeals to the Pope complaining against the unsympathetic and even hostile attitude of the episcopal authorities. Matters came to a head in 1890, when Peter Paul Cahensly sent a petition to the Holy See. He warned that the Church in the United States was suffering enormous leakage because it was not providing the German immigrant with a Church he could regard as his own. Cahensly urged the establishment of dioceses in the United States, not along geographical lines, but along lines of nationality and culture. In effect, it was a proposal to establish in America a system of independent national Catholic Churches, only loosely bound in any kind of federation. The American bishops united against this proposal, and it was rejected by the Vatican.

In addition to the Germans, Polish and Italian Catholics had now begun to seek new homes in the United States. To prevent the disintegration of American Catholicism into schismatic groups, the American bishops established "national parishes" in which these immigrants could feel at home. St. Francis Seminary at Milwaukee, Wisconsin, and the Josephinum Seminary in Ohio specialized in training German-speaking priests. SS. Cyril and Methodius Seminary at Orchard Lake, Michigan, began its work of training priests to minister to Polish Americans. Lay societies were encouraged along ethnic lines, and the language of the people was used in both churches and schools. Not all American bishops, however, were patient and prudent enough to let time take its course and to permit ethnic lines to dissolve gradually with second and third generations. In an effort to quickly "Americanize" the immigrants, some bishops tried to compel them to give up their European languages, customs, and traditions. Some schisms thus erupted, the largest of which was the establishment in 1897 of the Polish National Church. Father Francis Hodur led this schism and later had himself consecrated its first bishop by the Old Catholic Church of Utrecht, Holland. From Scranton, Pennsylvania, it spread to New England and Chicago. It lasts to this day, numbering some one-quarter of a million adherents.

Because of the marked Irish influences upon it, American Catholicism became "English speaking, puritanical, democratic, popular, and activistic." Coming from a country where the priest was virtually the only educated man in the community (apart from the bitterly resented British overlords), Irish immigrants brought to American Catholicism an attitude of intense reverence for the clergy. The undisputed leadership which priests enjoyed in the Catholic community contributed significantly toward the survival of Irish American Catholicism. So, too, did the fusion of religion and nationalism. The result was that the large-scale defections which had troubled Catholic leaders in the early part of the 1800's had virtually ceased, despite Protestant revival movements and despite expenditures by Protestant Churches of millions of dollars toward religious and social efforts for the immigrants, most of whom were Catholic.

While winning comparatively few who were not traditionally of the faith, the Catholic Church succeeded by and large in retaining the allegiance of the great majority of Catholics who had come to the United States. It did this in great measure by the building up of an almost amazing network of schools, ranging from the primary to the university levels. The parochial school system served to transform the Catholic proletariat into a middle class, so that by the turn of the century the Catholic Church in this country had achieved a relatively secure status. With the Irish tradition playing the part of catalyst in the process, there was developing, out of a bewildering diversity of nationalities, a unified Catholic Church, urban, organized, newly middle-class and yet not entirely out of touch with the "lower" classes of society.

Judaism: A Cultural-Religious Heritage

The first Jews to come to the American colonies arrived at New Amsterdam in 1654. They were largely Sephardic Jews, Spanish and Portuguese. No great numbers came, however; by the time of the Revolution there were only some twenty-five thousand Jews in America. In New York and Philadelphia they built synagogues and established orthodox patterns of Jewish life in their new community. Attempts were made by some of the younger members to introduce reforms and modifications in the traditional Jewish patterns, but they met with little success.

In the 1820's there began a wave of Jewish immigrants from Germany, the Ashkenazim. Because of their great numbers, the Jews who came here from Central Europe—and who continued to come in great numbers until about 1880—remade the character of American Judaism. They dispersed quickly throughout the country and accommodated themselves with ease to the American way of life. They built synagogues and hospitals and launched philanthropic causes. By 1860 the Jewish fraternal organization, B'nai B'rith ("Sons of the Covenant"), had some fifty lodges, and settlements of Jews could be found in most every city in the land. This speedy dispersal and acculturation of German Jews contributed to a high proportion of intermarriage and defection from the Jewish community. There was a strong likelihood that, in their eagerness to become Americans, they would discard much of their immigrant heritage, including their religion. To stem the tide of dissolution, leaders of the Ashkenazim community began strenuous efforts to adapt Jewish patterns to American conditions. Thus began the Reform movement within American Judaism.

The great power of Reform Judaism in America was Rabbi Isaac Mayer Wise. From 1854 to 1900 he served as a rabbi in Cincinnati, a city which he succeeded in making the Mecca of Reform Judaism in this country. The liturgy was shortened and made more intelligible. English was introduced, and segregation of men from women was abolished by family pews. When some Jews called for the substitution of Sunday for Sabbath worship, Rabbi Wise compromised with a shift from Saturday worship to a Friday evening synagogue service, an innovation which has since become something of a common practice among American Jews. Dietary laws were simplified, and Sabbath prohibitions were relaxed. The Reform movement spread rapidly, and without problem, until 1885. In that year a dozen Reform congregations began drastic revisions of traditional Jewish teaching. Meeting in Pittsburgh and adopting what has come to be known as the Pittsburgh Platform, they rejected any expectation of a personal Messiah or any desire to seek a home in Palestine. Above all, they rejected the authority of the Talmud and relegated it to the margin of Jewish life. Under the leadership of Sabato Morais, a substantial party of Jews withdrew from the Reform movement and set up parallel institutions under the banner of "historical Judaism."

Beginning in 1870 another group of Jewish immigrants became part of the American scene. This group came from Russia, and by 1914 it would bring two million Jews to America. This sudden mass deluge of East European Jews upset the settled pattern of American Jewish life. They did not disperse and acculturate quickly like their German predecessors; instead, they settled in a few large cities and established ghettos. These Russian Jews were themselves divided into two groups, a small but influential minority of radical secularists who had rejected Judaism as a religion altogether and, in greater numbers, religious Jews who were attempting to transplant the old way of life on new soil. The East European Jews tended to identify "Jewish" with "Yiddish," their religion with their entire cultural background. The vast majority of them were desperately poor and without skills. The settled German Jews disliked the religiosity of the traditionalists among the newcomers, and they resented the Zionism of the radicals. As a consequence, conflict arose between the older and newer Jewish communities. Anti-Semitism at home and abroad, however, brought the two communities together; and, with the social advance of the Russian Jews, the cultural divergence between the two national groups gradually disappeared.

The American Reform Jews played a large part in helping these East European newcomers to adjust to American life. The Jewish Theological Seminary was reorganized for this purpose, and to head it there was brought from Cambridge, England, a noted rabbi who was himself of East European background, Solomon Schechter. Schechter was responsible for developing the historical Judaism of the previous century into the Conservative movement of American Judaism. In 1913 a federation of Conservative congregations was formed, taking a middle road between Traditional and Reform Judaism.

None of these religious movements within Judaism, whether Traditional, Conservative, or Reform, had any great impact on second-generation American Jews. In an age of militant secularism, they broke with the cultural-religious heritage of their fathers and became a generation of ardent radicals, some internationalists and others Zionists. Ever since Theodor Herzl's prophetic book, *The Jewish State,* Zionism had been a burning issue of debate. Orthodox and Conservative Jews, still imbued with the ancient expectations of the restoration of Israel, embraced the movement wholeheartedly. Reform Jews, on the other hand, were generally hostile to Zionism and advocated assimilation. The outbreak of anti-Semitism in Germany in the 1930's led the Reform Jews to take a more neutral stand on Zionism, and the establishment and subsequent history of the State of Israel has since rallied American Jews of every persuasion to endorse its survival.

The Contemporary Scene

Protestants Today

World War I marked the end of an era for American Protestants. Up to this time theirs had been the dominant religion, both in numbers and influence. Now, although they still occupied the majority position, they were splintered into denominations and felt threatened by the growing influence of American Catholics. They were a majority religion with minority fears. An influx of German immigrants brought up the number of Lutherans in America; and today, although there are some 250 Protestant bodies, the great bulk of Protestants belong to the seven top denominational families—Baptist, Methodist, Lutheran, Presbyterian, Episcopalian, United Church (Congregational), and Disciples of Christ. Some recent studies cite American Protestants as approximately 68% of the total population. This percentage, however, includes many who, not wishing to be regarded as unbelievers and yet not formally affiliated with any particular Church, distinguish themselves from Catholics, Orthodox, and Jews by retaining the title "Protestant."

The United States entered into the "war to end all wars" with a great deal of idealism. The war proved dirty and unheroic; enthusiasm waned, and Americans became disenchanted with crusades of any sort. The war was an uprooting experience, and as usually happens after a war, there followed a breakdown of public and private morals. The Jazz Age rebelled against what was termed America's "puritanism." Religion was dismissed as antiquated, sanctimonious, and repressive. Church attendance among Protestants declined sharply.

Protestant Churches were confronted, not only by the shifting mood of the nation, but by division in their own ranks. The classification of Protestants into denominations became far less significant than their division into Liberal and Conservative camps. Nearly every major Protestant body had both groups within its members. The Liberal Protestants had so accommodated their religion to the modern American temperament that the two became indistinguishable. They had made peace with the world and, as a result, lost their identity. Religion had become social service. There arose in reaction a "Back to God" movement, a Fundamentalism which equated patriotism with the "old-time religion." "Back to Christ, the Bible, and the Constitution" was its battle cry.

The crux of the Liberal-Conservative polemic among Protestants concerned the literal or figurative interpretation of scripture. The Fundamentalists insisted that every word of the Bible was literally and historically true. The Liberals disagreed, opting for a symbolic interpretation. The controversy came to a head in 1925 with the Scopes "monkey trial" in Tennessee, in which a Conservative Protestant champion, William Jennings Bryan, tangled with agnostic Clarence Darrow over the conflict between the Bible and evolution. The violent language and vituperation of the Fundamentalists alienated public opinion and prevented their winning control of any major Protestant denomination.

Conservative Protestantism today is strongest in the South and among small sects. In 1942 the National Association of Evangelicals was formed under the leadership of Harold Ockenga. The real champion of Conservative Protestantism today, however, is Billy Graham. He began as an itinerant evangelist in 1945 with his "Youth for Christ" movement. After proving his technique and appeal in Los Angeles in 1950, he has since toured the world with his evangelistic crusades. His success has been due in great part to the anxiety created by the current Cold War. Convinced that communism is masterminded by Satan, and attacking reds, pinks, and the U.N., Billy Graham preaches that the greatest single weapon against communism is a "born-again" Christian. The chief publication of Conservative Protestants is *Christianity Today*, edited by Carl F. H. Henry, father-in-law of Billy Graham.

Liberal Protestantism, having long suffered a theological erosion and robbed of any independent vision of life, had become a creature, rather than a creator, of American culture. In the 1930's a theological revival began in the seminaries, borrowing heavily from the personalism of Martin Buber and the existentialism of Sören Kierkegaard. Neo-Orthodoxy became widespread and ushered in a return to 16th-century Reformation theology as interpreted by Karl Barth; Paul Tillich, Dietrich Bonhoeffer, and Reinhold Niebuhr also had significant impact. From a popular standpoint, however, the most conspicuous exponent of the Liberal school was Norman Vincent Peale. His *Power of Positive Thinking,* published in 1952, proved an enormous success with its gospel of "do-it-yourself" faith. Replace negative attitudes with positive thinking, Peale advocated, and obtain peace of mind. The primary publication of Liberal Protestants today is *Christian Century.* A leading recent exponent has been Bishop James Pike, former Episcopal bishop of California, who attempted to prune Christianity of its archaic historical forms and to make it relevant to the 20th century with its humanistic and scientific bent.

The chief problem facing Protestant Churches in America today is still the city. Unlike Catholicism and Judaism, which immediately took root in America's cities, Protestantism is still faced with relating itself to urban society. Experiments have been made in Church-Labor associations and industrial chaplaincies. Particularly at the upper levels, Protestant Churches have shown genuine concern for the social problems of modern industrial society. Yet they have had little effect, at least in comparison to their numbers and the movements of the past.

The Supreme Court decision of 1954 outlawing segregation in public schools aroused Protestants, along with the rest of the nation, to an awareness of the plight of the Negro in America. In many areas Protestant Churches have since taken the lead in working for fair employment, housing, and opportunity for Negroes. Reverend Martin Luther King and his Southern Christian Leadership Conference became the guiding spirit for a major portion of the American Civil Rights movement.

Perhaps the most noteworthy aspect of Protestantism today is its involvement in the ecumenical movement. Although until very recently it was generally eschewed by Conservative Protestants, other Protestant Churches entered into the movement with wholehearted enthusiasm. Speaking at Grace Episcopal Cathedral, San Francisco, in 1960, at the invitation of Bishop James Pike, Dr. Eugene Carson Blake proposed discussions among Presbyterians, Episcopalians, Methodists, the United Church of Christ, and other interested denominations toward the formulation of a union that would be at the same time "both catholic and reformed." The Blake-Pike plan has since grown into the Consultation on Church Union and has embraced several other Churches.

Catholics Today

In June 1908, Pope Pius X brought an end to the missionary status of the Catholic Church in the United States. He thus recognized the American Catholic Church's coming of age. Restrictive legislation halted any further massive waves of immigration, but the Catholic Church had already become by far the largest single Church in the United States. In 1964 it counted some 45,000,000 adherents, 23% of the entire American population. American Catholics live in some 17,000 parishes and are served by over 200 bishops and 50,000 priests. Most of them live in large cities, where often enough they make up either a majority or a sizable minority—Buffalo, Boston, Newark, Chicago, Detroit. American Catholics maintain the largest private educational system anywhere in the world. In 1964 there were 10,902 elementary schools, 2,458 high schools, and 295 colleges and universities, all this with little or no direct aid from public taxation. With a vast system of hospitals, orphanages, and homes for the aged added to its parish churches and schools, the American Catholic Church is undoubtedly not only the largest grouping of Catholics anywhere in the world but also the most affluent.

The great majority of Catholics who immigrated to America came from the underprivileged classes of Europe. Many were illiterate, and most were without financial resources or skills. It took a span of several generations, therefore, before there was any notable Catholic influence on American public life. As Catholics moved out of their ghettos, self-imposed and otherwise, the lines of social and economic demarcation between them and the rest of the community began to vanish. Even more rapidly Catholics assumed political prominence, at least in urban areas where they had the greatest strength. In 1928 Alfred E. Smith won the Democratic nomination for the Presidency and actually fared better than any Democratic candidate in the previous two Presidential elections, obtaining over 40% of the popular vote. Catholic participation became commonplace after the election of 1932, and in 1960 John F. Kennedy put to rest the myth that a Catholic could not be elected President of the United States.

As the religion of the underprivileged and laboring classes, the Catholic Church had identified itself easily with social and labor movements. In 1921 the National Catholic Welfare Conference (NCWC) was established as a coordinating agency for Catholic affairs, including education, missions, and social action. The Conference had no independent authority, since it was controlled by the entire episcopate and served only to advise them, but it became an effective instrument for establishing national policy and issuing pronouncements in the name of the entire Catholic hierarchy. Its social teachings, formulated by the head of its Social Action Department, Monsignor John A. Ryan, had considerable impact upon the federal government; most of its recommendations were enacted into law as part of the New Deal legislation of the early Roosevelt years.

Catholics were active almost from the start in the American labor movement. Particularly through the efforts of several "labor priests," including a number of Jesuits, and such agencies as the Association of Catholic Trade Unionists, the Catholic Church has remained close to the labor movement and has imbued it with the spirit of the social encyclicals of Popes Leo XIII and Pius XI. In the 1930's the controversial Father Charles Coughlin won a large radio following because of his outspoken stands on political, social, and economic questions. In 1933 Dorothy Day helped to found the Catholic Worker movement, which remains to this day an exponent of semi-anarchistic socialism and Christian pacifism. In 1934 Jesuit Father John LaFarge organized the Catholic Interracial Council in a campaign against racial segregation; the movement bore fruit as the dioceses of St. Louis, Mo., Washington, D.C. and Raleigh, N.C., opened their schools to people of every race, even before the Supreme Court decision of 1954.

In the 1950's a religious revival affected the Catholic Church as well as other Churches. For Catholics two major symbols of religion's new popularity were Bishop Fulton J. Sheen and the

Trappist monk Thomas Merton. Bishop Sheen gained both fame and an avid following with his books and talks on a weekly television program. His appointment as National Director of the Society for the Propagation of the Faith made the Catholics of America more aware of their responsibility to the foreign mission program, and more generous; by 1957, 65% of the total budget for missions was being met by gifts from the United States. Thomas Merton, a disillusioned Greenwich Village sophisticate, entered a Trappist monastery in Kentucky and wrote his best-selling autobiography, *The Seven Storey Mountain*. Father Merton's steady stream of books placed a spotlight upon Catholic contemplative life, and Trappist monasteries witnessed a surge in interest and applications.

The most recent force to have an impact upon the Catholic Church in America was the very same one to rock the Church throughout the rest of the world, Pope John XXIII and the Second Vatican Council. Movements which prior to this time had been below the surface of the Church's public life suddenly erupted into sunlight—a liturgical and scriptural revival, the ecumenical movement, a drive to give laymen greater voice and participation in the affairs of the Church. The *aggiornamento* caught on quickly in certain areas of the United States. Liturgical reform was spearheaded in America by the Benedictine monks, particularly those in Collegeville, Minnesota, where the liturgical monthly magazine *Worship* is published. The Biblical movement in America was led by several celebrated Catholic scripture scholars whose efforts have resulted in numerous books on Biblical theology, a modern translation of the Bible, and a noteworthy publication edited for popular consumption, the *Bible Today*.

The entry of the Catholic Church into the ecumenical arena has served to further break down the separatism which often prevented Catholics from entering fully into American life. Because they previously had not been accepted and had often feared their predominantly Protestant environment, Catholics in America built a network of institutions and organizations paralleling those of the larger secular community. There are Catholic Boy Scouts and Catholic War Veterans; Catholic associations of doctors, lawyers, and philosophers; Catholic leagues of policemen, firemen, and sanitary workers; Catholic fraternities and luncheon clubs. As this self-contained world begins to crumble, Catholic resources are opening to the public at large and Catholic influence is extending beyond the confines of the former ghettos to the broader community.

An increase of lay activity in Church affairs also marks the modern American Catholic scene. The Christopher movement seeks to restore Christian ideals to public life. The Christian Family Movement (CFM) brings married couples together for discussion of family and community problems. Parent-teacher Guilds and school boards are providing lay Catholics with a greater voice in the management of the Catholic school system. A number of leading Catholic periodicals edited by laymen, including *Commonweal, Cross Currents,* and the *National Catholic Reporter,* have become vocal in expressing their opinions and have proved successful in making their influence felt among Catholics, occasionally to the dismay of some American bishops. Priests, too, have assumed a greater voice in forming diocesan policies. Priest senates have been elected by the clergy to represent them. Synods and diocesan congresses composed of priests and laymen are working to realize the spirit and decrees of Vatican Council II on the local level. The reorganization of the NCWC into the National Council of Bishops, with Archbishop John F. Dearden of Detroit as its President, assures a greater autonomy for the Church in America and the continuation of its *aggiornamento.*

Jews Today

There are today some 5,250,000 Jews living in America, about 3% of the total population. They are a highly urbanized group; 40% of them are to be found in New York alone; 75% live in five metropolitan communities. Jews are predominantly middle-class in economic and social structure. The Jewish proletariat was, for the most part, a one-generation phenomenon. The Jewish emphasis on education and scholarship has brought large numbers of American Jews to high levels in almost every profession and science. They are educators and psychologists, doctors and lawyers, Broadway entertainers and Hollywood producers; they are symphonic musicians, research scientists, bankers, and merchants. Their contributions to all of these fields have been remarkably extensive.

Sporadic attempts have been made to form the Jewish community into an organized unit with a central authority; they have always failed. American Jews are either unwilling or unable to organize into anything more than a number of loosely related autonomous groups. They refuse to imitate the example of the British Jews in establishing an authoritative Board of Deputies; instead, they follow closely the Protestant pattern of decentralization and voluntarism. There are, however, a number of all-inclusive bodies which cross divergent lines. The Synagogue Council of America works for the common interests of all three branches of Judaism, Traditional, Conservative, and Reform. The Jewish Welfare Board ministers to various religious and social needs within the Jewish community. B'nai B'rith is the largest Jewish fraternal organization in America, but its scope goes far beyond merely social interest. The Anti-Defamation League, a subsidiary of B'nai B'rith, ceaselessly attempts to combat anti-Semitism in particular, but works to protect all minority groups against discrimination. The American Jewish Congress and the American Jewish Committee also serve to bring Jews together for their common political, social, and cultural interests.

The closest thing to a single hierarchical structure embracing the entire Jewish community is the machinery of fund raising and allocation. The Jews contribute more per capita than any comparable group in the United States, and their technique for fund raising has reached an exceptionally high level of efficiency. The Council of Jewish Federations and Welfare Funds operates mainly through the United Jewish Appeal; it has established connections with all Jewish groups, even the smallest.

The Jewish community today suffers no little amount of perplexity and restlessness. It questions its individual identity and destiny. It is still a distinct social group with clearly marked boundaries. What binds it together and holds it separate from the rest of the American community, however, remains a mystery.

Conclusion:

Modern America, like old Gaul, is divided into three parts—
Protestant, Catholic, and Jewish. They constitute the three faces
of religion in America, and are recognized as three major subdivisions of the American people. While there are some very
obvious differences in these three groups, Americans belonging to
these faiths share a great deal in common—idealism, pragmatic
activism, and a broad tolerance of the beliefs of others. Americans,
however, have been characterized as believing more in believing
than believing in God, and it is a fact of contemporary life that
the influence of religion upon American life is waning. Secularity
and the city are having an impact, an impact which may very
well affect not only the future but the very existence of religion
in America. It is of immediate importance, therefore, that we take
a closer look at religion in the secular city of today.

Suggested Reading

Herberg, Will. *Protestant, Catholic, Jew.* Doubleday, 1955.
Hudson, Winthrop S. *Religion in America.* Scribner, 1965.
Rosten, Leo, ed. *Religions in America.* Simon and Schuster, 1963.
Thomas, John L. *Religion and the American People.* Newman, 1963.

II / Religion in the Secular City

We feel we must disagree with those prophets of gloom, who are always forecasting disaster, as though the end of the world were at hand. In the present order of things, Divine Providence is leading us to a new order of human relations which, by men's own efforts and even beyond their very expectations, are directed toward the fulfillment of God's superior and inscrutable designs.

—POPE JOHN XXIII,
Opening Address to Vatican Council II

All the "signs of the times" point to the fact that a new society is taking shape before us, and the basic shape of that society is thoroughly urban. The life and culture of America has come to be radically dominated by the metropolis, the secular city and its sprawling complex of suburbs. No less than other aspects of contemporary thought and activity, religion has been colored by our urban society. How has the city affected men's religious attitudes, their beliefs, their devotional practices? Is religion capable of having an impact on urban society? Does the Church have a special mission to the metropolis? How can the Church be relevant to the new society? These are questions with no easy answers. They imply problems with no easy solutions. Trying to find those answers and solutions, however, is of critical importance—both for the Church and the secular city.

Religion in Society Today

Surveys, Statistics, and Sociology

The Religious Revival. As recently as a generation ago, it seemed that religion was gasping its last. Darwin, Marx, and Freud had each contributed to the demise of Deity in general and Christianity in particular. Or so it was surmised. But in the 1940's and even more so the '50's, it became apparent that America was experiencing a religious revival. Church membership, along with attendance at services, increased throughout the United States. New churches rose in town and countryside; the best-seller lists, the writings of intellectuals, and popular articles in the mass media left no doubt about it—the American people were making a return to religion.

In the quarter of the century between 1926 and 1950, the population of the United States increased 28.6%; church membership, however, increased twice as rapidly. In 1940 church members in the United States constituted 49% of the population. In 1958 church memberhip was up to 63%. Other telling figures are the close-to $500,000,000 spent each year on new church buildings and an estimate of four new churches each week for the Catholic Church alone.

Religion in these years was very much in the public eye, with men in public office expected to attend church regularly and the professed atheist an unlikely candidate for either major political party for any office. Jukeboxes grinding out religious songs, popular magazine articles on theology, Hollywood spectaculars with Biblical themes, paperback editions of Tillich, Buber, Sheen, Maritain, and Merton—all marked the recent American scene. In 1957, 96.4% of the American population 14 years of age and over identified themselves with some religious denomination.

It cannot be denied that, following 1940, the United States witnessed a growth in "religiousness." It is difficult, however, to measure its extent or to evaluate its authenticity. Does one gauge these, for example, by people's orthodox beliefs or by their religious knowledge, by their religious feelings and the frequency with which they attend services or by the effect that religion has on their lives? In any case, if statistics of church membership are used as an indication of a religious revival, it must also be admitted that the long-term trend has leveled off. There has been no appreciable increase in church membership since 1958, when it was 63% of the American population. In 1962 it was but 63.4%.

Religious Orthodoxy. At the same time that religion in America was experiencing something of a revival, it was undergoing a change. The two trends are not necessarily unrelated. The skepticism and militant atheism of fifty years ago was directed primarily against certain Protestant Fundamentalist interpretations of Christianity, e.g., the creation accounts in Genesis. Such attacks are no longer in vogue, since Fundamentalist beliefs have ceased to have any serious influence on mainstream Protestantism. In fact, there is positive indication that the major Protestant denominations are becoming increasingly less orthodox in their approach to Christian doctrine. The historic schisms of Christianity were largely marked by disputes on creeds, organizational forms, and ritual. Surveys of grass-roots church members, however, indicate that these issues have lost much of their significance in contemporary America. They have lost their devisiveness, because they seem to have lost their importance.

Although the historic bases for denominational divisions among Protestants have for the most part subsided, new and perhaps far more devastating cleavages are taking place, cleavages which affect nearly every major Church. These new divergences concern the most fundamental Christian beliefs. No longer is the emphasis so much on worship; rather, it is on whether or not it makes sense to worship at all. No longer is the important question whether or not Christ is truly present in the Eucharist, but whether or not he is truly the eternal Son of God.

If asked whether they believe in God, 97% of all American adults respond yes. Of this number, however, not all believe in a personal God, some indicating belief only in a higher power of some kind. This includes 16% of the Congregationalists, 11% of the Methodists, and 12% of the Episcopalians. Only about 3% of the Catholics interviewed, and even less of the Conservative Protestant Churches, doubted the existence of a personal God. Of those Catholics and Protestants who admitted belief in a personal God, 17% of the total Protestants and 13% of the Catholics admitted having some doubts. In other words, while nearly all American Christians admit their belief in God, there is considerable variation as to the strength of their belief and the kind of God they believe in.

When asked whether they believed Jesus was truly the divine Son of God, 85% of all Protestants said yes, along with 94% of all Catholics. But of the Protestants professing this belief, only 68% of all Congregationalists and 76% of all Methodists are included, in comparison with 99% of the Southern Baptists and 98% of the Missouri Synod Lutherans. Between these two extremes, 84% of the Episcopalians, 84% of the Disciples of Christ, and 91% of the Presbyterians believe in Christ's divinity.

When asked if they believed Jesus was born of a virgin, 99% of the Southern Baptists said yes, but of the other Protestant major denominations an affirmative response came from only 21% of the Congregationalists, 34% of the Methodists, 39% of the Episcopalians, 62% of the Disciples of Christ, 57% of the Presbyterians, 66% of the American Lutherans, and 69% of the American Baptists. Of the remaining major Churches, 92% of the Missouri Synod Lutherans believed in the virgin birth of Christ, along with 96% of the small sects, and, interestingly enough, only 81% of the Catholics.

A belief in the existence of the devil has become something of a determining point between Liberal and Conservative Protestants. Of the Southern Baptists only 1% answered that it was probably or definitely not true that the devil exists. But 78% of the Congregationalists questioned were sure he doesn't exist, along with 66% of the Methodists, 60% of the Episcopalians, 38% of the Disciples of Christ, 48% of the Presbyterians, 26% of the American Lutherans, 29% of the American Baptists, and 10% of the Missouri Synod Lutherans. The total percentage of Protestants who rejected belief in the devil was 43%; this is compared to only 14% of the Catholics questioned.

The pattern repeats itself over and over again. In a number of Protestant denominations, the supernatural elements of traditional Christianity have been replaced by an ethical rather than theological religion. It seems safe to assume that the typical Episcopalian or Congregationalist in the mid-19th century believed in such doctrines as the Virgin Birth, the devil, original sin, and the miracles of Christ as recorded in scripture. Not so his counterpart today. Only a minority of Episcopalians and Congregationalists still adhere to these beliefs; the majority hold a more naturalistic view. This "secularization" of these two major Protestant Churches is in striking contrast to the Southern Baptists and small Protestant sects, groups which have shown themselves almost impervious to change. Among the various Protestant denominations, there seem to emerge three clearly identifiable theological camps. The *Liberals* include Congregationalists, Methodists, and Episcopalians; a majority of their members reject a firm belief in the central tenets of Christian orthodoxy. The *Moderates* are composed of the Disciples of Christ and the Presbyterians, who are somewhat to the left of center, and the American Lutherans and the American Baptists, who tend to be to the right of center. The *Conservatives* include Missouri Synod Lutherans, Southern Baptists, and a host of small sects such as Holiness and Pentecostal Churches.

The implications of these sociological surveys for the future of ecumenism are immense. Contrasts between Catholics and Protestants are often large enough to be notable, but quite often too they are remarkably small. They seem inconsequential, however, compared to the vast differences found among Protestants themselves. There really is no such thing as a typical Protestant. When Protestants of all persuasions are treated as a single group, the accumulated data actually refer to just a few denominations or to none at all.

In the light of this data, what is the likelihood of a unified Protestant Church, let alone of a unified Christian Church including Catholics as well as Protestants? It is ironic that such Churches as the Baptist and Missouri Synod Lutheran, with the greatest consensus of orthodoxy, are precisely those which are least amenable to ecumenical relations with fellow Protestants, much less with Catholics. The Churches which are showing the greatest ecumenical interest today are the Churches with a wide spectrum of views on theology.

Among Liberal Protestants, such as the Congregationalists, Episcopalians, Methodists, and some Presbyterians, a form of merger is quite possible in the not-too-distant future. Often, however, consensus is obtained by narrowing theological concerns down to their largest common denominator or putting doctrinal matters aside altogether. Given the Catholic Church's traditional emphasis on orthodoxy, the outlook, at least in the immediate future, for any doctrinal rapprochement between Catholics and

Liberal Protestants appears extremely dim. It would seem that the greatest ecumenical contribution the Catholic Church could make to Liberal Protestant Churches is to bring them to reconsider their historic and dogmatic roots. This would serve not only to make hopes of Christian reunion more likely; it might also generate a greater devotion and commitment among their members, for here too Liberal Protestant Churches display a wide disparity.

A substantial core of Protestants are found to be retaining traditional Protestant religious practices. Of the Baptists, 61% are regular churchgoers, 60% say night prayers, and 48% read the Bible regularly. Of the Episcopalians, 45% attend church, 57% say night prayers, and 34% read the Bible regularly. Of the Congregationalists, only 38% attend church regularly, 61% say night prayers, and 46% read the Bible regularly. Within the Liberal Protestant Churches, those members who are more active in the life of the Church and retain traditional religious practices are usually those who nevertheless hold on to a more traditional theology. It seems that traditional church activities are inappropriate or distasteful to persons who have a liberal, ethical interest, rather than a theological interest, in their church. Consequently, less orthodox Protestant Churches show a markedly lower level of commitment from their members, especially when compared to more conservative groups. Such findings indicate either that the old practices need to be converted to the new Christians or that the new Christians need to be converted back to the old theology and devotional practices. Otherwise, Churches with liberal theologies and traditional practices can expect to steadily lose the participation of their memberships.

Interfaith Attitudes. The Second Vatican Council, if it did nothing else, should have demonstrated compellingly that the Catholic Church is not a monolith, that it embraces any number of divergent attitudes and trends. The foregoing statistics indicate clearly that there is no such entity as a typical Protestant. Yet, despite such real differences within their memberships, Catholics and Protestants are still grouped together into their respective broad classifications. Such stereotypes, whether of Catholics or

Protestants, will not be easily brushed aside with a few social gatherings and exchanges of ecumenical pleasantries.

A survey taken in 1952 questioned a wide cross section of Americans concerning their attitudes toward members of other religions. While only a small percentage of either Catholics or Protestants admitted to harboring ill feelings themselves because of any personal unpleasant experience, 24% of the Protestants questioned believed that there was much ill feeling among Protestants against Catholics, and 11% of the Catholics questioned believed that there was much ill feeling among Catholics against Protestants. Furthermore, 34% of the Protestants questioned believed that Catholics looked down on them. Such beliefs, whether well-founded or not, indicate a sizable core of mutual suspicion if not resentment.

Investigation reveals, however, that Catholics and Protestants generally hold rather favorable views toward one another. Protestants are especially impressed by Catholics in the way they "live up to their religion" and "assist people of their own faith who need help." They are critical of Catholics, however, for "not respecting the beliefs of others," and they express some doubt about Catholic generosity toward public charities. Catholics, on the other hand, are also quite positive in their appraisal of Protestants, except for the fact that 24% of them do not believe that Protestants live up to their faith as well as most Catholics do.

Patterns of Change. The same survey of 1952 tried to uncover the stability of Americans in their religious preferences, their patterns of denominational change. It revealed that 74% of the Protestants questioned and 90% of the Catholics had never shifted their Church affiliation; they still belonged to the Church in which they were raised. In other words, one out of every four Protestants and one out of every ten Catholics is a "convert"; furthermore, most of these converts had been at least nominal members of some other denomination before joining the new Church. Converts seem to be exchanged rather uniformly by all denominations, and only rarely does the reason prompting such a change seem to be based on a religious conviction. About 28% of the converts changed their religion in order to adopt the faith of their marriage partner; about 20% changed because another

Church was more convenient. When asked what religion they preferred next to their own, the majority of Catholics (64%) had no opinion, indicating that they had never given much thought to even the possibility of belonging to another faith. On the other hand, nearly four-fifths of the Protestants expressed a definite alternative preference, generally another Protestant denomination. It would seem that a large percentage of American Protestants believe that one Church is as good as another, so long as it is Protestant.

The foregoing statistics indicate that religious pluralism is taken very much for granted by most Americans. They show, likewise, that American Protestants do not think of themselves as belonging to a universal Church but, rather, as belonging to diversified segments of a broader spiritual communion known as Christianity. Although most Protestants have a favorable attitude toward Catholics, a large portion of them (28%) named the Catholic Church as the religion they would be least inclined to join. In many instances, these are the same Protestants who have maintained the orthodox teachings of traditional Christianity. Doctrinally, at least, Catholics have most in common with the very Protestants who are least inclined toward the Catholic Church.

The Trend toward Secularism

Observers of the American religious scene have not been slow to note that, along with the revival of religion in America, there has also continued to develop a trend toward secularism. Religion may be popular, they say, but it bears little or no impact on people's lives. It does not seem to enter into their decision making. Americans buy Bibles, but they do not read them. They fill churches on Sundays, but when asked to rate the most significant dates in history, they give first place to Columbus' discovery of America and fourteenth place to the birth of Jesus Christ, ranking it on a par with the discovery of X rays.

A number of sociologists in recent years have attempted to explain the apparent paradox of a religious revival amid what appears to be a pervasive secularism. Among the most notable of these, Will Herberg offers the thesis that Americans are turning to religion as a form of self-identification. In an effort to purge themselves of all "foreignness," most second-generation Americans, he contends, were willing to cast off all their immigrant heritage, including their religion, in order to become fully American. It seemed in those years immediately after the vast waves of immigration that America would become the famous "melting pot" in which all national groups would be totally assimilated into one homogeneous mass, the American people. Contrary to the expectations of the cultural assimilationists, however, the third generation of Americans felt no need to prove their "Americanness." Instead, they felt a need to be different, to belong to a group, to be somehow identifiable. According to Professor Herberg, this generation would not or could not return to the linguistic and cultural heritage of its fathers, but it could and did return to its religious heritage. As a result, America has become, to use Herberg's description, a "triple melting pot" in which religion becomes little more than a psychological and cultural crutch, a symbol of tradition, a means of adjusting and belonging. In a changing, fluctuating world it provides a sense of security; along with the school and the home, it acts as a stabilizing element in society. Religion in America, according to Herberg, constitutes three diverse representations of the same spiritual values, Protestant, Catholic, and Jewish. It is part of the American way of life, identified with patriotism and loyalty. Americans believe in religion more than they believe in God, according to Professor Herberg, but it has no great significance in their lives.

Will Herberg's thesis has not gone without its critics. He was accused of limiting the impact of religion on society only to its effects on education, politics, and the economy. Even here, however, some sociologists point to an impact which religion has on society, not directly, but through the vast numbers of people it educates. Basing his thesis on a study made in 1958, Professor Gerhard Lenski contends that religious organizations today are not only still vigorous but influential in American society, and he foresees gains in their vitality in the immediate future. He found that religion is constantly influencing the daily lives of millions of Americans, and that these millions of people in turn make an impact on all the other institutions and patterns within their communities. Thus, indirectly but still influentially, religion operates at the social as well as the personal level.

Lenski found, for example, that Jews and white Protestants in America usually identify themselves with individualistic, competitive patterns of thought and action. American Catholics and Negro Protestants, on the other hand, are more often associated with collectivist, security-orientated, working-class patterns of thought and action. In the area of politics, Protestants were the only religious group to give the Republican Party a plurality. Catholics, however, in the 1958 survey, favored the Democratic Party (57%) over the Republican Party (19%), because of its traditional appeal to the workingman. Protestant families have traditionally been small, loosely knit, and inclined to place great emphasis on education and independent thinking. Catholic families have tended traditionally to be large, closely knit, inclined to place emphasis on obedience rather than independence, and less inclined to defer an immediate goal such as marriage or economic independence for the sake of a long-range goal such as a college education. Thus, according to Lenski, a man's religion will still tend to influence his attitudes toward a welfare state, installment buying, freedom of speech, saving, raising a large family, voting Republican, or trying to get ahead. This impact which religion has on American institutions results, not from any concentrated campaign or effort, but as a by-product of its influence on people, especially in their formative years.

History proves that really creative religious movements are invariably the work of lower levels of society. It likewise indicates that where Christians, whether Catholic or Protestant, have become bourgeois and alienated from the lower strata of society, as in Sweden, England, or France, participation in religious affairs has by and large declined to a mere fraction. But among white Protestants in America today, there are nearly twice as many of those earning $8,000 or more who attend church every Sunday as those earning less than $5,000. It is already true of Protestants. It is rapidly becoming true of Catholics. Christianity in America today is becoming middle-class, domesticated, "harmless." It has yet to face up to the problems and questions arising from that fascinating yet frightening phenomenon growing today before our very eyes, the exploding metropolis. It has yet to face up to the agonizing growing pains and needs of the secular city.

The Urban Complex

The City

In 1790 five out of a hundred people in the United States lived in urban areas. By the end of the Civil War, twenty-five out of a hundred lived in cities. By the end of World War I, cities came to contain half of the country's population. In 1950, 64% of all Americans lived in metropolitan areas. There can be little doubt that the city is now the primary milieu for American life. Super-cities have emerged in crazy-quilt, urban-suburban patterns from Boston to Newport, from San Francisco to San Diego, from Detroit to Chicago. They have brought together strange mixtures of slums and subdivisions, factories and shopping plazas, skyscrapers and expressways. Their emergence is probably the most significant social fact of our era. It poses some of the most serious problems Christianity has ever faced.

For the last two generations the preponderant growth of metropolitan areas has been in residential rings surrounding the central city. The needs of industry for labor brought streams of foreign-born immigrants to the city, where they sought jobs and homes. Reacting to these immigrants, established city-dwellers moved to the periphery of the city as soon as they were financially able to do so. At the turn of the century, when thousands of Catholic immigrants streamed into America's cities, white Protestants had risen high enough on the social scale to escape from the central city to the outlying residential areas. Whole Protestant congregations shifted outward to the suburbs, leaving their lower-class members in the city and adding newer, more affluent members from the residential districts. When, after World War I, foreign immigration was reduced to a mere trickle, rural white Protestants from the South were lured to the cities. They brought with them a style of life so different that they were regarded by both Catholics and urban Protestants as aliens. Despite the fact these Southern whites had been traditionally Protestant, they were left without adequate ministry to their religious needs; the established congregations continued their exodus to the suburbs.

The withdrawal of white Protestants from city to suburb accelerated with the influx of large numbers of Negroes. Since 1920 Negroes have become a major source of metropolitan growth, bringing with them even more complex problems to the urban situation. If they had been allowed to follow the pattern of social and economic upgrading which white Protestants and foreign-born white Catholics had experienced, Negroes would now be distributed over the entire spectrum of residential areas. Job discrimination, however, prevented Negroes from getting better jobs, confining them to unskilled and service occupations. Residential segregation further aggravated the already serious situation by confining to the central-city ghetto even those Negroes who were financially able to move out. As a result of segregation, the density of Negro population within the limited space of the central city has mounted to the extent that today's metropolis is rapidly becoming an all-Negro island, occasionally dotted by pockets of Puerto Ricans, Mexicans, and Southern whites, and surrounded by a sea of consistently white suburbs.

The *social effects* accompanying this city explosion have been far-reaching and profound. Because of almost constant shifts of population, nearly every urban community has entered into a state of flux. Transitions are always painful, and the newcomers to the city today are subjected to the same suspicion, contempt, and abuse that the Irish immigrants suffered a century ago at the hands of Yankee Protestants. Racial features, however, tend to prevent even second- and third-generation Negroes and Spanish-speaking peoples from becoming part of the general community. Their plight has been steadily aggravated rather than improved with time. A good portion of Americans today are compelled to live in conditions that are both inadequate and indefensible. Slums today are not confined to the inner city, but have begun to spread through the metropolis like a cancer. Neighborhood conservation has proved, thus far at least, to be a myth; most people are more interested in escaping minority groups by moving to the suburbs than in staying and saving an old neighborhood. Urban renewal has proved to be more adept in building superhighways and luxury apartment buildings than in providing the kind of public housing which will prevent a project from becoming just a new site for another slum.

The *religious effects* of the metropolis explosion and exodus have been no less devastating. Transplanting congregations to the suburbs has already impoverished the Protestant ministry to the central city. Major denominations have for the most part surrendered the inner-city ministry to Fundamentalist and storefront Churches. The areas of greatest physical and social need have received the least attention; they have received the fewest clergy, the poorest facilities, the most slipshod programs. The exodus to the suburbs was not wholly a matter of bad faith or irresponsible leadership; urban congregations were simply not psychologically prepared or physically equipped to meet the new problems. And the experience of white Protestantism a generation ago has become that of the Catholic Church today. The outcome is a schism no less religious than it is racial, social, and cultural.

In 1950 less than 5% of urban Negroes were living in suburbs. City-suburban boundary lines are serving to separate white ghettos from Negro ghettos. Equally distant from one another are the social classes, white-collar workers from blue-collar workers, upper and middle classes from the lower class. In the struggle for stability in their neighborhoods, in their eagerness for the comfortable, the familiar, the secure, white Americans have made segregation along racial and class lines the normal pattern of urban life. Because Churches, both Catholic and Protestant, have traditionally anchored themselves in parochial structures, and therefore in residential areas, they are affected today by the same pathology that assails the rest of the community. They are becoming insulated and thereby alienated from urban culture, from the lower classes that inhabit the inner city. It has been frequently noted before that eleven o'clock on Sunday is the most segregated hour of the week. Without conscious deliberation or intent, Christians have come to establish congregations that are socially and economically homogeneous. Once remarkable for its inclusiveness—rich and poor, Jew and Gentile, slave and freeman—the Christian Church has come to be characterized in today's metropolis by its exclusiveness.

The Church has grown together with the middle class. It has become, to use one author's description, "a captive of the suburbs."

The Suburbs

The suburbs in many ways represent values to which Americans have been deeply attached. Suburbia is somehow part of the American dream, the culmination of the American success story, an opportunity to which most Americans feel they have some sort of right. It poses as a happy compromise between the convenience of the city and the healthfulness of the countryside, an ideal place to raise a family. It's a place where one can escape the nuisances of industrial society and thus enjoy the simple things of life—golf, gardening, outdoor barbecuing, or just relaxing on a tailored lawn back of a pastel-colored house. Suburbia is a means of enjoying the fruits of metropolitan living without paying its full price. Above all, it is an ideal situation for togetherness, for the security of being with one's own. On the occupational level, the metropolis is very open to all people of every background, skin color, and style of life, but it is very impersonal. After five o'clock, however, the metropolis becomes fragmented as people gravitate toward members of their own ethnic and social background. Surveys have shown that suburbanites feel a keen need for the sense of belonging; suburbia has become an attempt to fabricate some semblance of a community bound by strong, personal ties.

Within this suburban milieu, Churches have had to confront several problems, new and in a way peculiar to this situation. There is the problem of affluence, the unprecedented material prosperity of suburbia. Christianity has never condemned ownership of goods. Neither is it opposed to technology, atomic energy, automation, or gadgets. Yet it is not always easy to harmonize the good life and all its luxuries with following One who said, "Blessed are the poor in spirit." Most suburbanites are not even aware that there may be a contradiction between a push-button life of comfort and "seeking first the kingdom of God and his justice." The meaning and value of asceticism has not really made an impact upon most churchgoing suburbanites. Few of them see any point in depriving themselves of anything they think they can afford.

For a parish in suburbia there is the problem of simply keeping up with the expanding community, providing all the required programs and facilities and obtaining all the finances necessary to provide them. A pastor has the problem of filling all the various roles which his congregation in the suburbs has come to expect of him—preacher, counselor, socializer, organizer, diplomat, builder, planner, athletic director, and chum to all the teenagers. But the chief problem for Christianity in the suburbs seems to be that, in the very fact that it is so thoroughly involved there, the Churches have invested in suburbia the greater amount of their finances and personnel. As a result, like the suburbs themselves, the Church has tended to become isolated from other aspects of life. Situated in a comfortable, affluent milieu, it is all too easy for Christians to forget about the poverty, the squalor, the racial and social schisms of the central city. The congregation in the suburbs can be so concerned with its own growth, so busy building up its own self-supporting community, that it is entirely divorced from the more desperate problems of the larger metropolitan community. The chief problem for a Christian in the suburbs is simply remaining Christian, that is, remaining open and concerned about the needs of others. Thus far the Church has provided suburbanites with a sense of identity, a sense of belonging, a sense of continuity with the past and its traditions. It has relieved them of the anxiety which comes with rootlessness. But the Church is not meant to be a psychological pacifier. It was established to be a community of men, joined together to witness to Christ through service. The Church in the surburbs is called to serve the needs and minister to the wounds of the entire city.

The affluence which Americans enjoy in the suburbs should not lead to the conclusion that they, including the churchgoers among them, are a crassly materialistic people. Most suburbanites do not pile up possessions simply for the sake of ownership; they are not avowedly greedy. On the contrary, Americans are noted for their financial generosity. It might not always be out of the most disinterested of motives, but, more often than not, the middle-class American reaches for his checkbook at the appeal of what is considered a worthy cause. Too few suburbanites realize, however, that money is not enough. True Christianity demands not only almsgiving but self-giving. Hands are needed in the inner city, not just handouts. Rather than a personal check, personal service is needed. Christians themselves are needed, willing to give of their time, talents, and energy, in active works of social justice and Christ-like charity. The Church's mission has always been that of reconciliation. In our day that mission appears to be specifically the reconciliation of city and suburb.

Too few people in the suburbs have yet realized either the need of their personal service to the central city or their responsibility to provide it. In their insulation from the squalor, they are unable to comprehend the discrimination and deprivation which proliferate there. When the anguish of the inner city leads to anger and then violence, the apathy and incomprehension of the suburbanite usually revolves into indignation and often into backlash. The suburbanite feels threatened, for himself and for those privileges he now takes to be his rights. He protests violence in the name of law and order, forgetting that entire masses of Americans feel themselves victimized rather than protected by the law and order of our existing social system. The increasing incidence of riots in America's cities are symptomatic of the malaise. They indicate compellingly that today's metropolis verges on the creation of two alien and inimical cultures. To the few who are willing to face the facts and accept them, it is increasingly apparent that the city is becoming a breeding ground for racial and social class war.

Catholics in this country have traditionally identified the work and mission of the Church with the clergy. They have not acquired, to any great degree, a lay missionary sense. Protestants, on the other hand, traditionally identify the Christian community with their own immediate fellowship, but the autonomy of the local church has too often developed into the isolation of the local church. Such clericalism and parochialism are great obstacles to Christian involvement in the problems and needs of the secular city. The Christian mission today demands not only emerging but involved laymen and an assortment of new structures and techniques above and beyond the parochial level to meet the problems of the new metropolis.

An active laity is absolutely vital for the very possibility, let alone the success, of the Christian mission to the metropolis. Just a few generations ago, a pastor could apprise himself of the personal and social needs in his community, and he was able to use considerable direct influence to answer those needs. In our own day, however, managerial bureaucracy has made any such direct influence by pastors almost impossible. The day of direct intervention by clergy in community life, except in small towns, is rapidly disappearing. Sensitive laymen, however, with a theological vision of life and a sense of Christian responsibility, can raise important questions and press vital issues. They can be trained to see the moral dimensions of the problems within the metropolis. In many instances they are in a more advantageous position to see such problems and needs than are members of the clergy. In most instances they are far better equipped to see what complex processes can be utilized to answer those needs. In almost all instances they alone are in a position to put those processes into action. It is becoming increasingly apparent that a theologically self-conscious and socially alert Christian laity is the only form through which the Church's witness and mission in metropolitan society can be realized.

The scope of the problems and needs in today's secular city and the complexity of its processes demonstrate rather convincingly that the parish church is simply not capable of meeting these demands. Mass communications media, racial justice, urban renewal, city planning, social and economic relations—all are problems beyond the competence of any single congregation. The parish cannot be the only level or even the primary level at which Christianity seeks to serve the world. New apostolates, new patterns, new structures, new techniques—all are necessary, in every area of metropolitan life, for the Church to meet the challenge of the secular city.

This does not mean that the parish congregation should disappear entirely as a viable structure within the Church. Just because it cannot do everything that is needed does not mean that the parish can do nothing. Indeed, the parish community can well take on a whole new and more profound importance, precisely as an educational structure for the urban apostolate. Although it must look after its own organizational needs, the suburban parish should not conceive of itself as an end in itself. It must realize that it exists to serve the larger community. To this end it should employ all of its educational facilities to form active, theologically mature lay apostles, drawing its strength for the accomplishment of its apostolic mission from its worship and liturgical devotion. Within this new concept of the parish, the pastor is not so much an ordained jack-of-all-trades as a theological specialist. His task is to form lay apostles by educating them for service, sharing with them his theological insight and fortifying them for this service by uniting them in active celebration of the liturgy.

Conclusion:

Throughout most of this discussion of the Church's mission in the secular city of today, a deliberate attempt has been made to avoid specific references to "Protestant" or "Catholic." The challenges to be met in the central city, and particularly in the inner city, are far too vast for Catholics or Protestants alone to contend with them successfully. And the situation of Protestant and Catholic congregations in the suburbs is such as to make superfluous any distinction between their problems. Ecumenical collaboration, if it is needed anywhere, is absolutely demanded by the Christian mission to the secular city.

Suggested Reading

Glock, Charles Y., and Rodney Stark. *Religion and Society in Tension*. Rand McNally, 1965.

Greeley, Andrew. *The Church and the Suburbs*. Paulist, 1953.

Herberg, Will. *Protestant, Catholic, Jew*. Doubleday, 1955.

Lenski, Gerhard. *The Religious Factor*. Doubleday, 1963.

Nelson, Claude D. *Religion and Society: The Ecumenical Impact*. Sheed and Ward, 1966.

Thomas, John L. *Religion and the American People*. Newman, 1963.

Winter, Gibson. *The New Creation as Metropolis*. Macmillan, 1963.

——— *The Suburban Captivity of the Churches*. Macmillan, 1962.

12 / Religion in the Inner City

Since in our times cooperation in social matters is very widely practiced, all men without exception are summoned to united effort. Those who believe in God have a stronger summons, but the strongest claims are laid on Christians, since they have been sealed with the name of Christ. Co-operation among all Christians vividly expresses that bond which already unites them, and it sets in clearer relief the features of Christ the Servant.

—DECREE ON ECUMENISM, NO. 12

Tens of millions of Americans enjoy the highest standard of living history has ever known. At the same time, however, there exists another America, a subculture of poverty whose inhabitants suffer deprivations every bit as real as those of any underdeveloped nation in Africa or Asia. And the poverty found in the United States inflicts a suffering all the more depressing and acute, precisely because it is in such contrast to the prosperity enjoyed by the general public. In this era of expanding urbanization, great masses of poverty-stricken Americans have gravitated to the inner cities of the vast metropolitan centers. Their numbers, together with the complexity of the urban situation, have made poverty a major social problem of our day, one which is further responsible for such problems as disease, alcoholism, substandard housing, crime, racial violence and discrimination.

Within this milieu, Christians are called to be witnesses to Christ. Moreover, the "least of his brethren" have a special claim upon the Church. The advent of the Messianic kingdom is marked by the gospel's being preached to the poor. Christ the Savior was also Christ the Servant and Christ the Physician. Ministering to the physical hunger of the poor is no less important than ministering to their spiritual needs; it is indeed prerequisite. Evangelizing and ministering to the poor in today's inner city is an immediate and gigantic task. It calls for a massive, unified effort by all Christians of every Church. It requires the fullest ecumenical collaboration. Furthermore, the cause of unity among Christians could not be better served than by their joint efforts to imitate more closely a Christ who himself was poor.

It is the task of a servant to listen. The Church cannot pretend to serve the inner-city poor unless it first listens to them, learns of their sorrows, becomes aware of their needs. It cannot speak to them of God until it learns what they know of God and what they think of themselves in terms of their relationship with God. The poor are not without religion, but it is a religion peculiar to the poor and their circumstances. It is a religion of storefront churches, handclapping, and Halleluias. It speaks strange tongues and sings of a freedom that's coming tomorrow. To serve the poor, it is necessary to know them and their religion. In many ways they cannot be known except together.

The Facts of Poverty

Depending on the criterion of low income that is adopted, there are somewhere between forty and fifty million people in America who are poor. They constitute about twenty-five percent of the total population. Although rural poverty is one of the major components of this culture of poverty, it is a declining percentage; it does not form the mass base. Today's poor cluster together in sprawling metropolitan slums—industrial rejects, migrant workers, large families, families without a father, people with little education, the aged. It comes as a surprise to many to learn that the majority of America's poor are white; the nonwhite minorities, however—Negroes, Mexicans, and Puerto Ricans—suffer from the most intense and concentrated impoverishment of any single group.

From the outset it should be made clear that these tens of millions of Americans are not starving. Because mass production has made good clothing a plentiful and inexpensive commodity, they are relatively well dressed. Yet they are poor, existing at levels beneath those of human decency, without adequate housing, education, or medical care. They are hungry. They are sometimes fat from hunger; that's what cheap foods like potatoes and macaroni do. They are thrown together and pressed in. In 1959 it was estimated that "if the population density in some of Harlem's worst blocks obtained in the rest of New York City, the entire population of the United States could fit into three of New York's boroughs." Because they are jammed in together in unhygienic conditions and suffer inadequate diets, the poor get sick more often than any other group in society. Because they are unable to afford adequate medical attention, they stay sick longer than anyone else. Because they get sick more often and stay sick longer, they lose both work and wages. Generally the poor find it difficult to find a steady job; hence, there is no money for adequate diet, housing, and medical attention. And the vicious circle continues.

Causes and Casualties

Today's poor have been left behind by progress. They missed the political and social gains of the New Deal. While unemployment compensation, social security, and other welfare programs were being enacted during the depression of the 1930's to assist today's middle-income group, today's poor were in the South, in unorganizable jobs, in minority groups, or in small factories that were low on capital and light on labor. They were in the wrong place, born to the wrong parents, in the wrong section of the country, in the wrong industry, or with the wrong color. Many of today's poor have no skills; if they find steady employment, it has to be in a factory, where they have no seniority, or in a kitchen. Others have skills which have been rendered useless by the advance of modern technology. Layoffs and plant closings result in thousands of men losing their jobs only to find themselves too old to find new jobs and too young to retire.

The main concentration of rural poverty has been in the South —Virginia, West Virginia, Kentucky, Tennessee, the Carolinas. These are the descendants of the yeoman who fought the American

War of Revolution and began the pioneer trek West, into the Appalachian frontier. Today they make up the so-called pockets of poverty, casualties of depleted mines and small farms. They had the misfortune of living in a section of the country which has become economically obsolete. During the 1950's some 1,500,000 left Appalachia. They headed for the cities, for St. Louis, Chicago, Detroit. Here these descendants of the early pioneers were considered little better than aliens; the backwoods had not fitted them for urban life. Without skills, without anything more than a rudimentary education, these masses of Southern whites immigrated to the city, precisely at a time when industry was undergoing the onslaught of automation and doing away with unskilled jobs.

Negroes constitute about one quarter of the nation's poor. About a third of them are still living in the rural South. The rest live in cities; here their lot is better than that of the sharecroppers, but still they are the last hired and the first fired. In 1960, 25.9% of America's whites were in professional and managerial occupations, only 6.7% of the Negroes; among the whites, 20% had high-skilled industrial jobs, only 9% of the Negroes. The reasons for these obvious disparities are not only discrimination against the Negro because he is colored, but also discrimination because he is poor. Even when he has a college education, a Negro's earnings are about 59% less in the North and 85% less in the South than that of his white counterpart. In 1960 Negroes made up only 1.69% of the total number of apprentices in the economy; the figure is disputed, but the fact is real—Negroes have been denied access to precisely those jobs which offer high salary and stability.

Housing is another crucial factor. Along with other minority groups, Negroes have been segregated into substandard housing, packed into run-down tenements where they must pay rents as high or higher than those in other areas of town. They pay whether they like it or not; racial discrimination elsewhere and a general urban housing shortage leave them no alternative. It has been estimated that it would cost some $125,000,000,000 of public and private investment to end slums in twenty-five years. Such an investment is not beyond the realm of possibility, but it does not seem soon forthcoming. As a consequence, the slums continue to breed despair and, along with it, every form of vice and crime.

Results

The greatest injustice done to today's inner-city poor is assuredly the maiming of their spirit. Life in the slums tends to create a peculiar type of personality, passive, devoid of hope, hostile, prone to occasional outbursts of violence. It is a conservative guess that three times as many of the poor are in need of psychiatric assistance than those in the middle and upper classes. Alcoholism, prostitution, families disrupted by desertion or divorce, have profound consequences on the personalities of the poor, particularly the young. They contribute to feelings of futility, a pessimistic fatalism. The satisfactions of the poor are few, so they are unlikely to postpone them. Because they prefer to live for the present and do not save, they are accused of being lazy and shiftless, unwilling to get ahead the hard way like everyone else. They are packed densely together, yet often they have few friends among themselves. They are twisted and defeated. Their aspirations to self-improvement have been snuffed out. The only avenues provided them for escape seem to be alcohol, drugs, sex—and religion.

Religion for the poor offers some small amount of surcease to their miseries. It helps them to forget. It offers a glimmer of hope, a promise of freedom from this earthly bondage, even though only hereafter. It provides the one institution where they can be equal, where they can be important. The religion of the poor can be identified with their needs—escape, hope, and equality. Like everything else in their lives, it too is rooted in their privation.

The Religion of the Poor

Holiness and Pentecostal Churches—
Opportunity for Escape

More than 2,000,000 Americans, most of them numbered among the poor, make up the membership of several dozen churches known as Holiness Churches or Pentecostal Churches. These religious bodies include the Church of the Nazarene, with 315,000 members; the Assemblies of God, with over 500,000 members; and the International Church of the Foursquare Gospel, enrolling almost 160,000 members. But scores of smaller distinct Churches and sects come under the category of Holiness or Pentecostal bodies, besides innumerable storefront Churches. They come and go, merge and split, assume new names. They are all characterized, however, by emotionalism, faith healing, revivals, and hymns that "swing." They are made up predominantly of the poor. In a world offering little comfort and less joy, the Holiness and Pentecostal Churches provide the poor with both ecstasy and escape.

The Holiness Churches, commonly though not kindly known as "Holy Rollers," grew out of several post-Civil War revivals. These revivals stressed the doctrine of complete holiness, or perfection, first taught by the founder of the Methodist Churches, John Wesley. According to this doctrine, a truly committed Christian can expect, after his baptism with water, a second baptism of the Holy Spirit, a deeply moving religious experience which would free him from all depravity, from all sinful desires. Over the years mainstream Methodist Churches came to pay less and less attention to this doctrine of entire sanctification. But after the Civil War a "Holiness movement" arose, emphasizing precisely this belief. Methodist bishops tried to constrain the movement, but without success. Thousands of Holiness adherents seceded to form their own Churches. Largest among those surviving is the Church of the Nazarene. Formed in 1908, the Church of the Nazarene dropped first the word "Pentecostal" from its official title and then the word "Holiness." It is now viewed as an excellent example of a religious body in transition from a sect to a Church; it is coming to resemble closely the Methodist Church from which it once broke. Before long it is expected to assume full status as a respectable, established Protestant denomination.

The Holiness Churches are all juridically distinct, but they are united in professing the same beliefs. Generally they accuse the larger Protestant denominations of abandoning true Biblical faith and compromising with the world. They adhere rigidly to scripture, upholding its literal interpretation particularly against any theory of evolution. They maintain firmly such doctrines as the Trinity, the divinity of Christ, the Virgin Birth, the Resurrection. Although they come closer to the Catholic Church than to most Liberal Protestant Churches, Holiness adherents usually regard Catholicism with distrust and regard it as a corruption of Biblical Christianity. The central teaching of the Holiness Churches is the "second blessing," an experience produced in the heart by the direct action of the Holy Spirit. It is an exalted feeling, a bodily emotion, an inner impression. It may require years of preparation; but once it comes, there's no mistaking it. It results in infallible awareness of God's presence and loving kindness.

For a Holiness body such as the Church of the Nazarene, this exhilarating experience of the Holy Spirit may be calm and subdued. Not so for the left wing of the Holiness movement, the Pentecostal Churches. For them the descent of the Holy Spirit is marked today, as it was at the first Pentecost, by the gift of speaking in tongues. According to the Pentecostals, when the Holy Spirit comes to perfect a soul, his advent is not merely invisible. Visible gifts, above all the *glossolalia,* mark his presence, even as it was recorded in the Acts of the Apostles: "And they were all filled with the Holy Spirit and began to speak in other tongues, as the Spirit gave them utterance" (Acts 2:4). Many of these languages, according to the Pentecostals, are no longer spoken in our times, and some of them are the languages of angels rather than of men. What is taken by an unbelieving observer to be nothing but incoherent mumbling is, to a Pentecostal, an earnestly sought-after gift of God. Most receive it only at their "second baptism"; some privileged few are permitted to exercise it all their lives. Still others receive the gift of interpreting these strange sounds for the rest of the congregation.

The largest Pentecostal association in America is the Assemblies of God. Along with its membership of 555,000 in the United States, it has nearly 1,500,000 adherents in other countries. It was organized in 1914 at Hot Springs, Arkansas. Since 1925 it has increased its membership ten times over. Its members are expected to tithe, abstain from liquor and tobacco, and avoid secret societies. Its members, like most Holiness and Pentecostal adherents, probably spend more time in church than Catholics and other Protestants; there are services on Sunday morning and

evenings, midweek services, and revivals which may last as long
as several weeks at a time. Such revivals are the specialty of the
best-known Pentecostal preacher in America, Oral Roberts. Both
an evangelist and a faith healer, Oral Roberts has made Tulsa,
Oklahoma, the headquarters both of the Oral Roberts Evangelistic
Association and the new Oral Roberts University. Weekly radio
and television broadcasts have brought him a prominence in
evangelistic circles second only to Billy Graham's.

The most colorful personality in the Pentecostal movement,
however, was Aimee Semple McPherson, the founder of the
International Church of the Foursquare Gospel. Her 5,000-seat
Angelus Temple in Los Angeles was opened in 1923, and she
was adept at filling it, using every device of oratory, lighting,
costuming, publicity, and dramatics to gain attention and win
converts. In her heyday she entered the Temple wearing a football
uniform and riding a motorcycle. Since her death the Foursquare
Gospel Church has become somewhat more subdued, but it has
continued to grow from 21,000 members in 1936 to 84,000 members in this country in 1962.

The mark of a good Pentecostal evangelist is his ability to
convey the Spirit to his hearers with fiery oratory. Gospel singing,
confessions of sins, statements of repentance, and long worship
services punctuated spontaneously by "Amens" and "Halleluias"
—all help provide an atmosphere of excitement and expectation.
Finally, one of the congregation, feeling especially blessed, rises
to testify; his words come faster and finally become incoherent.
A wave of emotion sweeps the assembly like an electric charge.
The Holy Spirit has become manifest.

The Holiness and Pentecostal Churches appeal mainly to people
who like their religion lively and informal, people with limited
education and social standing. A majority of those who belong
are women, with fifteen percent of them Negro. Surprisingly
enough, they conduct an extensive missionary program; a rigid
puritan morality forbids luxuries and enjoins upon their members
a frugality which enables them to afford widespread evangelizing.
In this they have a common bond with another form of religion
with special appeal to the poor, particularly Negroes, the exotic
and Nationalist sects.

The Exotic Sects—Opportunity for Hope

When transplanted from the rural South to the urban jungle of
the slums, many Negroes tended to look back with nostalgia to
the uninhibited emotionalism of their childhood religious experience. Like their white counterparts, they sought to reproduce the
intimacy of their rural churches in tiny storefronts. As a result,
there has proliferated throughout the inner city a host of tiny
Negro denominations—most of them of the Holiness and Pentecostal variety—the Church of God in Christ, the Apostolic Overcoming Holy Church of God, the Church of the Living God, and
the Bible Way Churches of Our Lord Jesus Christ. But, like the
urban whites who have toyed with exotic forms of religion, urban
Negroes, too, have developed a variety of exotic cults, among them
a number of Nationalist sects.

A phenomenon of the depression years was Bishop Charles
"Sweet Daddy" Grace. His House of Prayer for All Nations
emphasized nonracial brotherhood. His followers provided additional income to his movement through the purchase of Daddy
Grace cold cream, Daddy Grace toothpaste, and Daddy Grace
coffee. Even more bizarre, however, was the Peace Mission of
George Baker, better known as "Father Divine." Father Divine
claimed to be God. Making his headquarters in Harlem, he fed
the hungry and healed the sick. In return he demanded that his
followers refrain from stealing, smoking, drinking, gambling,
obscene language, bigotry, greed, and racial prejudice. His movement lost most of its momentum after World War II.

The cult which has attracted most attention in the 1960's is one
which repudiates both Christianity and the Caucasian culture,
turning instead to Asiatic culture and the religion of Islam, the
Black Muslims. Whereas most cults tend to emphasize the glory
and happiness of the hereafter as a solace to the miseries of the
here and now, the Black Muslims are very much a this-world
religion. They reject Christianity as a white man's religion. Instead,
Allah is worshiped. Honored as his messenger, prophet, and priest
is the founder of the Black Muslims, Elijah Muhammad. The
Black Muslims preach Negro superiority and urge withdrawal
from white society. They are an ardent segregationist cult, preach-

ing physical resistance against white discrimination and injustice. Like other cultic religions, the Black Muslims maintain an exacting moral code. They make a direct appeal to the racial pride of the most disadvantaged Negroes; as a result, the cult has proven remarkably adept in reforming the moral behavior of prostitutes, alcoholics, dope addicts, and convicts.

Aside from the Black Muslims, most exotic and Holiness sects concentrate on less worldly interests. They regard material comforts, possessions, and status as distractions from the more important pursuit of happiness in the next world. Seldom are they concerned with eradicating poverty and the social evils associated with it. These sufferings are accepted as nothing in comparison with the hereafter. The exotic cults and Holiness sects provide instant if temporary relief to the poor with their ecstatic rituals and gospel of hope. The pain of life in the slums becomes bearable, furthermore, in that it is shared. Togetherness provides an opportunity for some limited sense of equality and a feeling of belonging, of being important. Togetherness provides relief from the pain of being poor; providing this togetherness is another one of the functions of religion in the inner city.

The Denominations—Opportunity for Equality and Fellowship

Although they are becoming increasingly important as a factor in the American religious scene, the Holiness Churches and exotic sects are still only on the fringe of the American religious life. The majority of the inner-city poor, both white and Negro, still adhere to the religion their fathers held to in the rural South, the Methodist and, above all, the Baptist Churches. These lack the extravagance and unashamed emotionalism of the smaller sects, but they share with them their informality and their emphasis on fellowship. They provide the poor with the one major institution in their lives in which they can find social acceptance. Religion for the poor is not only an opportunity for worship or for learning the Word of God; for most of them it is not even primarily so. A church is rather a meeting place, a focal point for sociability. Excluded from wider, community organizations, the poor find identity in the smaller, more intimate fellowship of a congregation. Because of this function religion has in their lives, many of the poor spend a considerably high percentage of their leisure time participating in church-related activities, especially in comparison with people of better education and greater means.

Church fellowship provides the poor, not only with recreation, but also with recognition. Because most inner-city congregations are small and their activities are many and varied, positions of leadership need to be filled. They offer the opportunity for holding an office and gaining a sense of personal importance. To be a trustee, a deacon, an officer in the ladies' auxiliary, a member of the chorus or even a soloist, a chairman of a committee, or a teacher at the Sunday School—these are opportunities for significant and meaningful activity. Meaningfulness and significance are not commodities easily come by for the poor. Their church-related activities provide one such opportunity.

The religious institutions of the poor exist as a refuge for the disinherited. In a paternalistic society where they are manifestly unequal, religion provides them with a closed structure within which they can find some semblance of both equality and fraternity. This has been particularly true for Negroes. Some six out of ten Negro churchgoers belong to large Protestant denominations, primarily Baptist and Methodist. But theirs have been segregated groups, allowed to develop their own spirit and form of folk religion, quite distinct from the rest of American Protestantism. The religious institutions of the Negro poor, like those of the white poor, provide opportunity for escape, hope for the hereafter, and equality. They do so, however, with a distinctive Negro character, one rooted in the history of Negroes in America. These Negro Churches have come to assume, in the light of the recent ferment in Civil Rights, an important and even central role.

Religion and the Negroes

History

The religion of the Negroes represents a peculiar form of Protestantism. It has developed outside the mainstream of American Protestantism from its very beginning. The Africans brought to

America as slaves by Dutch traders posed a problem to the Anglican planters of Virginia. Should they be exposed to Christianity?
Would baptism necessitate their emancipation? When it was decided
that being a Christian and a slave involved no inherent contradiction, slave owners proved quite willing to have the Negroes
evangelized, particularly when they decided that Christianity
rendered the African slaves more obedient and servile. Religion
was seen as beneficial to the planters in this world and to the slaves
in the next. The Puritans in New England owned few slaves themselves, but found participation in the slave trade a vital aspect of
their economy. They justified their activities with the belief that
slavery was a proper method for bringing these cursed people
within the reach of God's grace. With some few isolated exceptions, the religious training given the Negroes was minimal, barely
enough to justify their baptism.

The Society for the Propagation of the Gospel was founded in
England in 1701 in an effort to expand the Anglican Church,
particularly in the colonies. It focused upon Indians and Negroes.
The Christianity taught them was one which concentrated wholly
on the hereafter; it fitted into the framework of institutional slavery
quite nicely. Of those colonial Churches which took any real
interest in the religious condition of the Negroes, the Quakers
were unique in combining social concern with religious conversion.
They inculcated the Negroes with a sense of their human dignity,
exposing them to the Christian doctrines of liberty, justice, and
equality. Along with the Great Awakening and the spirit of independence fostered by the War of Revolution, the Quakers succeeded in promoting the Abolition movement in the North. In
time the Christians of the North became more vocal in their
condemnation of slavery in the South; at the same time, however,
they were already compelling the freed Negroes in their midst to
form separate congregations. As early as 1794, segregation of
Churches in the North on the basis of race was an accomplished
fact.

In the first years after the Revolutionary War, Methodists and
Baptists were exceptionally outspoken in their denunciation of
slavery. In 1800, however, the Second Great Awakening began to
sweep the nation in a feverish religious revival, one which em-

phasized personal conversion and morality. It was extremely moralistic in its approach, losing sight almost completely of any social dimensions to Christianity. Soon Baptist and Methodist missionaries pressed into the plantations of the South, urging the Negroes to accept their lot for the sake of the future and to become the best possible slaves they could. Camp meetings became the basic tool for this massive evangelization program. They were protracted week after week, providing a festive break in the monotony of the Negro's existence but, at the same time, equating religion with emotion. The fundamentals of Christian doctrine were ignored; instead, the evangelicals encouraged the slaves to gauge their faith and the assurance of their salvation by the intensity of their feelings. For the Negro slaves, faith became identified with frenzy; Christian morality consisted essentially of humility and obedience.

Before long the slaves learned the techniques of revivalism from the white evangelicals. Baptists, particularly, encouraged Negroes to become preachers. The only qualifications they required were the feeling of an inner call and evidence of an ability to preach; theological training was considered unnecessary. The whites looked benignly upon the Negro preachers. They did not realize that religion was contributing to the development of an invisible institution: it provided the slaves with their first real opportunity for organization and leadership. And the religion of the slaves grew more and more to concentrate on the Biblical themes of exodus and freedom. In an atmosphere of bondage there arose the Negro spirituals, thinly veiled songs of defiance, revolt, and escape. In the 1820's a number of insurrections arose out of the religious meetings of the slaves. Laws were subsequently passed forbidding any Negro meeting which was not adequately monitored. Before the insurrections, camp meetings and revivals had been the means to bring Negroes together to hear about freedom more than about the Promised Land. After the insurrections, meetings had to be held in secret at midnight. The spirituals served to call the meetings, to protest the Negro's desperate circumstances, and to lull the white community into a false sense of security as one and then another slave would steal away to the North via the "underground railroad."

The white men of the South used religion as a tool to make Negroes docile. The Negroes used religion as a tool to find freedom. With the Civil War and the defeat of the South, religion assumed a new function for the newly emancipated Negroes. The Negroes of the South withdrew in masses from the Churches of their former masters. Their exodus became a symbol of their new freedom; furthermore, the former slaves were tired of being urged to live lives of humble submission. Negro Episcopalians and Presbyterians left the congregations in which they had been consigned to back rows and to separated galleries. In 1860 the Methodist Episcopal Church, South, claimed a Negro membership of over 200,000; ten years later its membership was totally white.

The greatest harvest of Negro Methodists was reaped by the African Methodist Episcopal (AME) Church. It had been organized in Philadelphia in 1816 as a protest against the inferior status that had been inflicted on the freed Negroes in the North. From 20,000 members in 1864, the AME Church grew within twenty years to almost 400,000. The largest number of Negroes, however, were Baptists. Because of the Baptist tradition of local autonomy, separate Negro Baptist congregations were formed with ease. Within a few years after the Civil War, every Southern state had its own Negro Baptist Convention. In 1886 the majority of Negro Baptists were brought together as members of the National Baptist Convention. During this period after the Civil War, the Negro Churches made striking gains in membership. Prior to the war only about 11% of the American Negro population were church members. By 1916 it had increased to some 43%. Cut off from most areas of political and social life, Negroes found opportunity for self-expression and leadership in their religious associations. These proved to make up one of the few institutions that a Negro could regard as exclusively his own.

Problems of the Present

The rapid growth of independent Negro congregations and their undisputed success led to the present situation of religion in America whereby Sunday morning, eleven o'clock, is the most segregated period of the entire week. After the Civil War, white

Protestants almost completely ignored Negroes as prospects for conversion and membership in their congregations. The rationale behind their attitude was that it was not only natural but right for Negroes to go their own separate way in religion. Since whites would not accept Negroes in large masses and Negroes would not accept segregation by whites within congregations, there seemed to be no alternative. Negroes segregated themselves voluntarily with the blessings of the white majority. Provoked by whites and perpetuated by Negroes, the belief persisted that Negroes would be integrated into society as they increased in ability and that this improvement could best be accomplished by the separation of the races. Thus ironically, religion, which before the Civil War had been instrumental in gaining freedom for Negroes, came to be instrumental in perpetuating the myth of white superiority. The Negro Church became, at one and the same time, the most important cultural institution created by Negroes and the greatest single institutional obstacle to the integration and assimilation of Negroes into American society.

The passage of time has demonstrated the baneful results of racial segregation in all areas of life, above all, in the area of worship and religious brotherhood. At the national level, most major Protestant Churches have gone on record as opposing segregation in their own congregations. Segregation persists *de facto* as a religious pattern, however, because it remains the normal pattern as regards housing. Even with the best will of its ministers and leading lay people, Protestantism has not succeeded widely in integrating its Churches. Most Protestant denominations lack the influence of higher ecclesiastical authority; they must allow each local congregation to determine its own course of action or inaction. Likewise, many large and influential groups of Negroes have both an emotional and social self-interest in maintaining separate Churches; they are not always eager or willing to accept integration and thereby lose their identity.

The Catholic Church has fared somewhat better than Protestants at integrating Negroes into the mainstream of its life. Catholics have more often than not followed local patterns in providing separate facilities for Negroes, but there have always been some Negroes who attend services in white parishes and whites who attend services in Negro parishes. Despite this greater integration within Catholic congregations, however, the Catholic Church in America has remained almost exclusively a white Church; even with its high rate of urban conversions, only about five percent of the Negro population is Catholic. Ironically, the reason for the low percentage of Negro Catholics and the greater ease of Catholic congregations to integrate is probably the same. The typical Catholic parish does not have the close social bonds of fellowship that one finds in Protestant congregations. A Negro can become a member of a Catholic congregation without entering into any intimate, personal association with his white co-parishioners. And yet, historically, it is just this form of close association that Negroes have come to expect from religion as a fulfillment of their personal and social needs.

Because of its roots in the camp meetings of the past and its subsequent history of separateness, the religion of American Negroes is peculiar to them and their problems. It has a character all its own, cutting across denominational barriers. Born in slavery and reared in segregation, religion for Negroes became a means both of protest and relief, a bond which brought them together for the purpose of obtaining freedom and equality in a white society. Negro congregations have traditionally concentrated less on doctrine and liturgy, emphasizing instead religious fellowship. The popularity of a given church normally hinges upon the quality of the singing and the showmanship of the preacher. A full program of dramas, musicales, pageants, suppers, meetings, and gospel singing offers diversion as well as devotion. Amusement is expected of religion no less today than at the pre-Civil War camp meetings.

Religion provides today's Negroes with a meeting house for political gatherings and discussion. Although the influence of Negro clergymen has at times been ambiguous, there can be no doubt that today they provide not only the leadership but also the ideology and techniques for the current struggle by Negroes for full exercise of their civil rights. The Freedom movement has come to be symbolized by a minister, the Reverend Martin Luther King.

In the tradition of the preachers who led the slave insurrections before the Civil War, King is responsible for expanding the 1955 bus boycott in Montgomery, Alabama, into a nationwide Civil Rights movement. He has not worked alone, however; many well-trained, articulate Negro ministers can be found with him in the vanguard of the Negro struggle for civil rights. Together with Martin Luther King, they deserve the credit for developing the nonviolent technique of civil protest and for widening the scope of the present racial situation in America; they have expanded it from a political and legal matter to an issue of the gravest religious and moral concern.

Precisely because they had to act both as social centers and political forums, Negro Churches have suffered several religious deficiencies. The hallmark of religion among Negroes is still emotionalism and otherworldliness. Among those Negroes who have succeeded in moving into the middle class, there has been a tendency to integrate faith with life. With the masses of Negro poor, however, religion is still an escape from an intolerable this-world situation. Negro Churches suffer a real theological poverty; they accept the Lordship of Jesus Christ, but this affirmation of faith holds them together less than the bond of race. There is, by and large, little sense of tradition and history within Negro Churches; emphasis is given to moral concerns instead. Because their bonds have been racial more than doctrinal, Negro Churches have shown little or no involvement or interest in the ecumenical movement. Because they have been separated from the mainstream of Protestant life, Negro Christians have contributed little to the mission of the Church, except in their denominational approach to other Negroes.

The absence of Negroes from theological faculties, ecumenical activities, and the mission fields points up, not their blame, but their need. It is not so much an indictment of Negro religion as of white religion. Excluded from full participation in the broader life of the Christian community, Negroes have been forced to imitate traditional Christian institutions and forms. The result too often has been merely a substitute, a limited facsimile of a Christian community.

Irreligion among the Poor

A consideration of the inner city and the religion of the poor would not be complete without at least a word about the irreligion of the poor. Holiness Churches, storefronts and sects, segregated Negro denominations, do not tell the whole story. Large numbers of the poor have disassociated themselves almost entirely from any religion; they prefer to find their escape and emotional catharsis by other less spiritual means. Contrary to popular belief, recent surveys show that the poor are less likely than the middle class to attend church services regularly. They likewise demonstrate that religious affiliation decreases when members of the lower classes become involved with social or political movements bent upon bettering their worldly lot. Religion has perennially counseled the poor to accept their deprivation for the sake of an otherworldly reward; more immediate solutions attainable through political and social organization are increasingly becoming a more attractive alternative to the "other America."

For youth especially, religion has come to mean very little in the life of the inner city. Christianity is being regarded by them more and more as a failure, even as a shackle. It seems to be just one more means whereby society maintains a status quo they find intolerable. Exposed to modern scientific thought, they reject the fundamentalism of their parents. Likewise discarded is the puritan moral code which seems only to limit their freedom and to prevent them from enjoying the material success their more affluent counterparts take for granted.

Conclusion:

The problems of the inner city are too complicated and intense to attempt to solve them with anything less than a massive, all-out ecumenical effort by all Churches. A truly Christian concern for the poor must be at once both natural and supernatural, committed to the here as well as the hereafter. For the clarity of its witness and the effectiveness of its service, it cannot afford to be denominational or sectarian. In a ministry to the inner city, ecumenical inclusiveness is an absolute necessity.

To bear any relevance at all to the lives of the poor in the inner city, Christians must be prepared to meet the many, varied, and in some instances desperate needs which they suffer. Whether Negro or white, the poor would seem to stand in need of a more orthodox and encompassing approach to religion. They need a sense of history, an appreciation of their own roots, a conviction of personal dignity. And their material needs must be satisfied—adequate food, housing, medical care, social security. Above all, the members of the "other America" require a sense of pride, a belief in themselves along with their belief in God. Only when they are convinced that they have something to give in return can the poor receive the charity of others without resentment.

In approaching the problems and needs of the inner city, there is a very real danger that middle-class Christians will do so with something of a patronizing air. Not only for the sake of charity but for the sake of truth, every effort needs to be taken to prevent the contamination of Christian service and social action by paternalism. Middle-class Christianity suffers from a spiritual poverty just as real and possibly more alarming than the material poverty of the inner city. If for no other reason, its active involvement in serving the entire metropolis is required by the Church, so that it may continue to claim the title of Christian.

Furthermore, we Christians need to be reminded of some rather vexing historical data. The almost phenomenal success of the early Christian Church was due, in great measure, to the fact that the poor received the gospel from men who were, like them, poor. The religious revival which swept Protestantism in the early 19th century made an impact upon the American frontier because the men who carried the Christian message West were of the same social and cultural conditions as the rest of the pioneers. In apprising these facts, the question inevitably arises, Can a materially comfortable, middle-class Christianity relate at all to the poor, no matter how keen its moral sensibilities? Perhaps herein is the greatest challenge of all to American Christianity. "Sell all you own, distribute it to the poor, and come follow me" has rarely been given a literal interpretation by individual Christians; almost never has it been so interpreted by institutions. And yet it may well prove the only way of making the gospel meaningful to the inner city. In working together to bind up the wounds of a society torn apart by racial, social, and economic inequalities, we Christians may find our own wounds of separation being healed. The cost of such healing, however, may well prove greater than any of us suspects.

Suggested Reading

Fichter, Joseph. "American Religion and the Negro," *Daedelus, Journal of the American Academy of Arts and Sciences,* Vol. 94, No. 4, Fall 1965, pp. 1085–1106.

Frazier, Franklin. *The Negro Church in America.* Schocken, 1964.

Hardon, John A. *The Protestant Churches of America.* Newman, 1958.

Harrington, Michael. *The Other America.* Penguin, 1963.

Luzbeth, Louis, ed. *The Church in the Changing City.* Divine Word Publications, 1966.

Washington, Joseph R. *Black Religion: The Negro and Christianity in the United States.* Beacon Press, 1964.

Whalen, William. *Separated Brethren.* Bruce, 1958.

13 / The Church in the World of Tomorrow

> *This most sacred Synod urgently desires that the initiatives of the sons of the Catholic Church, joined with those of the separated brethren, go forward without obstructing the ways of divine Providence and without prejudging the future inspiration of the Holy Spirit. Further, this Synod declares its realization that the holy task of reconciling all Christians in the unity of the one and only Church of Christ transcends human energies and abilities. It therefore places its hope entirely in the prayer of Christ for the Church, in the love of the Father for us, and in the power of the Holy Spirit.*
> —DECREE ON ECUMENISM, NO. 24

On October 4, 1957, Sputnik I broke the bonds of gravity, and human history was catapulted into the Space Age. Twelve months later, in October of 1958, Angelo Roncalli became Pope John XXIII, and the Catholic Church was ushered into an age just as shattering and just as new. Presumably chosen because of his advanced age to be a transition between Popes, he became instead a transition between eras. The Johannine spirit of openness and dialogue affected not only Catholics, but all Christians. It injected new hope into the world for a brotherhood which can overcome barriers of history, suspicion, and guilt.

These two incidents, so close in time, so apparently different in character, have come to typify both Christianity and society today. Both events serve as watersheds, separating the static from the dynamic, the "has been" from the "what will be." They symbolize a changing Church in a changing world, often uneasy at what seems impending but directed and committed irrevocably to the future.

When change is the foremost characteristic of an institution or an age, any attempt to predict its future becomes not only precarious but foolhardy. And yet, after assessing carefully the facts of the past and the trends of the present, a certain prospective seems warranted: certain directions can be discerned. In its mighty effort to be relevant to the 20th century, Christianity cannot forget to begin preparing for the 21st. It has been suggested that Vatican Council II served neither as a new springtime for the Church nor an autumn harvest, but rather as a prewinter planting, a planting whose seeds will not bear fruit until some time in the distant future. If this proves true, then the Council, like the Pope who summoned it, was transitional. Its full implications will not be realized until a Third Vatican Council or even a Fourth.

It is precisely to such a council, perhaps in another century, that the ecumenical movement directs its efforts. No honest or perceptive observer of the ecumenical scene presumes to date just when the quest for Christian unity might be realized. To predict the specifics of such a union runs the risk of precluding an avenue of approach not yet opened by God to the vision of men. Christian unity is primarily a work of God, one which demands of all Christians a willingness to search and to learn. Ecumenism looks to tomorrow, confident that both the Church of tomorrow and the world of tomorrow will be considerably changed from what they are today. Ecumenism requires an openness not only to a faith but to a future different from one's own. Without attempting to direct the hand of God, it is worthwhile—for the sake of openness to the future and, perhaps in certain aspects, of preparation for it—to search the horizon for some of the possibilities it offers.

A Changing World

Population

In 1740, for the first time in history, the human race came to number one billion people. In the next two hundred years, by 1940, that figure doubled to two billion. Twenty years later, in 1960, the world's population amounted to three billion; the fourth billion is expected to be reached by 1977. An increased birthrate is not the only cause for this phenomenal rate of acceleration. Medical science has vastly decreased the number of deaths occurring in early childhood and has extended life expectancy to an average of 70 years. By the year 2000 the average life-span is expected to reach 100 years. The rate of increase of world population has accelerated from 3.7 million people per year in 1740 to 45 million people per year in 1960; there is no sign of an early decline. The world is becoming more crowded, more complex. More people means more minds, more ideas, inventions, and skills. Time and the population explosion are together bringing the human race to the point where we are living in a society that is changing not only rapidly but constantly.

Growth in the world's population has been co-relative to an increase in the size and number of cities. The population of the United States today is estimated at 200 million; two-thirds of these Americans live in cities and suburbs, only some 10% of U.S. land area. By the year 2000 the U.S. population is forecast at 300 million, and 80% of these are expected to be jammed into urban areas. Overcrowding will become a major problem of the future, bringing with it a host of other technical and social problems. Population density in metropolitan areas today is about 400 persons per square mile; by the year 2000 it will be up to 700 persons. How will these masses of people be provided with housing, food, clean water, fresh air, suitable recreation facilities? The swelling urban population will require huge rebuilding projects in our present cities and the creation of totally new ones. In each year of the coming generation, the United States will build the equivalent of 15 cities of 200,000 people each. The forecast, however, is a continuation of today's trend toward supercities, cities and suburbs melding together into population belts. City planners see a nearly solid development from San Diego to San Francisco, from Buffalo and Cleveland to Detroit, from Miami to Houston.

What will life be like in the supercity of tomorrow? High-rise apartment dwellings seem to offer one solution to the housing problem. One planner foresees one-hundred-story apartment dwellings encircling a city like the rim of a wheel; in its center would be a park area—golf courses, streams, lakes, bicycle paths, and no automobiles. Commercial areas, schools, theaters, and public buildings would be located throughout the rest of the complex, with transportation provided by automated monorail, subway, and moving sidewalks.

Because of advances in medical science, the world of tomorrow will have millions more senior citizens than we do today. Yet the accent, if only by sheer weight of numbers, will be on youth. Over half of the American population is already under 30 years of age, and the average is becoming younger all the time. A constantly changing society requires the ability to adjust quickly to new conditions and situations, a capacity peculiar to youth. Ability, however, more than youth or old age, will determine leadership in tomorrow's world. In a pretechnical and relatively stable society, one with a high value placed upon tradition, old age brought with itself the right to leadership. In a technical world, leadership falls to the most gifted people in their particular field, whether young or old. Some study has already been devoted to the problems of older people and how to enable them to play an active and contributing role in community life; these problems will be multiplied in the not-too-distant future. But even more critical is the study of the situation where an entire society is dominated numerically by youth. Today's culture already suffers the problems of adolescence, its doubts, anxieties, and neuroses. So heavy is the emphasis placed upon youthful vigor and its values that the awareness of growing old is becoming for many people a severe psychic trauma.

Science

An expanding manpower has been accompanied by brainpower accelerating at much the same rate. Science and invention have created a knowledge explosion equal in its proportions to that of the world population. All the knowledge accumulated from the dawn of mankind to the year 1700 was duplicated in the next two hundred years, from 1700 to 1900. It was duplicated again, but this time within fifty years, from 1900 to 1950. It was duplicated a fourth time within the ten-year span from 1950 to 1960. It has been possible for a man in one lifetime to witness the invention of the electric light bulb and the launching of a manned rocket into outer space.

Underlying this growth in man's knowledge is the undeniable magnitude of scientific research. Some ninety percent of the scientists who ever lived are alive today. Armed with their microscopes and test tubes, this army in white coats looks forward to the virtual elimination of all bacterial and viral diseases, from pneumonia to the common cold. Physicians will be transplanting hearts, kidneys, and other vital organs as a matter of routine by the mid-1970's. And the drug industry is already experimenting with a pill that can control or modify the human personality. The secrets of the chromosomes should be unraveled by the year 2000, opening up the possibility of science preventing hereditary birth defects. Scientists are confident, too, that by that time they will have created in a test tube primitive forms of artificial life.

Technology

The most startling advances made by science are those applied to industry, the conquest of nature and the harnessing of its energies into a tool for material progress and convenience. Modern technology has brought with it jobs, products, and problems unheard of before our time.

In 1830 the world production of energy was 200 billion kilowatts; in 1960 it was 30,000 billion kilowatts. In 1830 the maximum speed attainable by man was about 12 miles an hour; today space travel can attain 17,500 miles per hour, twenty times the speed of sound. In 1910 the production of plastic was zero; today it amounts to 3,000 billion tons a year. The rate of technological progress will continue. It has been estimated that at least half of all the children born today will eventually be employed in jobs that don't as yet exist and that half of the products they will be using have not as yet been invented.

Technology, in the not-too-distant future, will permit the control of weather, at least on a regional scale. Astronauts are expected to land, before the end of the century, not only on the moon but on Mars. Minerals, gas, oil, and sulphur will be obtained from the sea. Half of America's electricity will be provided by nuclear power. But the technological advance most likely to have the greatest impact on tomorrow's world will be cybernation, the coupling together of computers and machines into fully automatic productive systems requiring little or no manpower.

Some 30,000 computers are already at work in the United States today; some 6,000 computers are being added to this number each year. These devices are already being used to ferret out dishonest income tax returns, to analyze stock markets, forecast elections, figure out traffic programs, play chess, and write television dramas. Computers are expected to revolutionize education, replacing the textbook as a deposit for information, in many instances replacing even the teacher. They may very well replace currency, checkbooks, and credit cards with a system whereby a computer will record a man's bank balance, debit his account with every purchase he makes, and add to it with every sale, bonus, or payday.

Cybernation means that fewer people will be needed to produce more goods. Today one out of two workers is still needed for production jobs. By 1990 only one out of four will be needed. And not only blue-collar workers will be affected by automation; computers are replacing men in middle managerial positions as well. Twenty-hour, rather than forty-hour, work weeks will be commonplace in tomorrow's world, together with thirteen-week vacations. And yet the output of goods will increase steadily. The income of the average U.S. family today is about $6,000. By 1990, measured in buying power of today's dollar, the average income will be up to $12,000.

Advances in transportation and communication will bring tomorrow's billions of people even closer together than they are now. Supertrains that whiz between cities at 200 miles per hour, planes that take off vertically and then level off to increase speed, helicopters that carry several hundred people, even missiles that shoot freight across a continent in several minutes—all will serve to make the world little more than a village. Television will continue to connect the most outlying areas with wherever the action is. And video phones will make both business and gossip even more of a button-to-button confrontation.

Implications for the Future

The implications of these changes are far-reaching and profound. They are psychological, social, and religious. They provide the material for high hopes and, at the same time, the gravest fears. The advances in population, science, and technology offer the possibility for creating a world civilization at once utopian and humane. They also imply, however, a capacity for destructiveness far beyond the nightmares of Orwell's *1984* or Huxley's *Brave New World*. Human life, dignity, freedom, all the values we have come to hold important, could be raised to new heights of meaning and expression or virtually wiped out. Both are distinct possibilities for the changing world of tomorrow.

The accelerated *increase in population* exposes modern man to a loss of identity, a disappearance of his selfhood. In exchange for his name, he receives a pattern of holes on an IBM card. Such is the apparent danger when a man is but a unit amid a homogeneous mass. Urban society requires entering into a vast network of impersonal, functional relationships—with salesmen, waitresses, bank tellers, to name but a few. It would be impossible to enter into an I-Thou relationship with each one of these people, and it would be disastrous on the nervous system to try. Yet the very number of these public, occupational relationships heightens the need for private, personal relationships as well. There is no loneliness like that of being alone in a crowd. Urban living, however, enables a person to form close bonds of friendship with far greater freedom of choice than he had before. A city-dweller is not compelled to enter into personal relationships with his immediate neighbors. Proximity of residence is no longer the only basis for establishing a community; similarity of occupation, interests, talents, hobbies, now serve just as well for bringing people together.

Urban living requires a collective existence. No longer is it possible for any one person, organization, or institution to be all things to all men or to isolate itself from the rest of society. Interdependence is coming to characterize all areas of social life—political, educational, recreational, and religious, not only on the local and national but also on the international level. In such a society, structures are not expendable; they are all the more necessary. Teamwork and sensitivity to the needs of the broad community are absolute requisites for making any impact upon society. Isolation of an individual or institution from the needs of the community works to the detriment of the individual and the institution as well as to that of the community.

The phenomenal success of *science* in unlocking the secrets of nature and improving at least the material aspects of our human condition has earned for science something of a religious aura. Scientists, for many people, have become the high priests of a new faith which holds that time and test tubes are enough for man to work any miracle, cure any ill. And even those who do not go to this extent honor science by accepting its methods and conclusions without question. Modern man has become not only imbued but identified with a scientific mentality and culture. The future portends an intensification of this influence, and this raises a serious challenge to religious faith.

There is no inherent conflict between science and religion. Christianity has traditionally taught that there can be no contradiction between nature and revelation, since God is the author of both. Yet the perspectives of science and religion, their methods and values, are very different. Modern surveys show that, at the level of human behavior, religion is found together with scientific scholarship only with great infrequency. Men of strong religious convictions are either not attracted toward the sciences or else tend to lose those convictions if they do enter them. The implication is a practical, if not essential, competition between science and religion. Given the hero status of today's scientists and their continuing influence on the popular mind, the future portends either a society less oriented toward religion or else a kind of Christianity considerably modified from what it has been. A scientific mind, constantly searching, probing, is unlikely to espouse any eternal verity which claims to be comprehensive or all-sufficient.

The impact of *technology* upon the world of tomorrow will be such that all the implications have not been even conceived of as yet. In our present culture a man is identified by his function. "What's your name?" is invariably followed by the question, "What do you do for a living?" But, in the cybernated world of tomorrow, many men may very well be doing nothing for a living. In the production of goods, automation reduces the human role to programming computers and maintaining the equipment. A high percentage of the population will be needed, of course, in the professions and sciences. But what about those without the intellectual acumen for such occupations? Millions of men may well look forward to a lifetime without work. Others will spend most of their lives in classrooms as students. Still others will have only token jobs. How will this affect the way people look upon life and their purpose in it? How prepared will people be for leisure? It is apparent that a new definition of work will have to be found, new dimensions of purposefulness, and new outlets for creative activity.

Advances in transportation and communications media have rendered modern man more mobile. People no longer live where they reside. Telecommunications will soon permit any spot on earth to be brought directly and instantly into any man's living room or, for that matter, into his jungle hut. As a result, the style of the city will continue to invade and eventually imbue the farthest outposts of civilization. That style will become the common property of the entire race. But, in the meantime, the meeting of contradictory cultures will result either in clash or capitulation. Differing values do not always complement each other; and when they don't, and yet cannot remain in isolation from one another, the law of natural selection takes over, the survival of the fittest. The not-too-distant future will inevitably witness the collapse of countless traditions and cultures. Whole civilizations will be preempted by the style of the metropolis.

Freedom is a value to which modern man has attached great importance. It is that singular quality which most makes him an individual. What chance does it have to survive in a society where interdependence is the keynote for existence, where mass communications media can create a world consensus, a common mind, where a pill can modify a man's personality? When society, its structures, and interrelationships become so complex that only great and complex minds can coordinate it, what role does democracy play? What amount of self-determination will be per-

mitted to lesser intelligences? These are some of the perplexing
questions facing modern society.

Some of the implications of the changes taking place in society
are more important than others; some are more probable than
others. One, however, is undeniable: the world of tomorrow will
be very different from the world of today. Times are changing and
institutions must change along with them or else find themselves
little more than relics, curiosities hanging over from another age.
In a constantly changing world, such as that of tomorrow, the
greatest single value may well be the capacity for adaptation. Constant revision, renewal, and reform will be the price any organization will have to pay in order to be contemporary, to claim
relevance. It is a high price, and painful. And it is a claim from
which no institution is exempted, least of all the Church. A changing world requires a changing Church. The world is not waiting
for tomorrow to begin its transformation. The Church cannot afford to wait either.

A Changing Church

A New Theology

The Church, from its apostolic beginnings, has been a community
of faith. Christians are united to one another by faith, then by
worship. Theology is an attempt to understand that faith, to sound
its depths, to ferret out its implications. It is burdened further with
the task of translating its understanding of God's revelation in
terms intelligible to its age. This demands knowing the age, its
problems and needs.

Christianity holds that God's revelation has not ceased but,
rather, has reached its fullness with Christ in the Church. God
continues to reveal himself in history, in and through the events
that mark our times and mold our lives. But these events must
be understood in the light of faith. If this be so, if theology must
speak of faith in terms relevant to its times, if it must seek to understand God's workings in the present as well as the past, then
Christianity is in need of a new theology—not a new faith, but a
new understanding of that faith.

The theology which has characterized Christianity for the last fifteen hundred years was a product of its time. It was born and nurtured in a static culture given to eternal verities and immutable principles. Stability marked both life and mankind's approach to it. But all that is now coming to an end; we are entering into an age in which dynamic change will be the status quo. As a result, the Church is in need of a theology of change, an understanding of how God works today, how and in what way he reveals himself today. The Church must become open to a development of its understanding of God. And it must acquire some sense of how and why this development takes place. In short, the Church needs to develop a theology of developing doctrine, of an evolving Church, of a changing world. Not that it might foretell where we are going, but it might well help us to understand who we are and where we've been. And that is no mean contribution.

A new theology, open to development and striving to understand its own dynamism, will invariably be less dogmatic. Not that it will do away with all elements of stability. What God has revealed and is continuing to reveal through Christ, now in the Church, will remain. "Jesus Christ is the same yesterday and today and for ever" (Heb. 13:8). "And lo, I am with you always . . ." (Matt. 28:20). But Christianity will be less inclined to equate its perennial faith with its less-than-perfect understanding of it. It will be less inclined to confuse creed with comprehension, less inclined to measure mysteries. God revealing himself through Christ in the Church will become the principle object of Christian belief rather than a set of formulized doctrines. Pope John's celebrated distinction between the substance of faith and the way it is presented will have further implications than the updating of theological terminology. It will see the whittling away of historical accretions, understandings, and misunderstandings in an effort to arrive at the primary substance of Christian faith.

The changing Church of tomorrow will need to understand itself not only as changing but also as small. Gone for anything like the foreseeable future is the cultural synthesis of the Middle Ages in which the role of the Church was dominant. Christianity is entering into what has been called a diaspora situation, that of a small community in a crowded world. The cultural influence and temporal power of the Church will diminish to the extent that the culture in which Christians will be living tomorrow will be characteristically post-Christian. As a result, the faith of tomorrow's Christians will have to depend radically upon their individual commitment together with grace; external support of institutions and social pressures will be lacking. Because of its diaspora situation, the Church may have to consider itself, as Karl Rahner has suggested, not as the ordinary means for attaining salvation, but as the extraordinary means. The former Mistress of Nations will quite likely find itself not only a servant but a suffering servant, a small Messianic community by whose wounds the many will be healed.

Laymen

The Second Vatican Council has described the Church as the pilgrim people of God. It will have to become such not only in theory but in fact. For too long the layman in the pew has been described in negative terms, as being neither a cleric nor a religious. Recent Catholic theology has returned to the early Christian conviction so popular with the 16th-century Reformers, that faith and Baptism together constitute a man as belonging to the priesthood of the faithful. In virtue of Baptism and Confirmation, he shares in the privileges and responsibilities of the Church's mission to the world—the mission to witness to Christ in the world, to enter into a community, and to serve. His participation in the Eucharist is meant precisely to strengthen him in the accomplishment of his mission.

The layman has both the right and the responsibility of assuming an active role in the expansion and organization of the Church. This role has not always been admitted or, if admitted, has rarely been permitted exercise. Leadership in the Catholic Church has long been synonymous with the clergy. Laymen have had to be satisfied with being shepherded. Those who have entered into the active lay apostolate have been considerd as assisting the hierarchy in their mission of bringing Christ to the world. By rights, however, the roles should be reversed. Examination of the relationship of the ministerial priesthood of the hierarchy to the lay priesthood of the faithful shows that the clergy are meant to assist the laity in their mission of bringing Christ to the world. Restoring the proper relationship between clergy and laity within the Church would be a difficult task if it were not for present trends which are making such a reversal of roles absolutely necessary. Despite the rise in population and therefore in the number of Christian laymen, religious vocations are suffering a definite decline. This sharp falling off of vocations can be read in different ways. Some see it as a crisis; others see it as a providential act of God, compelling the clergy to give up roles which are not theirs and restoring to laymen their proper function of activity and even leadership within the Church.

Among the effects of modern, technological civilization is the emancipation of women. Women have entered into the professions, the business world, the faculties of major universities. They have proved their equality to men in both leadership and intellectual capacities. But they have not yet been permitted to assume such leadership within the Church. Despite the fact that women make up half of the Church, they have been accorded little more than second-class citizenship. There are some one million women religious in the Catholic Church today, relegated ordinarily to tasks of scrubbing, taking temperatures, and teaching ABC's. The emergence of the layman in the Church today is already resulting in the emergence of the Sister. Religious women have begun to make their voices heard in the Church, demonstrating unusual intelligence, sensitivity, and creativeness. The convent and the classroom will no longer provide the sole area for their apostolic efforts. The Church of tomorrow will see women religious assuming new roles, engaging in specialized apostolates. They will be teachers of adults as well as children. They will be on the sidewalks as well as in the schoolrooms, organizing social action programs as well as school lunch projects. And in various capacities they will be exercising leadership. Ordaining women to the priesthood in the Church of the future is not too much to conceive; in fact, it has already been conceived and is being argued for compellingly.

Even more likely in tomorrow's Church is seeing women ordained to the diaconate or, at least, appointed to its equivalent. Long dormant in the Western Catholic Church, the permanent diaconate has been reinstituted by Vatican Council II. Its restoration will see laymen serving in roles of leadership in conjunction with priests. They will preach, baptize, officiate at non-Eucharistic liturgical ceremonies, distribute Holy Communion, and help to manage whatever temporalities the Church has at its disposal. The permanent diaconate can be expected to become a part of American Catholic life within the next decade. It will serve to bridge the present gap which exists between clergy and laity, clarifying the respective roles of each. It could serve as well to prepare the way for a priesthood which serves the Christian community without being part of a Brahmin caste, a priesthood of married men as well as bachelors.

Priests

The Church of tomorrow will require priests to study the Word of God professionally, preach it relevantly, and celebrate it liturgically. The apostles established the order of diaconate because, they said, "It is not right that we should give up preaching the word of God to serve tables" (Acts 6:2). Yet pastoral work, at least in recent years, has taken priests out of the study and put them into the roles of marriage counselor, football coach, janitor, bookkeeper, administrator, roles which could be filled by laymen and filled better. The task of the priest in the Church of tomorrow will be to know the mind of Christ, to become expert in the sacred sciences, and to share his expertise with the rest of the Church. He will exercise leadership principally through the formation of lay apostles. Assisted by his lay deacons, the priest will form a local congregation through the Word and the sacraments, and he will prepare the members of his congregation for their own ministry of service. The priest of tomorrow will not be all things to all men; he will be a theologian, a preacher, a liturgist.

Today's large urban parishes need breaking up, not consolidation. But each congregation requires an ordained leader to officiate at the Eucharist. Couldn't the role of liturgist be filled by a semiprofessional priest, one who is married, raising a family, employed in some secular task, yet trained and ordained to lead Eucharistic worship? It has been adequately demonstrated by the Eastern Catholic and Orthodox Churches that marriage and the priesthood are not incompatible. It has yet to be proven adequately that the priesthood and a full-time secular occupation are contradictory or mutually exclusive. St. Paul's tent-making pursuits and the apostolate of the French priest-workers argue a strong case for compatibility.

This is not to say, however, that celibacy will not remain as an institution within the Church, the religious life, or the priesthood. There will always be those who devote their lives entirely to the Christian community and free themselves to work at their task full-time by giving up the responsibilities and joys of married life. Such people, men and women, will probably although not necessarily assume the responsibility of serving on a higher organizational level. They will fill the role of specialists within the Church and serve the broader Christian community on the diocesan or national level. They will be the professionals, the coordinators. They will be the servants of the people of God, not only in name but in fact.

The Parish

The basic unit of tomorrow's changing Church will still be the local congregation, the parish, if you will; but it too, like the world, will be a changing parish. The residential parish is no longer the all-sufficient or even primary structure for the mission of the Church in an urban society. It was the natural structure for another age with a different culture, one in which men worked, congregated, and played in the same place they slept. This is no longer true. New social conditions have arisen, and the Church will have to devise patterns commensurate with them. The Church of tomorrow will have to create worshiping congregations within nonresidential social structures—communities of people drawn together by common interests, occupations, backgrounds, and even such needs as alcohol or drug addiction. Rather than supplant them, these nonresidential communities will coexist with residential parishes. But even territorial communities will be smaller, more intimate, less formal. The large urban parishes of today with their several thousand members will be subdivided in the future into much smaller, more intimate units.

A highly differentiated society will require differentiated parishes. Just as the religious expression of cultures and nations already differ from one another, so too will the religious expression of particular communities and groups differ. There is no reason why the worship of a group of teen-agers should be identical to that of their parents. There is no reason why, within a general framework, senior citizens, artists, members of Alcoholics Anonymous, or a group of nurses cannot worship differently from one another. Just as they differ from one another as a community of people, so too will they differ from one another in their liturgical expression of worship. It is for worship that they will gather together, and for service. Here too, local communities will be able to differ from one another by specializing in one ministry, fulfilling one particular need, providing one particular form of assistance to the general community.

Although the parishes of the future will be differentiated from one another in their liturgy, in the service they render, in the basis they have for forming a community, there are several things they will probably hold in common. They will be small, their temporal properties minimal, their mode of operation experimental, flexible. They will probably gather in homes, in halls, in rented storefronts; their liturgical leader will be one of them, a family man sharing their particular interest, need, or occupation. But they will not exist in total isolation from other local communities, lest their parochialism be as bad as, or even worse than, our own. Rather, they will maintain close relationships with the general community.

The Diocese

The urban diocese of today resembles a major corporation more than a local Church. It attempts to serve several hundred thousand people with a staff made up of a bishop, a few auxiliary bishops, and several hundred pastors and assistants. Its assets usually amount to several millions of dollars in church buildings, schools, hospitals, and various agencies. It is often so big that many priests have never met their bishop personally, and most laymen in the diocese look upon their bishop as a figure remote from them, a celebrity of sorts, but certainly not one of their own. Not so in the Church of the future.

Tomorrow's diocese will be small, consisting of a single segment of a metropolitan area. It will resemble a present-day deanery with twenty parishes or thereabouts under its jurisdiction. The bishop of such a diocese will be able to know his priests intimately, both those married and celibate. He will be readily accessible to the people of his diocese, since these will number only several thousand at most. His primary duty will be to teach, first and foremost his priests, but also his people. For major holy days and functions, he will gather his priests and people around him for worship in his cathedral, a building about the size of today's urban parish church. Here the liturgy will be somewhat more formal than that which characterizes the informal worship of tomorrow's parish, when people will gather in homes or storefronts.

The bishop of a diocese will be chosen by the priests and people in a more or less general election. Most probably he will be celibate, in accordance with the most ancient traditions of the Church, even in the East. His unique function, distinguishing him most from his fellow priests, will be to establish strong bonds between local congregations, to prevent them from becoming insulated from one another. A bishop will work to orient his priests and people to the needs of the entire metropolis, coordinating their efforts with congregations of other dioceses and thus militating against any form of parochialism. The diocese will be responsible for providing certain services and agencies which are beyond the scope of a local parish, schools for lay catechists, for example, social and recreation centers, adult education programs geared toward training parents to teach the faith effectively to their own children in their homes. Many agencies and services now associated with parishes will be managed by dioceses. Those that we associate with our present diocesan structure will be handled by a supradiocesan structure, the archdiocese or metrodiocese.

Like the diocese of tomorrow, the metro-diocese will function primarily as a coordinating agency, encompassing, however, an entire metropolitan area. It will provide the services which no parish nor even a single diocese could manage—a seminary, for instance, a school for the preparation of permanent lay deacons, a college of theology for laymen, social service agencies. The metro-diocese will be responsible for constantly reviewing the work being done by the Church within the individual dioceses and throughout the entire metropolis, updating it, renewing and re-forming it. A large staff of laymen will be among the features of the metro-diocesan structure, since its functions are largely administrative. The ultimate authority in the metro-diocese, however, will be vested in a synod of bishops, a council composed of the bishops of the individual dioceses which make up the metropolis. Serving as the chairman of the board, as it were, of this metro-politan synod of bishops will be an archbishop or metropolitan. His primary task will be to call the synod together and to represent it at national and world conferences of the episcopate. His personal jurisdiction, however, will affect only his own individual diocese directly. In affairs concerning the entire metropolis, his vote will be but one of several on the metro-diocesan synod.

The Papacy and Universal Episcopacy

In the world of tomorrow, the interdependence of nations will be such that world coordinating—and, in certain areas, even governing—agencies will be absolutely necessary for maintaining peace and promoting world welfare. And the Church of tomorrow, although marked by considerable decentralization in comparison to our own day, will still require a universal authority. National conferences of bishops or metropolitans will manage most of the Church's concerns on the national level; they will represent their individual synods of bishops from each city. Collegiality will be the hallmark of these episcopal conferences. They will speak the mind of the Church on national issues and represent the concerns of the Church to national governing bodies. They will have at their service the finest theologians, social scientists, intellectuals, and creative minds affiliated with the Church or its interests.

Meeting regularly as duly elected representatives of these national conferences will be the universal Synod of Bishops under the leadership of the Papacy, or whatever title may be given to this office. The Church of tomorrow will not look upon the holder of this office as a universal and absolute monarch. Instead, there will shine through more clearly the Pope's title of Servant of the Servants of God. He will not act arbitrarily or of his own accord, but completely in conjunction with the universal Synod of Bishops; on this level above all will collegiality characterize the relationships among the Church's leaders of tomorrow, including those with the successor of St. Peter. Gone will be the pomp and splendor, the medieval pageantry which has come to be associated with the Papacy. Poverty, simplicity, and servanthood will mark the Church of tomorrow on all levels, identifying the Church no longer with Constantine but rather with the carpenter of Nazareth. The ministry of the Church on the universal level will be to maintain unity within the Church and to serve the world community at large, particularly those areas marked by poverty, affected by a particular need, or struck by some unforeseen calamity. The new nations of Africa and the "have-not" nations of Asia will be of particular concern to the universal Church for a long time in the future.

In our vision of the Church of the future, we see much that is unfamiliar—nonresidential parishes, semiprofessional married priests, community dioceses, permanent lay deacons, laymen assuming roles of leadership and impressing a Christian vision and Christian principles upon a complex urban society. Some details of this vision of tomorrow are more likely than others. All are based upon conjecture, an attempt to discern trends and anticipate needs. The only sure detail of tomorrow's Church will be that, like the society it finds itself living in, it will be different from our own.

The Question of Christian Unity

Will the Christian Church of tomorrow be united? What is the likelihood of the ecumenical movement ever attaining its goal? From the vantage point of today, these are questions which elude even an attempt at an easy answer. It is quite probable that the present ecumenical movement will see some convergence among Protestant Churches of the same theological temperament. A reunion among Catholic and Orthodox Churches may well mark

Christianity's entrance into the 21st century. A reunion between Catholics and Protestants would seem more remote. But who can say, especially since the Churches of tomorrow, Catholic, Protestant, and Orthodox, will be different from what they are today. They will not only be changed, but changing, renewing and reforming themselves by the twin measures of Christianity's apostolic beginnings and its contemporary mission.

The Orthodox and Protestant Churches, no less than the Catholic Church, are in need of renewal. The Protestant principle calling for constant reformation, *ecclesia semper reformanda,* has been honored, as many Protestants will admit, more in the breach than the observance. A Protestant Church burdened with 16th-century attitudes, forms, and structures is really not much more relevant to the 20th century than a 13th-century Catholic Church or an 8th-century Orthodox Church. The 21st century requires relevance of all Christians. It demands radical self-examination and evaluation, the pruning away of anything which misrepresents the substance of 1st-century Christianity or does not meet the needs of a 21st-century world. It might be noted that in some ways Protestants and Orthodox may have a more difficult time updating their Churches, since they are bound by customs no less than Catholics have been bound by laws. Unwritten traditions can often be more restrictive of renewal than laws; they are more difficult to break away from. The successful renewal of any Church, Catholic, Protestant, or Orthodox, can best be accomplished with a strong respect for history as well as a sense for the present. Thomas Fuller, a 17th-century English divine, put it this way: "History makes a man old, without either wrinkles or gray hairs; privileging him with the experience of age, without the infirmities or inconveniences thereof." In order to be united, the Christian Church of tomorrow requires both the wisdom of age and the vigor, perhaps even the recklessness, of youth.

The reconciliation of Christians into a united Christian Church is preeminently a work of God. In the words of the Second Vatican Council, it "transcends human energies and abilities." Our task is to work for the removal of unnecessary obstacles to the cause of Christian unity and to join our prayers to those of Christ for that same purpose. The forces and factors militating against Christian unity are many and varied. Quite possibly there are some we don't even envision yet. The magnitude of the task would be too discouraging for one to even begin if it were not for the promise given by Christ to the Church, "And lo, I am with you always . . ."

Armed with little else but this promise, the Church sets out into the desert of the unfamiliar and untried, much like Abraham four thousand years ago. It takes a great deal of faith and courage to leave some of the comfortable ways and ideas we cherished so long. In many ways they're not much, but they're all we know. Both our faith and our courage will be tested in the years ahead, quite possibly to a point of endurance we cannot imagine. But faith and courage give rise to another quality necessary for a Christian dedicated to the cause of ecumenism, a quality which is itself a sign of faith and courage and proves the authenticity of both—optimism. Pope John XXIII gave not only Catholics but all men some striking lessons on how to extend a hand to others in brotherhood. It is not accidental that he also gave the world an example of how to laugh.

Suggested Reading

Bordelon, Marvin. *The Parish in the Time of Change.* Fides, 1966.

Cox, Harvey. *The Secular City.* Macmillan, 1966.

Elias, C. E., Jr. *Metropolis: Values in Conflict.* Wadsworth, 1966.

Houtart, François. *The Challenge to Change.* Sheed and Ward, 1964.

McLuhan, Marshall. *Understanding Media: The Extensions of Man.* New American Library, 1964.

White, Hugh C., Jr. *Christians in a Technological Era.* Seabury, 1964.

Appendix / Practical Ecumenism

Ecumenical dialogue on a wide scale is a relatively recent phenomenon. Yet the benefits which derive from it are already visible. Talking together has created an atmosphere of openness, warmth, and a willingness to work together. Much of the scandal stemming from Christian antagonisms has been removed. Doors have been opened in the Catholic Church that some men thought were closed forever. Reforms have been started that once were considered unthinkable. But the Church is still primarily a community of faith, and a union of Catholics, Protestants, and Orthodox can never be possible until there is more accord in what we believe.

Catholic and Protestant theologians have already come to realize that much of what seemed contradictory in our respective faiths is actually complementary. Dialogue has brought about a greater understanding of one another's categories, thought patterns, and vocabulary; and this in turn has eliminated considerable misunderstanding. But it is naïve to believe that mere talk will dissolve all that divides us. There are areas of seemingly ultimate disagreement between Catholics and Protestants, differences which cannot be ignored and cannot be "talked away." Ecumenical dialogue, particularly among theologians, must be directed toward those areas which seem to offer the greatest resistance to Christian unity, namely, authority within the Church, the development of doctrine, and concepts of personal and communal spirituality. These differences must be confronted with courage and with confidence in the Holy Spirit that, although we cannot achieve unity by ourselves, "with God all things are possible."

The quest for Christian unity is a task for and a challenge to *all* Christians. It requires the interest, enthusiasm, and involvement of the whole Church, the people of God. Businessmen and factory workers, professionals and technicians, teachers and students, housewives and young adults—every individual who takes Christ and Christianity seriously—can contribute to the cause of unity in some way, however "small," *and in a way that no one else can.*

Contemporary Favorable Influences

The ecumenical movement has not developed within a vacuum. It is but one aspect of a reawakening which has affected practically every phase of Christian life in our day: scripture study, liturgy, theology, social awareness and concern, the ecumenical impetus within Protestantism, the convocation and decrees of the Second Vatican Council. Activity in all these areas is proving beneficial to the vitality of the entire Church and to the development of ecumenical dialogue and encounter.

The Biblical Movement

The last twenty years have seen a remarkable resurgence in Catholic Biblical scholarship. This renaissance has accompanied a movement to make sacred scripture the center and source of Catholic worship, piety, and education. Since scripture forms the foundation of the Protestant spirit, the Catholic Biblical movement has removed a serious barrier obstructing ecumenical dialogue. No longer is the Bible considered the primary source of the differences between Catholics and Protestants. Today Catholic and Protestant scripture scholars work side by side, doing archaeological and linguistic research on such projects as the Dead Sea Scrolls and producing such monumental works of scholarship as the Anchor Bible. The Revised Standard Version of the Bible, produced by Protestant biblical scholarship, has already been approved for Catholics. It is no exaggeration to say that there remain no major differences among recognized Catholic and Protestant scripture scholars concerning the literal meaning of the sacred text. What differences do remain are in the realm of dogmatic interpretation.

The Liturgical Movement

Recent years have seen, both within the Catholic Church and several Protestant Churches, a startling increase of liturgical studies and a movement for renewal of worship. Both of these movements have proven to be complementary. In the Catholic Church, liturgical reform has placed heavy emphasis on such traditionally Protestant concerns as the reading of scripture and the preaching of the Word of God. In many Protestant Churches, liturgical reform has emphasized the traditionally Catholic idea of the liturgy as a sacrament. Catholic liturgical studies have highlighted sacred scripture as a presence of Christ, and not only a deposit of truths. They have also come to emphasize the sacraments, not only as sources of grace, but as true signs of faith and real encounters with Christ. Such words as "scripture," "faith," and "encounter" are not lost upon Protestant ears. The Catholic liturgical movement has already spearheaded the translation of the liturgy into the vernacular for fuller lay participation. In popularizing scripture services to take the place of theologically off-center devotions, it has helped to make even private prayers more Christ-centered and Biblically orientated. The liturgical movement has already given to Catholic church architecture an evangelical simplicity which avoids ornateness and concentrates on essentials, the altar and pulpit. Longer scripture readings at Mass and a greater variety of them, the practice of homilies (i.e., commentary on scripture read at Mass), and the congregational singing of hymns are all striving to make Catholic worship more intelligible, attractive, and meaningful.

Protestant liturgical studies, on the other hand, are taking a second look at the meaning and place of sacraments within the Church. The Anglican Church in the last century returned to an understanding of the Lord's Supper as having a sacrificial nature. It is influencing other Protestant Churches to give serious consideration to the same question. This is an outstanding reversal of the more traditional Protestant position which emphatically denied that the Mass is a sacrifice. In coming to stress sacramental life and common worship, the Protestant liturgical movement has returned the altar to many sanctuaries, together with candles, vestments, and the practice of more frequent Communion. A resurge of monasticism is also beginning to make itself felt in both the Lutheran and Calvinist traditions.

Theological and Historical Studies

Dialogue between Catholic and Protestant theologians has already gone beyond the stage of merely explaining their relative positions to one another. Catholic and Protestant scholars have begun instead to work alongside one another in doing theological research, using one another's seminaries and colleges, writing for one another's journals and magazines. No longer is it an oddity to see a Catholic priest or layman studying Protestant theology at Harvard, Princeton, the University of Chicago, or Union Theological Seminary.

Ecumenical cooperation has proved unusually productive in the area of Reformation studies. Contemporary historians, both Catholic and Protestant, have come to virtual agreement in their assessment of the 16th-century Reformation, its causes and characters. No longer are Luther and Calvin extolled as saints or condemned as sinners. They are, rather, viewed realistically and sympathetically with an acknowledgment of their genius as well as their failings. Catholic scholars no longer try to whitewash the Church's desperate need for reform in the 16th century, and Protestants no longer close their eyes to the considerable Catholic influences found in Luther, Calvin, and their early followers.

Protestant Ecumenism

A most important impetus to dialogue among all Christians is the dialogue of Protestant Churches among themselves. Attitudes of openness and self-examination and a deeper delving into the sources of Christian doctrine have all resulted from Protestant ecumenism. A movement toward greater consolidation and centralization is already beginning to counteract the traditional Protestant tendency toward fragmentation. A few years ago there were over fifty different Lutheran Churches in the United States; today there are only three, and the near future may see a merging of these into one. The Consultation on Church Union is seeking to lay the groundwork for a union of the Episcopalian, Methodist, United Presbyterian, United Church of Christ, Disciples of Christ, and Evangelical United Brethren Churches, as well as several others. The World Council of Churches continues to keep ecumenism before the eyes of Protestants. In 1966 the World Congress of Evangelism, held in Berlin, brought together for the first time into an ecumenical situation leaders of conservative, evangelical Protestant Churches who have traditionally disavowed the World Council, ecumenism, and anything that would tend to smack of a super-Church.

Social and Civic Concerns

Catholic-Protestant dialogue among priests, ministers, sisters, and laymen has been fostered considerably by their common concern and collaboration in trying to answer the social and economic needs of our day. Integration, better housing, equal voting rights, and fair employment practices all call for a Christian involvement which transcends dogmatic differences. One such example is Project Equality, a program begun in the Archdiocese of Detroit and now active throughout the United States; it places the combined buying power of Catholic and Protestant Churches firmly behind the cause of fair employment. Numerous projects such as this are becoming increasingly active and effective. Civil rights demonstrations, human relations councils, and community improvement organizations are serving to bring together in common cause Christians of every theological background. As a result, the stereotyped images have begun to shatter and barriers of prejudice have begun to fall.

The Decrees of the Second Vatican Council

Avenues for fruitful consideration and dialogue were opened for Catholics and Protestants alike by many of the decrees of Vatican Council II. This is true not only of the Decree on Ecumenism, which provided a charter for Catholic ecumenical concern, but it is also true of many other documents promulgated by the Council.

The *Dogmatic Constitution on the Church* stresses the inner, invisible aspect of the Church's nature and admits the need of the Church for constant renewal and reform according to the mind of Christ. The Council espoused the so-called "Protestant principle" of *ecclesia semper reformanda,* "the Church must be ever reformed." Perhaps the most ecumenically significant doctrine to come from the Council is its teaching on the collegiality of bishops, the union of all the bishops responsible together for the welfare of all the Church, with the Pope as their spokesman and source of unity. This understanding certainly coincides better with the New Testament description of authority within the Church than a purely Papal monarchy. And it is far more acceptable to Orthodox Churches, which are united by their emphasis on the episcopacy, and also to Protestant Churches, which are democratically inclined. The establishment of national councils of bishops and the restoration of the permanent married diaconate will further serve to decentralize authority in the Catholic Church.

The *Constitution on Divine Revelation* emphasizes the centrality of sacred scripture in Christian worship, life, and spirituality. It opened the way to theological consideration of the development of doctrine within the Church, an all-important area of ecumenical dialogue.

The *Constitution on the Sacred Liturgy* underlines the sacraments as the worshiping acts of the Risen Christ within the Church. Its rejection of a mechanistic understanding of the sacraments for a more personalist interpretation finds sympathetic accord among Protestants. So, too, does the emphasis the document places on scripture, preaching, lay participation, and the reception of Holy Communion by the laity under both forms of bread and wine.

The *Pastoral Constitution on the Church in the Modern World* brings the Catholic Church into dialogue not only with separated Christians but also with atheistic humanists. It upholds the dignity of the human person and calls upon Christians to enter into a common concern with all men of good will for the causes of peace, international solidarity, and the socioeconomic development of the entire family of man.

The *Decree on the Apostolate of the Laity* recognizes that laymen are not only a part of the Church, but they are the Church.

The decree calls upon all baptized Christians to take a responsible and active part in the mission of witnessing their faith, of serving mankind and making Christ's presence felt in the world. Active and intelligent participation by laymen in the mission of the Church provides a healthy antidote to the clericalism which so many have criticized in the Catholic Church.

The *Decree on the Bishops' Pastoral Office in the Church* expands on the doctrine of episcopal collegiality and stresses the fact that bishops are not mere administrators, but teachers of the Word and pastors of the people. It calls for presbyteral senates in all dioceses, permitting more democratic processes in their regulations.

The *Declaration on Religious Freedom* upholds the sacredness of the individual conscience and rejects the idea of privileged union between Church and State. It thus alleviates the fears and suspicions of many people outside the Church concerning Catholic sincerity, a *sine qua non* for forthright dialogue.

The Problem of Interfaith Worship

The canon law of the Catholic Church has traditionally forbidden its members to actively participate in the official public worship of other Churches. A Catholic may attend a wedding or a funeral in another Church, and certainly he can pray with anyone of any faith in private. But he is not allowed to act in an official capacity at the worship of another Church, for example, as a minister or a godparent. And neither may he receive the sacraments in such a Church. Likewise, under ordinary circumstances, non-Catholic Christians are prohibited from receiving the sacraments within the Catholic Church, even when they request them.

There are several reasons for these prohibitions against interfaith worship, particularly against inter-Communion.

1. To take part in the worship of a Church is ordinarily understood as an expression of acceptance of that Church and all that it teaches. Its official worship, after all, is the deepest expression of the faith of any Church.

2. Since worshiping together, particularly by receiving the Eucharist, is a unique and even conclusive sign of oneness, for

Christians of different Churches to participate completely together in worship would be a deception. It does no good to pretend that a unity exists which simply does not.

3. Participating in the worship of other Churches can sometimes cause scandal and lead to religious indifferentism. There is often a danger that a Catholic's sharing in worship with those of another faith will be misunderstood as an act of disloyalty to his own Church. There is the further possibility that such worship in common would lead to the idea that one religion is as good as another.

To avoid these dangers and misunderstandings, Catholics have sometimes gone to extremes in avoiding any form of prayer with people of other faiths. The Church laws prohibiting worship in common were couched in such negative terms that many Catholics thought that any form of sharing in worship or prayer with others was sinful of its very nature. This, of course, is not true; and the Catholic Church has traditionally permitted certain exceptions to its general rule of nonparticipation. The sacraments of Penance and Anointing may be given to baptized non-Catholic Christians when they are in serious danger of death. And, likewise, a Catholic, when in danger of death and in the absence of a Catholic priest, may receive the sacraments from an ordained priest of another Church. Thus, for many centuries in the East and even today, Catholics attend Orthodox worship when no Catholic priest is available, and Orthodox Christians attend Catholic worship when no Orthodox priest is available.

The reason for these obvious exceptions to the rule of nonparticipation is that the sacraments are not only signs of unity; they are also means of grace. Liturgical worship is the instrument chosen by God to make men holy, to draw men to himself. Furthermore, participation in the worship of another is a means of furthering charity and Christian unity, expressing that partial unity of grace and baptism which already exists among Christians, even those separated by certain beliefs. Therefore, while worship in common among Christians of other faiths is ordinarily prohibited for a Catholic, when there is danger of death without the sacraments from one's own priest or where worship in common would foster charity and Christian unity, interfaith worship can be permitted because of the greater need. This presumes, however, that such worship or participation implies no danger of scandal or indifferentism.

These, then, are the basic principles that govern interfaith worship. Regarding worship as an intrinsic sign of unity, interfaith worship is forbidden, not because it is wrong in itself, but because it leads to misunderstanding, indifferentism, and scandal. On the other hand, regarding worship as a means of grace and of fostering Christian charity and unity, interfaith worship may not only be permitted but commended and encouraged. In an individual instance, which principle deserves the stricter adherence? The answer is a matter of prudent judgment, of finding the proper balance between the two principles. As summarized by Vatican Council II in the Decree on Ecumenism:

In certain special circumstances, such as in prayer services "for unity" and during ecumenical gatherings, it is allowable, indeed desirable, that Catholics should join in prayer with their separated brethren. Such prayers in common are certainly a very effective means of petitioning for the grace of unity, and they are a genuine expression of the ties which even now bind Catholics to their separated brethren. "For where two or three are gathered together for my sake, there am I in the midst of them" (Mt. 18:20).

As for common worship, however, it may not be regarded as a means to be used indiscriminately for the restoration of unity among Christians. Such worship depends chiefly on two principles: it should signify the unity of the Church; it should provide a sharing in the means of grace. The fact that it should signify unity generally rules out common worship. Yet the gaining of a needed grace sometimes commends it.

The practical course to be adopted, after due regard has been given to all the circumstances of time, place, and personage, is left to the prudent decision of the local episcopal authority, unless the Bishops' Conference according to its own statutes, or the Holy See, has determined otherwise. (No. 8)[1]

[1] For further information on guidelines for interfaith worship and common prayer, consult specific guidelines issued by local ecumenical commissions; or consult the "Interim Guidelines for Prayer in Common

Programs and Projects

Ecumenical concern must fill the heart of every Christian before God will work in us his purpose. Getting this concern to the grass-roots level is a primary task today for the ecumenical movement. A practical program is needed in every area of the Church's activity to make ecumenism not only a word but a vital, meaning-ful reality. Although such a program will vary according to the background and capacity of its participants, the elements which make it up will still be the same—prayer, study, dialogue, and cooperative service.

Working within his own community, a layman can employ these elements toward bringing ecumenism into his home, his parish, and the organizations to which he belongs. Invaluable assistance can be provided by already existing structures and agencies. The parish is a ready-made outlet for ecumenical activity, although both smaller, more personal groups and larger, more community-wide groups can also be used for ecumenical programming. The following is a selected list of projects open to any layman, and practical on a neighborhood, parish, or community level. It makes no pretense at being either exhaustive or restrictive. In ecumenical programming the only limits are those of imagination, enthusiasm, and the Holy Spirit.

Education

Study is required in order to understand the principles of ecumenism as well as to understand the history and doctrines of other faiths. Such study, however, involves far too much for one book, one lecture, or one course to even begin to provide real competence. A willingness to read and ponder is required. The titles given in the "Suggested Reading" lists at the end of each chapter of this book, and particularly those included in the "General Introductory Reading List" at the end of the book, should prove

---

and *Communicatio in Sacris* of the Bishops' Commission for Ecumenical Affairs," issued by the National Conference of Catholic Bishops, Committee on Ecumenical and Interreligious Affairs, 1312 Massachusetts Avenue, N.W., Washington, D.C. 20005.

interesting and helpful as starting points. In addition to education
through reading, there are several other easily available means.

Lecturers and Speakers. Parish societies, civic and social organizations and fraternities, from the Kiwanis Club to the Holy Name
Society, often sponsor lecturers and after-dinner speakers. Leaders
in the ecumenical movement, ministers, priests, rabbis, or laymen
can provide an evening which is both informative and stimulating.
Suggestions for speakers can be obtained from local ecumenical
commissions. Often a good choice is the pastor of a nearby congregation.

Film Programs. Films of an ecumenical nature are available for
rental and purchase, and these can be used as part of regular
meetings or for special showings. The National Council of Catholic Men, in conjunction with their NBC television program "The
Catholic Hour," has produced several such films, each thirty
minutes long.[2] Another recommendation is the sound film-strip
"A Foundation for Dialogue," which gives an insight into the
beliefs and practices of the major Christian Churches.[3] Such films
and film-strips are informative and provocative, and audiences can
subsequently be broken up into small groups for discussion
purposes.

Study Groups. Parish study groups can bring people together
to read and discuss the Bible, the documents of Vatican II, or
other pertinent books and articles. Several possibilities for background material for such groups are listed in the "General Introductory Reading List."

Encounter

Interfaith understanding comes through study, but education is incomplete until it is followed by ecumenical encounter. Meetings
and dialogues among Christians of different faiths can help the

[2] For catalog of films on ecumenism available for rental, write to: National Council of Catholic Men, Film Center, 405 Lexington Avenue, New
York, New York 10017.

[3] For further information, write to: Dominican Sisters, 2440 Atwood
Avenue, Madison, Wisconsin 53704.

participants to better understand both their own faith and the faith of others. Such encounters should not be mere occasions for social amenities. Rather, they should be opportunities for meaningful communication in an atmosphere of prayer, respect, and Christian affection. The following are a number of formats which can be used for sponsoring ecumenical encounter.

A Week of Prayer for Christian Unity. For over fifty years the Church Unity Octave, from January 18 to 25, has been observed by Catholics and Protestants alike as a time of prayer for Christian unity. This octave can be an occasion for any number of interfaith programs. One idea is a series of ecumenical Bible and prayer services, preferably held each time in different Churches. The clergy and laity can share roles of leadership in reading the scripture, leading prayers, and presenting a homily or meditation. Preparations for such an observance should begin early in the autumn. A leaflet prepared by the National Council of Churches together with the Graymoor Fathers, and recommended by the Catholic Bishops' Commission for Ecumenical Affairs, provides suggestions for hymns, prayers, and scripture readings, all following the same ecumenical theme.[4]

Informal Dialogues. Conversation among people of different faiths may take place in parish halls, community centers, or living rooms. Dialogue need not be so theologically profound that it demands expertise from the participants. Marriage, religion, science, social justice, peace, problems of Church and State—all are topics which call for mutual understanding among men of all faiths and, wherever possible, cooperative action. Helpful in preparing the format for such dialogues and in providing material for conversation is the book *Living Room Dialogues,* a guide for lay discussion, Catholic-Orthodox-Protestant.[5] Small informal groups of laymen can also meet regularly to read and study the Bible,

[4] For further information write to: Graymoor Fathers, Garrison, New York 10524.

[5] *Living Room Dialogues* was coedited by a Catholic, Father William Greenspun, C.S.P., and an officer of the National Council of Churches, William Norgren. For further information, write to: Paulist Press, Harristown Road, Glen Rock, New Jersey 07452.

using one or two commentaries recognized by Catholics and Protestants alike, or to study and discuss the Council documents, books on ecumenism, etc.

Interchurch Visits. A parish could sponsor for its members a visit to a nearby church of another faith. Arrangements should be made ahead of time with the pastor of that church. Visiting at the time of a regular service would provide the opportunity to witness its spirit of prayer and worship. A tour of the parish plant, a meeting with some of its members, and a fellowship hour are all possible features of such a visit. The hosts of such a tour would justifiably expect a return invitation, an opportunity to visit the church of their guests.

Exchange among Organizations. Catholic parish organizations have their counterparts in Jewish, Orthodox, and Protestant congregations. Their program activities often reflect the same concerns. It would be mutually rewarding for these groups to get to know one another. Within a given neighborhood, the lay officers of a parish organization could extend an invitation to the board members of parallel organizations in other churches. They could meet on an experimental basis to discuss their mutual needs as well as those of the community. Such an exchange could arrange for reciprocal invitations when one organization or another is sponsoring a special program or speaker. It could also explore the possibility of cooperative programs beneficial to the entire community.

Interreligious Concerts, Dramas, Art Exhibits. Music, drama, and art have all been used to enrich the religious heritage of mankind. They express in a universal language the sentiments and ideals upheld by all men who love God. They transcend theological barriers as no other means can. Collaborative sponsorship of a concert of religious music by several church choirs is an easy and attractive way of bringing men of different faiths together. A choir director or pastor can consult his counterparts in neighboring churches to learn the feasibility of such a project, and a committee composed of choir directors and lay leaders can arrange the program. Young people's clubs of various churches in the same neighborhood might cooperate in a similar way to sponsor an ecumenical play. A religious art exhibit can be planned in the same manner. The Advent-Christmas and Lent-Easter seasons lend themselves most readily to this type of cooperative venture. Performances can be given in the auditoriums or churches of the parishes involved, with admission open to the general public. Programs of this nature, especially when they include scripture reading and prayer, provide an outstanding witness to faith and charity, a veritable testimony to the sincerity of the movement toward Christian unity.

Involvement in Community Affairs

The Church has a mission to the world, in the words of Vatican Council II, to set "in clearer relief the features of Christ the Servant." Christians are called to express that bond which already unites them by working together "to relieve the afflictions of our times, such as famine and natural disasters, illiteracy and poverty, lack of housing, and the unequal distribution of wealth." This mission, common to all who profess to take Christ seriously, requires a vision which goes beyond all the usual boundaries. It demands a willingness to serve the larger community by recognizing and supporting all those who manifest zeal and charity in such efforts.

Interreligious Conferences on Human Relations and Civil Rights. It was the moral cancer of racial discrimination which first brought ecumenism in the United States out of the calm logic of theological discussion and into the sweaty thick of the picket line. Catholics, Protestants, Orthodox, Jews, and secular humanists banded together in trying to overcome discrimination in housing, employment, health, education, and the administration of justice. Where community human relations organizations already exist, a serious attempt should be made to make them truly representative of Christians and Christian Churches in that area. Where no such organizations exist, they can be formed through the joint sponsorship of Churches, organizations, and individuals with the help of human relations experts.

Interreligious Conferences on Poverty. Religious communities have historically upheld the dignity of the human person regardless of his economic condition; they have concerned themselves with the needs of the poor and preached against their exploitation. The vastness and complexity of society today, however, is such that only a united voice raised by all men of good will can prick the conscience of our age. And protest must be joined by action in behalf of the economically disenfranchised, particularly in such areas as employment, education, housing, health and welfare, legal services, and recreation. A committee made up of lay leaders of the Churches in any wide area can co-sponsor conferences which aim at community awareness of the problems of poverty, commitment to facing those problems, and involvement in overcoming them.

Do's and Don'ts for Dialogue

Communication is an art. It requires a talent and know-how not only for speaking but also, and often more important, for listening. Ecumenical dialogue demands both. The professionals at speaking have already entered into dialogue—prelates, priests, and professors of theology with rabbis, ministers, and doctors of divinity. But ecumenism will never attain its ends until the people in the pew enter into the exchange of ideas and attitudes.

At one time, discussing religion inevitably produced an atmosphere of argument. The result was that conversation suffered, and so too did religion. This attitude has changed rapidly in the last few years. Dialogue has replaced debate, as men of different faiths have stopped talking at each other and begun speaking to each other, and, even more important, listening and trying to understand each other.

Amateurs should not feel hesitant about entering into ecumenical dialogue. Interfaith dialogue is, after all, something of a novelty for everyone involved—even for the professionals. From their limited experience, however, some guidelines for dialogue have already been tried and found successful. They are offered here in order to provide both incentive and encouragement to would-be ecumenists.

*Presume that your partner in dialogue has as
much good faith as you do.*

It is a prerequisite for any kind of communication, but particularly
so for ecumenical dialogue, to assume truthfulness and good will.
Honesty forbids deceptiveness, and charity prohibits imputing false
motives or insincerity. Especially among Christians, dialogue
demands a devotion to truth and to him who said, "I am the way,
the truth, and the life." Unless the participants in ecumenical
dialogue are confident of one another's best intentions and good
will, it would be better for them not even to attempt it.

*Know your faith and be prepared to
learn more about it.*

An ecumenical dialogue in which the participants are unfamiliar
with their respective faiths proves to be little more than a pooling
of ignorance. A man need not be an expert in theology in order
to discuss his faith, but he should have some confidence that he
knows what he is talking about; otherwise, he speaks only for
himself rather than as a representative of his tradition. Knowledge
is necessary for ecumenical dialogue, and this requires a willingness to study and to read. Interfaith exchange has sent more than
a few of its participants back to the books and has given them a
greater understanding and appreciation of their own faith. A
degree in theology is not required for intelligent ecumenical
discussion, but it is inevitable that questions will arise which one
or another participant cannot answer. In such an instance, he
should admit his ignorance and promise to look up the answer.
Above all, conclusive statements or even good guesses should be
avoided, lest any doors are closed that needn't be.

*Know the faults and needs of your Church
and admit them.*

The history of almost every Church and religious association reveals the weakness and sinfulness of its all-too-human members.
Intolerance and persecution have characterized our relationships

with one another. The cruelty committed in the name of religion, whether by Catholics or Protestants, need not be defended, and it cannot be excused. Attempts can be made only to understand and acknowledge it. Following the example of the Second Vatican Council, all Christians ought to confess their past faults and present weaknesses, repent of them, and resolve with God's help to amend them. Before even gathering together with one another, participants in interfaith dialogue must be willing to seek forgiveness and extend it in return. Only then can we honestly ask God to "forgive us our trespasses."

Listen and try to understand the faith of your partner in dialogue.

Words can at times conceal more than they reveal. A great deal of misunderstanding has resulted from not listening carefully enough to a speaker's definition of terms. The same words can often have a variety of different meanings for people, words like "grace," "faith," and "sin." In interfaith discussion the participants need to see each other's position and to understand each other's point of view. They need to listen carefully to the way words are used in order to understand the meaning they are meant to convey. This demands that a man be willing and able to constantly revise his understanding of his partner's faith, or rather his misunderstanding of it. Dialogue can be healthfully destructive of caricatures. But this requires sympathetic listening, an effort to see similarities instead of differences, and the willingness to see another man's faith in the most favorable light possible.

Realize the issues that separate us and face up to them.

Charity should never be sacrificed for the sake of truth. But neither should truth be sacrificed for the sake of charity. To pretend that there is nothing that divides Christians, or at least nothing of any consequence, would be dishonest. Dialogue is serving not only to indicate where no serious differences exist between Christians, but it is also serving to show where the real cleavages lie. It may eventually show that our differences are greater and deeper than we ever dreamed. Making believe that barriers aren't there doesn't soften the shock when we finally meet up with them.

Cultivate a sense of reverence and a sense of humor.

The ecumenical movement has not been with us long enough to toughen our skins. After a long history of insult and argument, there is still a great deal of sensitivity on all sides of the discussion table. Care must be taken not to offend those sensitivities. Participants in dialogue need to acquire a sense of reverence and respect for what their partners consider holy. Good manners are required when visiting the church of another faith, and good taste is necessary when discussing the rituals, customs, and eccentricities of another faith. Before engaging in any ecumenical dialogue or activity, inquiry should be made from a knowledgeable source concerning such amenities as proper titles for the clergy, regulations and attitudes regarding food, drink, smoking, etc. Mutual planning serves not only to obviate minor problems and irritations, but helps to bring about the maximum involvement of all participants. Despite the best of intentions, however, inculpable ignorance or inadvertence may lead to some awkward situation or to a remark that could cause hurt feelings. To alleviate the embarrassment in such cases, a sense of humor is an invaluable asset. In any venture as new as ecumenical dialogue, there are bound to be a few toes stepped on. Such indiscretions should not be taken as insults.

Look upon dialogue as an opportunity, not for conquering, but for learning and sharing.

All the participants in ecumenical dialogue enter into the exchange with personal religious needs. A mutual concern for one another's needs should pervade the atmosphere together with an admission of one's own. Dialogue should never become a platform for displaying knowledge or making an exhibition of overpowering logic. A man should look upon his partner in dialogue, not as an opponent whom he can conquer, but as someone with whom he can share and from whom he can profit. He should look, not to victory, but to a mutual growing in love for God and for people, as the fruit of sincere ecumenical dialogue. Winning arguments does not necessarily win friends.

Never talk together without praying together.

A gathering for ecumenical dialogue should open and close with an awareness of God's presence together with sincere and humble prayer. The differences between us are such that mere good will and talk, as indispensable as they may be, simply are not enough. It is false optimism, bound to be shattered, which expects that union is around the corner. Such optimism can be dangerous; when its hopes are not immediately realized, it often becomes disillusionment, pessimism, and even cynicism. What we should strive for, rather, is the patient perseverance that comes with faith —faith in ourselves and in others, based on our faith in God. Prayer, the dialogue itself, and the pain of our separations should be offered to God with faith and confidence that what our mere human endeavors cannot achieve God in his might can accomplish.

General Introductory Reading List

PAPERBACKS

Abbot, Walter M., ed., *The Documents of Vatican II*. Complete texts of all of the documents promulgated by the Second Vatican Council, with notes and commentaries by Catholic, Protestant, and Orthodox authorities. Guild Press.

Baum, Gregory, ed., *Ecumenical Theology Today*. Reprints from *The Ecumenist* covering a wide range of topics. Paulist Press.

Blueprints for Action. Part of the Grass-roots Ecumenism Program. National Council of Catholic Men (Washington, D.C.).

Brown, Robert McAfee, *The Spirit of Protestantism*. A parallel to Karl Adam's *Spirit of Catholicism*. Well suited for dialogue and study groups. Galaxy Books.

Brown, Robert McAfee, and Gustave Weigel, *An American Dialogue*. A Protestant looks at Catholicism and a Catholic looks at Protestantism. Anchor Books.

Tavard, George H., *Understanding Protestantism*. A popular introduction to the history, development, and theology of Protestantism. Paulist Press.

PERIODICALS

Christian Century, 407 South Dearborn Street, Chicago, Illinois 60605. A weekly journal of liberal Protestant opinion, comparable to *Commonweal*.

Christianity Today, 375 West Center Street, Marion, Ohio 43302. A biweekly journal of conservative Protestant opinion.

The Ecumenist, Harristown Road, Glen Rock, New Jersey 07452. A bimonthly publication promoting Christian unity, published by the Paulist Fathers.